Natural Resources, Inequality and Conflict

Hamid E. Ali · Lars-Erik Cederman
Editors

Natural Resources, Inequality and Conflict

Editors
Hamid E. Ali
School of Public Administration and
Development Economics
Doha Institute for Graduates Studies
Doha, Qatar

Lars-Erik Cederman
International Conflict Research
ETH Zürich
Zürich, Switzerland

ISBN 978-3-030-73557-9   ISBN 978-3-030-73558-6 (eBook)
https://doi.org/10.1007/978-3-030-73558-6

© The Editor(s) (if applicable) and The Author(s), under exclusive license to Springer Nature Switzerland AG 2022
This work is subject to copyright. All rights are solely and exclusively licensed by the Publisher, whether the whole or part of the material is concerned, specifically the rights of translation, reprinting, reuse of illustrations, recitation, broadcasting, reproduction on microfilms or in any other physical way, and transmission or information storage and retrieval, electronic adaptation, computer software, or by similar or dissimilar methodology now known or hereafter developed.
The use of general descriptive names, registered names, trademarks, service marks, etc. in this publication does not imply, even in the absence of a specific statement, that such names are exempt from the relevant protective laws and regulations and therefore free for general use.
The publisher, the authors and the editors are safe to assume that the advice and information in this book are believed to be true and accurate at the date of publication. Neither the publisher nor the authors or the editors give a warranty, expressed or implied, with respect to the material contained herein or for any errors or omissions that may have been made. The publisher remains neutral with regard to jurisdictional claims in published maps and institutional affiliations.

This Palgrave Macmillan imprint is published by the registered company Springer Nature Switzerland AG
The registered company address is: Gewerbestrasse 11, 6330 Cham, Switzerland

Acknowledgments

This book is one of the main outputs from the collaborative project "Ethnic Power Relations and Conflict in Fragile States," which included researchers from Côte d'Ivoire, Egypt, Guatemala, India, Switzerland, and Zambia. The project was generously funded by the Research for Development (R4D) program of the Swiss National Science Foundation and the Swiss Agency for Development and Cooperation (Grant 171175). In particular, we would like to thank Claudia Zingerli at the Swiss National Science Foundation for her unflinching support.

We held two book workshops, the first one at the Tata Institute of Social Science in January 2019 and the second one at the University of Geneva the same year. We would like to thank Madhu Sekher and Simon Hug for organizing these events. Several of the R4D team members offered excellent comments and advice that helped us improve the book, including Simon Hug, Seraina Rüegger, and Manuel Vogt, who also contributed greatly to the management of the project as a whole. In addition, we are grateful to Ravi Bhavnani for extremely valuable feedback on several of the chapters. Finally, we would like to thank our publisher Palgrave Macmillan, who have supported this project with great enthusiasm and professionalism.

Contents

Part I Theories and Concepts

1 Introduction 3
   Hamid E. Ali and Lars-Erik Cederman

2 Mineral Resources and Conflict: An Analytical
   Overview 11
   Hamid E. Ali, Lars-Erik Cederman,
   and Yaron A. Weissberg

Part II Statistical Studies

3 No Extraction Without Representation: The
   Ethno-Regional Oil Curse and Secessionist Conflict 37
   Philipp Hunziker and Lars-Erik Cederman

4 Digging Deeper: On the Role of Grievances in African
   Mining Conflicts 71
   Yannick Pengl and Lars-Erik Cederman

Part III Case Studies

5 Ethnic Mobilization and Collective Grievances
   in the Copper Mining Areas of Zambia 97
   Robby Kapesa, John Bwalya, and Owen Sichone

6 Resource Extraction and Conflict in India   129
   Madhushree Sekher, Mansi Awasthi, Subhankar Nayak,
   and Rajesh Kumar

7 Indigenous Mobilization and Resource Extraction
   in Guatemala   151
   Alejandro Quiñonez and Ricardo Sáenz de Tejada

8 Fueling Conflicts by Sharing Benefits? Qualitative
   Evidence from a Mining Conflict in Burkina Faso   185
   Selina Bezzola

Part IV Conclusions

9 Conclusions for Theory and Policy   219
   Hamid E. Ali, Lars-Erik Cederman,
   and Yaron A. Weissberg

Index   229

Notes on Contributors

Hamid E. Ali is Associate Professor of Economics and Public Policy, Doha Institute for Graduate Studies, and the author of *Darfur Political Economy: A Quest for Development* (Routledge, 2014) and co-author with Christos Kollias of *Defense Spending, Natural Resources, and Conflict* (Routledge, 2017). He is also the author and co-author of articles in scholarly journals.

Mansi Awasthi has a Ph.D. in Economics from Tata Institute of Social Sciences, India, and currently is an Assistant Professor at the same institute.

Selina Bezzola is a Junior Programme Officer at the Swiss Agency for Development and Cooperation. She completed her Ph.D. at the Center for Development and Cooperation, ETH Zürich, in 2020. In her Ph.D. dissertation, she examined socio-political effects of Corporate Social Responsibility in the mining industry on state legitimacy and on conflict dynamics in sub-Saharan Africa.

John Bwalya is Associate Professor and Director of the Dag Hammarskjöld Institute of Peace and Conflict Studies at Copperbelt University, Zambia. He has researched and published on race relations in urban residential space in South Africa. He currently researches on ethnicity, electoral politics, and urban dialectics.

Lars-Erik Cederman is Professor of International Conflict Research, ETH Zürich, and the author of *Emergent Actors in World Politics: How States and Nations Develop and Dissolve* (Princeton University Press, 1997) and co-author of *Inequality, Grievances and Civil War* (Cambridge University Press, 2013), as well as numerous articles in scientific journals.

Ricardo Sáenz de Tejada is Professor of Anthropology, Universidad de San Carlos de Guatemala, and the autor of *Democracias de posguerra en Centroamérica: política, desigualdad y pobreza en Guatemala, El Salvador y Nicaragua (1979–2005)*, as well as other books and articles.

Philipp Hunziker is Data Scientist at Google and Post Doctoral fellow, Institute for Quantitative Social Science, Harvard University.

Robby Kapesa is a Peace and Conflict Scholar at the Dag Hammarskjöld Institute for Peace and Conflict Studies, Copperbelt University, Zambia. He has published on horizontal inequalities, ethnic mobilization, and political violence. His current research explores how exploitation of mineral resources fuels local grievances, ethnic tensions, and violence.

Rajesh Kumar worked as a Research Associate in the R4D Research Project on "Ethnic Power Relations" at Tata Institute of Social Sciences, India. He has a Masters in Development Studies.

Subhankar Nayak worked as a Senior Research Associate in the R4D Research Project on "Ethnic Power Relations" at Tata Institute of Social Sciences, India. He has a Masters in Rural Development.

Yannick Pengl is a Postdoctoral Researcher at ETH Zurich's International Conflict Research Group. His research interests include economic inequalities, political identities, ethnic politics, and armed conflict with a regional focus on sub-Saharan Africa.

Alejandro Quiñonez is Anthropologist and Professor, Universidad de San Carlos de Guatemala. Co-Founder, Social and Environmental Innovation Lab Sapiens. @laboratoriosapiens.

Madhushree Sekher is Professor (Political Science) in the Centre for the Study of Social Exclusion and Inclusive Policies at Tata Institute of Social Sciences, India. She has authored numerous research articles and books, including *Feeding India: Livelihoods, Entitlements and Capabilities* (Earthscan, 2013), *Governance and Governed* (Springer, 2017), and *Including the Excluded in South Asia* (Springer, 2019).

Owen Sichone is a member of the Electoral Eminent Persons Group advising the Electoral Commission of Zambia on peace and conflict matters. Currently in retirement after serving as Inaugural Dean of the School of Humanities Social Sciences, and as Director of the Dag Hammarsjköld Institute for Peace and Conflict Studies at Copperbelt University.

Yaron A. Weissberg is a Ph.D. student in the International Conflict Research group at ETH Zürich.

LIST OF FIGURES

Fig. 2.1	Visual illustration of our four-step approach and the important distinctions discussed in each step	23
Fig. 3.1	Sedimentary thickness (in km) from the CRUST 1.0 dataset	49
Fig. 3.2	Sedimentary thickness (in km) and ACOR fields (white/black dots) in Nigeria (left) and Burma (right)	49
Fig. 3.3	Comparison of ACOR and PETRODATA data of discovered Burmese petroleum fields in 1982	51
Fig. 3.4	Estimated increase in probability of civil conflict when moving from 0 to the median value of petroleum fields among producers. Panel D reports results for petroleum fields in populated areas. Density estimates reflect sampling variance. Based on Table I	57
Fig. 3.5	Marginal effect of (logged) populated petroleum fields on the probability of group-level territorial conflict, conditional on exclusion (Panel A) and group size (Panel B). Black vertical lines (Panel A) and dashed lines (Panel B) indicate 95% confidence intervals. Based on Columns 6 and 8 of Table II	63
Fig. 4.1	The African mining boom	72
Fig. 4.2	Results from cell-level analysis of conflict event data	82
Fig. 4.3	Results from cell-level analysis of conflict event data	86
Fig. 4.4	Results from group-level analysis of ethnic conflict onset data (Based on Models 1–4 in Table 1)	89
Fig. 5.1	Map of North-Western province and Solwezi district	101

Fig. 6.1	Rayagada district in Odisha. Highlighted are the bauxite mines in the area	137
Fig. 6.2	Context, stakeholders and power relations in natural resource conflicts	138
Fig. 7.1	Mining and hydroelectric projects analyzed in this chapter	158
Fig. 8.1	Map of Sanguié-Province in the Center-Western Region of Burkina Faso in which the department of Réo and the Perkoa mine is located	197
Fig. 8.2	Timeline of conflict in Perkoa	199

List of Tables

Table 3.1	(Instrumented) petroleum and civil conflict, country-level, 1991–2013	55
Table 3.2	(Instrumented) petroleum and territorial conflict, group-level, 1991–2013	60
Table 4.1	Mining and conflict events	83
Table 4.2	Mining, exclusion and conflict events	84
Table 4.3	Mining and conflict issues	84
Table 4.4	Mining, exclusion and conflict issues	85
Table 4.5	Group-level specifications	88
Table 5.1	Total copper production and contribution of the Solwezi mines, 2016	106
Table 5.2	Contribution to export earnings by metal exports, 2016	107
Table 5.3	Corporate social responsibility spending in the mining sector, 2016	108
Table 5.4	Employment figures in the mining sector and contributions of Solwezi mines, 2016	109

PART I

Theories and Concepts

CHAPTER 1

Introduction

Hamid E. Ali and Lars-Erik Cederman

Since the turn of the century, a veritable mining boom has swept through large parts of the world (Le Billon 2012). Extractive operations have entered production at a rate unparalleled in recent history in both Latin America (Bebbington and Bury 2013) and Africa (Chunan-Pole 2017). Driven by the industry's rapidly increasing demands for minerals and metals, coming especially from China and the growing demand for clean energy technologies (Hund et al. 2020; Bazilian 2018), this impressive wave of foreign direct investment has done much to accelerate development in previously underdeveloped regions.

Yet, there is a dark side to these positive developments. As minerals are extracted at a rapid pace, new problems emerge that may block, and even reverse, the benefits of mining. Academic pioneers have anticipated such complications for a long time. Under the heading of the

---

H. E. Ali
School of Public Administration and Development Economics, Doha Institute for Graduates Studies, Doha, Qatar
e-mail: hamid.ali@dohainstitute.edu.qa

L.-E. Cederman (✉)
International Conflict Research, ETH Zürich, Zürich, Switzerland
e-mail: lcederman@ethz.ch

© The Author(s), under exclusive license to Springer Nature Switzerland AG 2022
H. E. Ali and L.-E. Cederman (eds.), *Natural Resources, Inequality and Conflict*, https://doi.org/10.1007/978-3-030-73558-6_1

"resource curse" (Sachs and Warner 2001), scholars have been warning that resource abundance may thwart growth, destabilize democracy and trigger violent conflict (Ross 2015). Focusing on the final aspect of the resource curse, this volume evaluates the link between mineral resources and conflict. The main objective is to produce relevant insights into the socio-political contexts in which extraction takes place to inform policies and reforms that harness the developmental potential of resource wealth. In many ways, peace plays a crucial role in development and democratization processes, because it constitutes a necessary condition without which good governance becomes impossible.

There is already a rich literature on the link between resources and civil conflict, arguing that resource-dependence undermines good governance and increases the risk of political violence. An emerging scholarly consensus tells us that such a resource-conflict nexus does exist (see, e.g., Koubi et al. 2014), but despite the intensity of scholarly interest, several issues remain wide open. First, there is little agreement on what specific causal mechanisms underpin the resource-conflict link (Humphreys 2005; Koubi et al. 2014). Second, conflict researchers still struggle with the fact that resource exploitation cannot be considered exogenous to conflict (see, e.g., Koubi et al. 2014). Third, and finally, much of the literature has so far focused on oil (see, e.g., Ross 2015), although more recently, studies that analyze the link between non-fuel minerals and conflict have become more common (see, e.g., Le Billon 2012; Berman et al. 2017).

The contributions to the current volume address these points head-on:

First, whereas most scholarship in this area assumes that the resource curse derives from mobilization opportunities and greed-related factors, we consider the possibility that *inequality and grievances* play a central role in the resource-conflict nexus. Beyond evaluating negative externalities related to environmental degradation and expropriation, this volume analyzes how resource extraction creates or reinforces political and economic inequalities, typically along ethnic lines, which in turn increases the risk of protest and possibly political violence. Thus, we join a growing number of scholars who are interested in knowing how inequality and grievances interact with greedy motives and mobilization processes rather than viewing one set of factors as mutually exclusive of the other (Cederman and Vogt 2017).

Second, whereas the first generation of quantitative civil war studies tended to treat resource variables as if they were exogenous, scholars have more recently become aware of the *endogeneity* of resource extraction. Rather than being a natural phenomenon, extractive activities are highly dependent on local political and economic conditions, which means that reverse causation cannot be safely ruled out. Therefore, a number of solutions have been proposed to deal with this problem (see, e.g., Brunnschweiler and Bulte 2009; Cotet and Tsui 2013). Our approach is to combine quantitative analysis based on research designs that take endogeneity into account with a series of case studies that offer detailed information on the causal process at work. In this way, we are able to shed light on whether natural resources cause civil conflict.

Third, instead of limiting ourselves to petroleum extraction, our volume enlarges the empirical scope to encompass a wider set of natural resources, including various *non-fuel minerals*, such as bauxite, copper and zinc. Rather than merely extrapolating findings from the literature on petroleum-induced conflict, we consider whether the link between mining and civil conflict is different from the one linking petroleum to rebellion. Furthermore, we explicitly study how mining operations in these areas may trigger protest and civil conflict, and how the risks vary among the different types of mineral resources.

Much of our thinking has been inspired by studying the resource conflict in Aceh, the gas-rich province of Indonesia. This predominantly rural area, inhabited primarily by ethnic Acehnese, experienced profound structural changes as a consequence of the discovery of the Arun supergiant gas field in 1971. In cooperation with major petroleum companies, the Indonesian government quickly established extraction facilities and downstream petrochemical industry near the city of Lhokseumawe (Kell 2010, 35). This development had massive economic and societal impacts for the entire region. The establishment of the Lhokseumawe industrial zone involved large-scale land expropriation and caused significant in-migration and urbanization. Along with these structural changes came targeted efforts by the central government to establish more direct rule over the region. As the industrial resource sector in Aceh became a key contributor to the state budget, Jakarta began to foster a narrow local class of technocrats to be placed in the provincial government in order to execute the central government's policy in cooperation with the "ubiquitous" armed forces. The combination of rapid industrialization with little or no governance institutions in place to manage this development has led to land expropriation and catastrophic pollution (Kell 2010, 35ff). The case of Aceh demonstrates that by pushing the establishment of an extractive infrastructure in its periphery, the state of Indonesia effectively took over policy making in regions where it was lacking capacity and incentives to ensure public welfare. In response, separatist rebels could appeal directly to those who have had their livelihood and daily lives disrupted through expropriation and environmental damage, arguing that secession would lead to much needed redistribution in favor of the local population.

Yet, other prominent cases involving the extraction of non-fuel minerals exhibit a similar pattern. One example is the secessionist war involving Katanga, a province in the Democratic Republic of Congo, where the main resource in question was copper rather than petroleum. When the state became independent in 1960, representatives of the province of Katanga seceded with initial Belgian support. The secessionist bid was motivated by the regional politicians' fear that their political influence would be eclipsed by the country's center after independence. In particular, the objective was to secure as much as possible of the revenues from the province's large-scale copper-mining operations (Larmer and Kennes 2014, 746ff). Since the government opposed the secessionist attempt, a civil war broke out that prompted UN intervention.

Apart from distributional grievances related to the fear of losing privileged access to the lucrative mines, which emerged at the time of independence, political as well as migration-based grievances also played a central role. Political grievances developed parallel to the distribution fears and were based on the assumption that local leaders will lose political clout as a result of independence and the centralization of power that accompanied it. The privileged position which Katanga enjoyed during colonial times, the region was placed under the administration of the Comité Spécial du Katanga (CSK) instead of being ruled directly by Belgium (Larmer and Kennes 2014, 744), was at stake. This fear was again connected to the natural resources: not only was the special status aligned with mining interests, the presence of these resources had in addition hindered a national integration of the region since its infrastructure connected it more with southern Africa as opposed to the rest of Congo (Ibid.). This might also explain why Moïse Tshombe, the leader of the secessionist movement, pushed for a more federal political system within Congo, a plan which Patrice Lumumba, the first Prime Minister of the Republic of Congo, rejected (Arnold 2017, 22). Migration-based grievances were also prominent. The mining industry within Katanga brought in immigrant labor, thereby adding to the fears which fueled the secessionist project (Larmer and Kennes 2019, 388). This development increased the hostility toward Kasaian in-migration, which is an issue that remains relevant to this day (Larmer and Kennes 2019, 362).

Both the cases of Aceh and Katanga illustrate how grievances can lead to violent campaigns within resource-rich regions. To test this explanation on a larger scale and in order to delve deeper into how these grievances matter, the following volume is structured in four parts:

Part I introduces the theories and concepts of the entire volume. Specifically, Chapter 2 offers an overview of the literature on the link between natural resources and conflict. We elaborate on the three main themes introduced above and briefly discuss our *multi-method* research strategy.

Offering statistical analyses of the link between resources and conflict, Part II of the book is composed of two main chapters. As a reference point for the empirical chapters of the entire volume, Chapter 3 is devoted to a large-N study of oil extraction and civil war worldwide. Based on a geological identification strategy that addresses endogeneity, the analysis comes to the conclusion that petroleum extraction has an effect on rebellion in ethnic regions that are peripheral to the state. Going beyond petroleum extraction, Chapter 4, shifts the discussion towards non-fuel minerals. The chapter emphasizes ethnic exclusion from political power, a contextual factor that is shown to make resource-related grievances particularly conflict-prone.

Based on qualitative methods, Part III presents a series of case studies in order to investigate the mechanisms between the extraction of non-fuel minerals and violent conflict. Following up the statistical findings of Part II, we are particularly interested in whether the postulated link between mineral extraction and conflict runs through mechanisms that hinge on ethnic inequalities and grievances.

Chapter 5 investigates resource extraction in Zambia. Drawing on micro-level evidence from the North-Western regions of the country, it analyzes to what extent the region's booming copper-mining industry provoked grievances among the local population, and whether such grievances engender ethnic mobilization, tension, and clashes. The chapter specifically teases out distributive, migration, political, and environmental grievances introduced in the theoretical chapter and demonstrates how they can emerge in the context of low-value resource extraction.

Shifting the main focus to mobilization, Chapter 6 investigates the links between natural resource extraction and its impact on the local communities within resource-rich states in India. Shedding light on the negative consequences of mining, the chapter focuses on the state of Odisha which is one of the least developed regions within India but lies at the center of the country's new mining boom. Although a rise of foreign direct investments would be welcomed, mining investments are shown to cause grievances related to the eviction of tribal communities from their lands. Opportunist actors such as the Naxalites have taken advantage of such grievances and thereby find new recruits for their ideological struggle.

Also highlighting the plight of marginalized groups, Chapter 7 analyzes the indigenous response to extractive projects in Guatemala. In the mid-1990s and in the context of the peace negotiations between the government and the guerrilla, the country started to recognize itself as a multi-ethnic nation, thereby acknowledging the existence of indigenous communities. Despite this formal recognition, those communities increasingly face the threat of extractive projects which limit their access to strategic resources needed to sustain their livelihoods (e.g., water, forests, and land). The chapter analyzes how this threat has contributed to the unification and mobilization of the affected groups which has led to community consultations, peaceful resistance, and strategic litigations. With the latter allowing courts to rule in their favor, some substantial gains can be shown to emerge as a result of these peaceful forms of protest.

The final country study, presented in Chapter 8, evaluates the effectiveness of conflict prevention measures, or the lack thereof. Focusing on a mining conflict in Burkina Faso, the chapter discusses whether and how mining companies' attempts to share benefits with mining-affected communities can perversely backfire by contributing to grievances and conflict. The analysis combines grievance-based accounts of social mobilization with insights from the private politics literature. It argues that company-led benefit-sharing activities risk triggering grievances and conflict especially in fragmented societies, where companies have an interest to target their activities to certain powerful groups.

Finally, Part IV provides a summary of the previous analyses in the form of Chapter 9. Returning to our three main themes of grievances and inequality, mineral types and endogeneity, we discuss the overall trends and patterns for the benefit of future research, and even more importantly, for policy making.

REFERENCES

Arnold, Guy. 2017. *Africa A Modern History: 1945–2015*. London: Atlantic Books.
Bazilian, Morgan D. 2018. "The Mineral Foundation of the Energy Transition." *The Extractive Industries and Society* 5 (1): 93–97.
Bebbington, Andrew, and Jeffrey Bury. 2013. *Subterranean Struggles: New Dynamics of Mining, Oil, and Gas in Latin America*. Austin, TX: University of Texas Press.
Berman, Nicolas, Mathieu Couttenier, Dominic Rohner, and Mathias Thoenig. 2017. "This Mine Is Mine! How Minerals Fuel Conflicts in Africa." *American Economic Review* 107 (6): 1564–1610.
Brunnschweiler, Christa N., and Erwin H. Bulte. 2009. "Natural Resources and Violent Conflict: Resource Abundance, Dependence and the Onset of Civil Wars." *Oxford Economic Papers* 61 (4): 651–674.
Cederman, Lars-Erik., and Manuel Vogt. 2017. "Dynamics and Logics of Civil War." *Journal of Conflict Resolution* 61: 1992–2016.
Chunan-Pole, P., A. L. Dabalen, and B. C. Land. 2017. "Mining in Africa: Are Local Communities Better Off?" The World Bank.
Cotet, Anca M., and Kevin K. Tsui. 2013. "Oil and Conflict: What Does the Cross Country Evidence Really Show?" *American Economic Journal: Macroeconomics* 5 (1): 49–80.
Humphreys, Macartan. 2005. "Natural Resources, Conflict, and Conflict Resolution: Uncovering the Mechanisms." *Journal of Conflict Resolution* 49 (4): 508–537.
Hund, K., D. L., Porta, T. P., Fabregas, T., Laing, & J. Drexhage. 2020. "Minerals for Climate Action: The Mineral Intensity of the Clean Energy Transition." Climate Smart Mining. Washington D.C.: World Bank Group.
Kell, Tim. 2010. *The Roots of Acehnese Rebellion: 1989–1992*. Singapore: Equinox Publishing.
Koubi, Vally, Gabriele Spilker, Tobias Böhmelt, and Thomas Bernauer. 2014. "Do Natural Resources Matter for Interstate and Intrastate Armed Conflict?" *Journal of Peace Research* 51 (2): 227–243.
Larmer, Miles, and Erik Kennes. 2014. "Rethinking the Katangese Secession." *The Journal of Imperial and Commonwealth History* 42 (4): 741–761.
Larmer, Miles, and Erik Kennes. 2019. "Katanga's Secessionism in the Democratic Republic of Congo." In *Secessionism in African Politics*, eds. Lotje De Vries, Pierre Englebert and Mareike Schomerus.
Le Billon, Philippe. 2012. *Wars of Plunder: Conflicts, Profits and the Politics of Resources*. New York: Columbia University Press.

Ross, Michael L. 2015. "What Have We Learned About the Resource Curse?" *Annual Review of Political Science* 18: 239–259.

Sachs, Jeffrey D, and Andrew M. Warner. 2001. "The Curse of Natural Resources." *European Economic Review* 45 (4–6): 827–838.

CHAPTER 2

Mineral Resources and Conflict: An Analytical Overview

Hamid E. Ali, Lars-Erik Cederman, and Yaron A. Weissberg

As shown in the previous chapter, many regions in the developing world are currently undergoing a sweeping commodity boom. Data on foreign direct investments and the number of annual openings of mining operations in Africa confirm this picture (e.g. Christensen 2019) and highlight the global reach of these trends (see e.g. Andrews et al. 2018). However, this surge in extractive activity has triggered plenty of resistance and conflict (e.g. Kirsch 2014). Indeed, we are currently witnessing a worldwide wave of protest targeting both governments and companies involved in mining operations (Andrews et al. 2018).

This volume introduces causes and mechanisms that drive the surge of conflict. In the present chapter, we revisit the three main gaps in

---

H. E. Ali
School of Public Administration and Development Economics, Doha Institute for Graduates Studies, Doha, Qatar
e-mail: hamid.ali@dohainstitute.edu.qa

L.-E. Cederman (✉) · Y. A. Weissberg
International Conflict Research, ETH Zürich, Zürich, Switzerland
e-mail: lcederman@ethz.ch

© The Author(s), under exclusive license to Springer Nature Switzerland AG 2022
H. E. Ali and L.-E. Cederman (Eds.), *Natural Resources, Inequality and Conflict*, https://doi.org/10.1007/978-3-030-73558-6_2

the literature that we pointed to in the previous chapter. Since these violent reactions appear to express various forms of grievances, we start by considering what we know about how resource extraction may affect the link between inequality and conflict (see Sect. 2.1 below). Addressing the challenge of empirical analysis, Sect. 2.3 revisits the thorny issue of endogeneity, because, as we have argued above, resource extraction, in its full social and political form, cannot be considered exogenously given. This is an important point, because naïve analysis that does not take into account when and where mining occurs in the first place may turn out to be misleading with respect to its effects on conflict. Ultimately, without reasonably robust causal knowledge it will prove impossible to design reliable strategies for conflict mitigation. Finally, because of petroleum's high economic value, much of the literature has focused on this type of resource rather than minerals in general. Thus, based on recent, emerging scholarship on mining and conflict, Sect. 2.2 prepares the analytical ground for a widening of the topical scope to non-fuel minerals. The question is whether the lessons learned from petroleum-related conflict travel beyond this specific category of mineral resources.

2.1 The Role of Inequality and Grievances, Introducing Our Approach in Four-Steps

Despite the apparent prominence of grievances in conflict processes, such as civil war and less intense cases of political violence, most of the literature has tended to downplay such factors. This tendency has its roots in how the economic scholarship that emerged in the late 1990s accounted for civil war. In their pioneering contribution, Collier and Hoeffler (1998) argued that such political violence is caused by economic factors, including most prominently, natural resource abundance. Analyzing the statistical determinants of the outbreak of civil war at the country level, these authors claim that primary commodity exports, including agricultural goods and natural resources, are associated with a higher risk of conflict. Their main explanatory logic hinges on a simple opportunity cost argument according to which potential rebels will feel inclined to join the fight in case combat promises to yield financial gain, for example through looting of natural resources.

Challenging this account, Fearon and Laitin (2003) contend that natural resource production causes civil war not through "greedy" rebellion, but through a version of the resource curse logic that highlights how opportunistic governments rely on petroleum extraction rather than providing public goods and good governance to their countries' entire populations. State weakness of this type creates ideal conditions for military insurgencies that quickly escalate to large-scale conflicts due to the governments' ham-fisted response.

While these two seminal accounts differ with respect to specific causal mechanisms, they are agreeing with the fact that grievances do not cause internal conflict. Collier and Hoeffler (2004) brought this to the point by arguing that civil wars are due to "greed" rather than "grievances."[1] In their view, grievances are ubiquitous and therefore cannot serve as explanations of low-probability events, such as civil wars. Moreover, Collier and Hoeffler argue that even where grievances appear to be connected to conflict, they are much more likely to serve as an ideological cover for rebel leaders' greedy motivations.

Since these seminal contributions, the literature has grown enormously (for recent reviews, see Koubi et al., 2014; Ross 2015). In an important move, researchers have sought to gain firmer causal ground by relying on disaggregated and explicitly spatial data (e.g. Lujala 2010; Cederman and Gleditsch 2009). Moreover, attempts have been made to consider a wider set of causal mechanisms than those initially proposed by the first wave of writings (Ross 2006; Humphreys 2005). Yet, in their skepticism toward inequality and grievances as explanations of internal conflict, most scholars have followed the intellectual lead of Collier and Hoeffler as well as that of Fearon and Laitin.

By taking inequality and grievances seriously, this volume parts company from this tendency of grievance skepticism. We thus join a minority of quantitative scholars who have trod this path, including Murshed and Gates (2005) and Østby, Nordas & Rød (2009). Much of this scholarship rests on Stewart's (2009) notion of "horizontal inequalities," among culturally or ethnically defined groups, as opposed to "vertical inequalities," which compare individuals. Stewart, Brown and Langer (2009, 294–295) argue that natural resources tend to augment the effect of such ethnic differences on conflict:

The discovery of natural resources can generate sharp increases in regional inequality, and where these resources are located in ethnically or religiously distinct regions of the country, separatist conflict may emerge, particularly if the groups are relatively underdeveloped or feel that they are not benefiting from the exploitation of the resources.

To trace the modifying effect of resources, we use Cederman, Gleditsch and Buhaug's (2013) study of inequality, grievances and civil war as our theoretical point of departure. Without focusing on resources per se, this book articulates and evaluates a stylized grievance-based process that connects horizontal inequality with the outbreak of internal conflict. In the following, we postulate ways in which resource extraction may affect the specific stages of this process.

The interplay between horizontal inequalities and natural resource extraction has until recently received little attention and therefore constitutes an overarching gap in the literature to which this volume tries to contribute. Ross (2007, 251) has identified this research gap already more than a decade ago but with an emphasis on how new horizontal inequalities, resulting from resource extraction, can be avoided through governmental action. This volume however focuses on the potential for conflict resulting through the interplay between these inequalities and resource extraction as well as on how such conflicts can be reduced or even avoided.

We therefore assume that the link between extraction and conflict depends on how extractors, that is the actors responsible for extraction, and the affected communities interact. Depending on the political context and the nature of the resource, governments as well as foreign or domestic firms may play the role of extractors. In some cases, even rebel organizations can assume such a role.

Where extractors introduce or reinforce inequalities there is a higher risk that unhappiness among the affected local communities will prompt major mobilization against the extracting parties. Yet, if the extractors consciously try to reduce political and economic inequality, the affected communities are more likely to seek peaceful avenues to express their preferences, thus circumventing serious conflict.

Building on Cederman, Gleditsch and Buhaug (2013, Ch. 3), and without assuming any determinism, we postulate that the pathway from resource extraction to conflict runs through the following four steps.

Step 1: Identification of the extractors and the local community

The proposed approach to the resource-conflict nexus deviates from much of the literature, which has tended to highlight individual-level inequalities (see e.g. Collier and Hoeffler 1998, 2004). As hinted at above, the main attention in this volume centers on group-level comparisons, especially among ethnic groups, but can be generalized to identity-based differences that are not strictly ethnic, such as those based on region. Ethnic or horizontal inequalities presuppose the existence of distinctive ethnic communities, that are often geographically separated. On the side of the incumbent power wielders, state elites represent "ethnic groups in power," that monopolize state power along ethnic lines. These state-controlling ethnic elites typically serve as extractors themselves through their state agencies, especially in cases where high investment costs require direct state involvement. Yet, even in cases where a "neoliberal" opening of markets grants a direct role to domestic and foreign companies, it can be assumed that ethnic elites profit from these extractive activities through lucrative granting of extractive concessions.

Opposing communities are most easily formed if there is a clear ethnic difference between them and the extractors, but it is also possible that regional differences play this role. For this reason, most of the volume will be focusing on ethnic or regional cases. The critical issue here is the expression of collective property rights through historical claims based on long-standing settlements.

Step 2: Articulation of grievances by community leaders

For resource extraction to become politically consequential, activists need to articulate resource-related grievances to be acted on and they need to identify a target for their "framing" and "blaming" campaign. Targeting either the state and/or extracting firms, they can refer to different types of real or perceived resource-related injustices. Here is a taxonomy of four distinctive types of such grievances that are at least potentially linked to inequalities:

- Distributive grievances: Complaints of this kind depict the extractors as "outsiders" who unfairly siphon off resource revenues that should have benefited the local, rightful owners of the resources. Clearly, this requires the affected community to advance collective ownership claims with historical roots. In particular, state-driven resource extraction in ethno-regions where the state has previously been absent is very likely to cause a skewed rent allocation bypassing the peripheral group. This is due to the fact that the central state will initially face little incentives to allocate a significant portion of resource rents to the local population. In such settings, governing elites typically prefer to allocate revenue towards their core constituency in order to stay in power. As a rule, the population of the resource-rich region is hardly part of the central government's core constituency, especially if it had relatively little direct interaction with the central state prior to resource discovery. This is all the more pressing in multiethnic societies where the resource-abundant region is inhabited by an ethnic minority, as access to state benefits typically run along patronage networks that are based on ethnic ties (Scott 1972).[2] Resource extraction without commensurate compensation for the local population will disappoint citizens' expectations of impending windfalls. This sets the stage for ethno-nationalist agitation arguing that the center is "stealing" the valuable resources of their rightful owners. Ethnic nationalism thereby offers a well-known, robust and easily understandable script that can target the dominant ethnic elite through both "framing" and "blaming" (see e.g. Gamson, 1992).

- Migration-induced grievances: Extraction activities often take place in remote and impoverished regions. Given the level of underdevelopment and the lack of skilled labor, the extracting elites have little choice but to bring in members of the dominant group as well as foreign workers. This creates a situation that confronts the local population with a large inflow of ethnically distinct "intruders" who threaten to take over the local economy. Moreover, in-migration likely confronts the locals with large wealth differentials and make direct inter-ethnic comparisons virtually inevitable. In fact, this process can be conceptualized as an important special case of Weiner's (1978) notion of "sons of the soil." According to this logic, competition over the ethno-region's economic opportunities ensues between a peripherally located ethnic minority and ethnically distinct migrants. Here we are focusing on cases where the competition concerns employment in general, and jobs linked to the petroleum industry in particular, and where the state is triggering and controlling the migratory process.[3] Disruptive in-migration ensures that issues of fairness become salient. Daily confrontations and competition serve as conspicuous reminders of pervasive inequality. Grievances will thus resonate with the local population,

2 MINERAL RESOURCES AND CONFLICT: AN ANALYTICAL OVERVIEW   17

who cannot escape to notice that others profit handsomely from the oil riches.

- Political grievances: Especially where the state is engaged, extractive state penetration may pose a direct challenge to local ethnic elites. Large scale, industrialized resource production causes societal changes in favor of the state's capacity to control the local population more directly; in-migration, urbanization and a greater role of the state in the local economy all make government through a state bureaucracy easier as opposed to traditional modes of rule. Moreover, in order to ensure its access to extraction sites, the government is also likely to employ targeted policies to increase its control over the local populace leading to an increased feeling of marginalization among the local elites. As the local population is pressured to cooperate with state policies, be it through positive incentives, for example through the promise of welfare and employment benefits, or because non-collaboration is deterred through punishment, local power holders could find themselves increasingly unable to exercise autonomous power. In such situations, local elites have very little to lose from taking a lead in expressing separatist grievances and mobilizing against the state (Hechter, 2000, 71). The threat to their political status constitutes an incentive for local elites to mobilize political support against central rule by appealing to the community's right to "control its own destiny" (see e.g. Ballard and Banks 2003, p. 297). Sometimes, political grievances emanate from the extractor's repressive activities that may even include violent suppression of protest and targeted killings of activists (Ibid.).

- Environmental grievances: A final source of grievances are negative externalities associated with the resource extraction process itself. These threats to the local environment and the local community's livelihood are the negative consequences that have been relatively well covered in the literature so far (see e.g. Humphreys 2005). Without well-established local governance structures and an effective legal system, the establishment of an extractive industry is very likely to produce substantial costs for the surrounding population (Sexton 2020). For instance, in Aceh, the combination of rapid industrialization with little or no governance institutions in place to manage this development has led to land expropriation and catastrophic pollution

(Kell 2010, 35ff). Here too, state intrusion worsens the situation. By pushing the establishment of an extractive infrastructure in its periphery, the state effectively takes over policy making in regions where it lacks the governance capacity and incentives to ensure public welfare. In response, ethnic entrepreneurs can appeal directly to those who have had their livelihood and daily lives disrupted through expropriation and environmental damage.

Step 3: Community mobilization

Grievances held by the masses bring us a step closer to violent conflict, but there is no guarantee that such an outcome will materialize. Typically, conflict requires that the opposition to the extractors be organized politically involving large numbers of people and significant mobilizational resources (Tilly 1978). Without such organizational efforts, the extractors are able to crush the resistance relatively easily before it metastasizes into an effective armed campaign of rebellion.

The classical literature on resource abundance and conflict views this step in the chain as the central filter that dictates whether a conflict will erupt. Stressing how the rebels' opportunities to fight, rather than their grievances, determines the outcome, Fearon and Laitin (2003) and Collier et al. (2009) propose arguments that show how the power balance may tilt in the rebels' favor either through the resource curse's weakening the state or through resources boosting rebel finance.

This approach again highlights the economic or "greed" based arguments but neglects various other factors by which the presence and exploitation of natural resources can affect the mobilization of local communities. These grievances may serve as a focal point for coordinated protest and well-organized resistance (Emirbayer 1997; Cederman, Gleditsch and Buhaug 2013). In this sense, it is a mistake to see grievances and mobilizational opportunities as two independent, competing factors driving conflict. Indeed, their confluence can be expected to render resistance especially effective. Furthermore, while grievances without mobilizational efforts make little difference, widely held grievances may facilitate mobilization by boosting participation through emotional motivation.

In his study of conflict in Aceh, Aspinall (2007) shows how identity-based collective action plays a crucial role in mobilizing local communities for violent actions. Despite similar extraction processes in two other Indonesian regions (Riau and East Kalimantan) only Aceh experienced high levels of violence. The author explains this difference by highlighting how grievances are socially constructed: therefore, the grievances associated with resource extraction can only lead to mobilization of affected communities if there is a legacy of past conflicts, state institutionalization of ethnic identity as well as the ability of local political entrepreneurs to link these factors to the resource extraction process. Kuhn (2018) on the other hand, criticizes this reasoning because it fails to explain how resource extraction can produce new grievances instead of just amplifying existing ones.

Quantitative studies have established some evidence showing how ethnic fractionalization and the exclusion of ethnic groups from power can significantly increase the conflict risks associated with natural resources. Sorens (2011) finds that the presence of natural resources within an ethnically distinct region can foster secessionist or territorial conflict while having no effect on governmental conflict. This explanation builds on re-distributional arguments since it implies that the ethnic group can gain financially from independence by being able to keep all resource-related revenues for themselves. At the same time, past and current monetary payoffs of natural resources are assumed to have benefitted the defensive capabilities of the central state which is why territorial ambitions are limited to the objective of secession.

Focusing on a grievance-related mechanism, Basedau and Pierskalla (2014) as well as Asal et al. (2016) have made recent contributions which highlight the importance of the political status of ethnic groups living in the extraction region. Basedau and Pierskalla (2014) present a positive association between oil and conflict which disappears when the local population enjoys a monopoly over national-level political institutions. On the other hand, Asal et al. (2016) are able to find evidence in favor of a positive interaction effect between oil and exclusion which together raise the risk of conflict even more than the effect of political exclusion by itself.

Although these studies are able to present some evidence concerning the relevance of natural resources, and oil in particular, in explaining community mobilization, a consensus regarding the causal mechanisms linking resource production, mobilization and violence has yet to be established (Kuhn 2018). This is why qualitative analyses have become so important in this respect. As the case studies in chapters 5 through 8 of this volume will demonstrate, they are very useful in complementing the existing quantitative literature by highlighting the causal mechanisms at play.

Due to its stronger emphasis on the national context they allow a closer look at opportunity-based mechanisms. One example for this would be the study of Dube and Vargas (2013) which looks at conflict in Columbia and finds significant effects of price shocks on the level of conflict. Higher prices for natural resources can thereby enhance the opportunity of a rebel to take up arms, while higher prices for cash crops have the opposite effect by providing potential recruits a lucrative alternative source of income. Contrary to this "greed"-based argument, other opportunity-related mechanisms have also been explored. Engels (2017) identifies a "window of opportunity" in the case of Burkina Faso, where a regime change led to more protests in mining areas due to the fact that extraction companies lost crucial access to the governing elites as well as because national protests gave impetus for further demonstrations at the local level (Engels 2017, 164).

Apart from fluctuations of price levels and domestic political changes, shocks regarding transparency can also encourage mobilization. In this case NGOs as well as the action of foreign governments come into play, since they can ease access to information and thereby either increase awareness of injustices or change the facts on the ground by affecting the behavior of the extraction companies themselves.

So far, most case studies have again centered around the effects of oil and gas. One of the most prominent examples comes from Watts (2004) who looks at oil-rich regions in the Niger Delta. While highlighting the importance of pre-existing political dynamics he sees the associations between oil and conflict as stemming from the centralized resource revenues which accompany the extraction of oil. Other case studies such as Mähler and Pierskalla (2015), who study natural gas extraction and conflict in Bolivia, as well as Basedau, Mähler and Shabafrouz (2014) who look at Algeria, Nigeria, Iran and Venezuela, find similar observations: Mähler and Pierskalla (2015) stress that high-value natural resources combined with "local potential for indigenous mobilization" can encourage conflict to occur. Similarly, Basedau, Mähler and Shabafrouz (2014) find that national and subnational economic grievances, the cohesion of the opposition as well as the responsiveness of the political system play a major role in explaining the occurrence of violence. It remains however an open question whether the same observations hold true with regard to lower value non-fuel resources which often share quite different characteristics.[4]

Step 4: The extractors' reaction

Extractors faced with resistance activities have the choice of accommodating or repressing them (Cederman, Gleditsch and Buhaug 2013, Ch. 3). Violent conflict becomes especially likely in case extracting parties opt for a repressive response. Ruthless governments and extractive companies see no particular value in placating grievances, whether due to racism, ideological rigidity or a feeling that they can get away with it because of the local population's political weakness. Radical forms of laissez-faire free-market ideology can also contribute to conditions that remove constraints on extracting companies. In these cases, resource extraction typically goes hand in hand with a systematic campaign of marginalization and sometimes even outright repression, which may reach a higher level of intensity than was the case before the discovery of the resources (Aspinall 2007).

The resource curse literature warns that resource abundance often goes along with rent-seeking and bad governance, because extractive revenues offer ruling elites a source of income without having to rely on taxation and public good production (Karl 1997). In their much-cited article, Fearon and Laitin (2003) argue that in particular oil extraction tends to undermine the governments' knowledge about, and interest in, peripheral regions. This means that the rulers encounter difficulties separating rebels from other citizens, which may lead to brutal interventions that are prone to trigger violence.

More specifically related to mining, Steinberg (2018) finds that the location of mineral resource extraction matters. Her analysis shows that extractive activities in peripheral areas, far away from the capital, are more prone to trigger escalating protest than areas closer to the capital. According to this finding, governments are less likely to repress in more central areas of the country since the risk of resistance can be expected to be higher there. This mechanism resembles Roessler's (2011) general argument that governments in Sub-Saharan Africa have been prone to accept low-level civil war in the periphery rather than risking coups in the capital.

As argued above, however, repression of resistance is not the only response of extractors. In fact, resource revenues may enable governments to "buy off" potential protesters, for instance through generous investments in public goods (Ross 2001, Paine 2016). The Middle East, including especially oil-rich regimes in the Persian Gulf, offer good examples for this dynamic even though it remains contested as to how successful such strategies are in reducing dissent (Okruhlik 1999). From a less cynical but more general perspective, however, governmental brutality, especially in terms of one-sided violence, has become rarer around the world (Valentino 2014). Since the mid-1990s, an internal "accommodative regime" has yielded more inclusive politics and a willingness to engage in pragmatic compromises based on extended group rights, territorial and governmental power sharing and general democratization (Gurr 2000; Cederman, Gleditsch and Wucherpfennig 2017). This regime also extends to the private sector under the heading of "corporate social responsibility" (Campbell 2012) as the mining industry in particular has come under more scrutiny in their relations with affected populations (Conde and Le Billon 2017). This change has fortunately led to growing interest within the extractive industry in favor of cooperative solutions that serve to prevent violent conflict and are, in addition, often supported by international development community's efforts to encourage civil society organizations' defense of human rights (Franks 2012, IFC 2014; see also Bezzola 2020). Gradually, representatives of extracting elites have started to realize that cooperative solutions including compensation and empowerment of affected populations may be more cost effective than brutal suppression of protest (Frederiksen 2018, 497).

Whether these initiatives have been effective is still a matter of debate and it is still far from obvious if these measures have in fact managed to prevent resource conflict around the world. Based on a global sample from 1946 through 2006, Rustad and Binningsbø (2012) argue that the presence of natural resources in post-conflict situations increases the risk of conflict recurrence, because the resources' value is worth fighting for. Likewise, Frynas (2005) casts doubt on oil companies' commitment to corporate social responsibility and evidence from Peru shows that there is also no guarantee that redistribution of mining revenues through decentralization will prevent violent protest (Arellano-Yanguas 2011). Clearly, when it comes to effective implementation of specific schemes of revenue sharing, the devil is in the detail (Ross, Lujala and Rustad 2012).

2 MINERAL RESOURCES AND CONFLICT: AN ANALYTICAL OVERVIEW

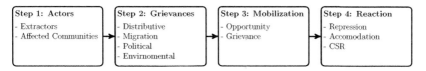

Fig. 2.1 Visual illustration of our four-step approach and the important distinctions discussed in each step

Given the inclusiveness of the literature, this volume attempts to further analyze what could reduce resource conflict. If the link between resources and conflict runs at least partly through inequality and grievances, then grievance-reduction may be a good avenue for conflict reduction (see Stewart 2018). These measures present promising opportunities regarding the key actors in these processes, including resident populations, governments and extraction companies (Fig. 2.1).

2.2 ENDOGENEITY AND OTHER METHODOLOGICAL CONSIDERATIONS

Regardless of the specific mechanism postulated, empirical researchers have to confront the difficult challenge of causal inference. Indeed, a growing number of scholars focusing primarily on petroleum extraction argue that many of the initial "resource curse" findings may be the result of spurious inference (see e.g. Brunnschweiler and Bulte 2009; Mitchell and Thies 2012; Cotet and Tsui 2013; Lei and Michaels 2014). In particular, there are several reasons to believe that whether, and to what degree a given country or region exhibits mineral resource production is not determined exogenously, but the result of socio-political and economic factors. One such confounding variable is the quality of political institutions.

Some authors argue that countries featuring poor institutions are more likely to rely on an oversized mining sector because they are unable to establish competitive manufacturing and service industries (Ross 2004; Haber and Menaldo, 2011). Since weak, inefficient states are also more likely to experience violence, this mechanism would imply that previous studies have overstated the resource-conflict link. Others suggest that weak institutions may be associated with fewer mining projects, as weak property rights disincentivize investments in extractive infrastructure (Cotet and Tsui, 2013; Torvik, 2009). In this case, previous studies would have underestimated the gravity of the resource curse.

Another potential threat to inference arises due to reverse causality. In particular, the mere prospect of political violence may deter investments in extractive infrastructure. In this alternative case, correlational analyses would underestimate the risks associated with mining, as the most dangerous locations never actually see mineral resource production. Several strategies have been proposed to address these endogeneity problems. One popular approach is to dismiss between-unit variance and focus solely on how resource extraction and political violence covary over time. This design eliminates bias caused by unmeasured time-invariant confounders such as political institutions (e.g. Cotet and Tsui 2013; Haber and Menaldo 2011). This is also the strategy Christensen (2019) relies on in his study of mineral resource production in Africa. In particular, following the standard diff-in-diff setup, he shows that areas with newly opened mines exhibit elevated levels of political protest, while featuring pre-treatment levels of protest comparable to non-mining areas. In a similar study, Berman et al. (2017) take a slightly different approach, using fluctuations in world commodity prices as an exogenous source of variation in the market value of local African mineral resource deposits. Hence, like Christensen (2019), they dismiss cross-sectional variation as potentially biased, and only compare levels of violence within a geographic unit over time, finding that conflict-related events are more frequent when the locally available resources are more valuable.

Lei and Michaels (2014) as well as Cotet and Tsui (2013) get around the problem of endogeneity by relying on giant oil discoveries. Their results are however not congruent which is why certain doubts regarding this specific method remain.

Taking advantage of a natural experiment, Vicente (2010) presents with a difference-in-difference estimation, another strategy for solving the same problem: Although focusing on the corruption side of the oil-curse, the author looks at two similar island nations, Sao Tome and Principe compared to Cape Verde, in order to detect the effects of oil discoveries in the former. The results emphasize that even in countries with relatively good institutions the sudden discovery of natural resources can reduce their quality (Van Der Ploeg and Poelhekke 2017, 208).

In addition, case studies can contribute helpful information about causal processes, especially when combined with quantitative studies

(Sambanis 2004). With their help, it becomes possible to investigate mechanism-based arguments that can only be superficially explored with large-N cross-sectional data and methods. Following up this idea in practice, Collier and Sambanis's (2005) two volumes expose Collier and Hoeffler's (2004) model of civil war to detailed scrutiny covering cases around the world. Rather than merely attempting to confirm the original model, the chapter authors critically evaluate the original theory and propose a series of modifications and amendments in response to empirical challenges.

Inspired by these advances, the current volume relies on a series of methodologies to cope with endogeneity. Focusing on a large number of cases across the world, the quantitative investigation in Chapters 3 introduces an instrumental-variable approach in order to improve causal inference. Following up this study and focusing on cases of mining in sub-Saharan Africa, Chapter 4 approximates a difference-in-differences setup only relying on within-case variation over time. The remaining, case-based chapters use qualitative techniques as a way to study resource extraction in specific countries. They thus add welcome context and detail to the sparser findings of Chapters 3 and 4.

2.3 Going Beyond the Oil-Conflict Nexus

The grievance-based scenarios sketched in Sect. 2.1 are primarily inspired by a series of prominent ethno-regional conflicts involving petroleum, as for example the secessionist civil war that pitted Aceh against Djakarta. Offering further elaboration of this logic while focusing on oil extraction, Chapter 3 offers a systematic test of these arguments. In these cases, the high cost and technical complexity of extraction call for major state involvement, with potentially far-reaching consequences for the grievance repertoire introduced above. In particular, it can be expected that extraction has repercussions that go well beyond environmental grievances.

To what extent can we generalize from this mostly petroleum-focused account to other types of natural resources, such as non-fuel minerals? So far, the systematic literature on mining and conflict has offered little evidence backing up the role of grievances in this context. For example, in their quantitative study of mining and conflict, Berman et al. (2017) exploits time trends and price shocks while discussing a series of possible mechanisms, including grievances, but put the most weight on an opportunity-driven mechanism based on rebel finance. In a similar study of the same causal link, Christensen (2019) explicitly rejects mechanisms operating through inequality and grievances. Contrary to this finding there are however qualitative studies of mining and conflict that put the blame on grievances, see for instance Hilson (2006).

In the following, we discuss the extent to which the extraction of non-fuel minerals affects conflict differently from the petroleum cases by using the four-step process. Since the literature on mining tends to be somewhat younger than its oil equivalent, this discussion has to be somewhat speculative. Despite this uncertainty, however, it is useful to form some theoretical expectations to guide the analysis in the empirical chapters of the book.

Starting with Step 1, concerning extractors, it can be expected that extraction of most non-fuel minerals requires somewhat less elaborate installations compared to those needed by the petroleum industry. This in turn implies that, on average, mining may involve less state involvement than does petroleum exploitation. Yet, this conjecture needs to be assessed against the backdrop of general state retrenchment since the 1990s that appears to have reduced governmental involvement in the extraction of both fuel and non-fuel minerals. For example, Campbell (2012) describes how a partly externally imposed reform process, led by the World Bank, has led to privatization of the mining industry in African countries.

In terms of Step 2, a plausible case can be made that all four types of grievances that were identified in petroleum-related cases such as Aceh also apply to extractive processes involving non-fuel minerals, although in some cases to a somewhat lesser extent:

- Distributional grievances: While the value of non-fuel resources is often lower than in the case of oil, there are good reasons to believe that they can also trigger distributional grievances. Conflicts over the ownership of major mineral deposits are known to have escalated to full-fledged civil war, as in the well-known case of Katanga in the 1960s (Larmer and Kennes 2019, 369). Indeed, if large-scale mining projects motivate state expansion into the region in question, this would tend to have far-reaching consequences for politics and social relations as well. For example, it would seem that there are clear parallels between the Indonesian state plunging into Aceh in its search for gas-driven profits, and the Indian state's state penetration project in Odisha (see Chapter 5), and possibly also in how the search for natural resources in Guatemala prompted the state to push into the northern area bordering Mexico.

- Migration-related grievances : It is also reasonable to assume that mining attracts foreign, or at least non-local, skilled labor who are typically better remunerated than the local population, which in turn may trigger grievances. However, compared to oil, it is possible that the required skill level is not quite on a par with fuel extraction, at least once the mining operation has entered service.

- Political grievances: If state involvement is less prominent in mining than in the oil industry, then we would expect local and regional political elites to be less threatened by extractive projects, although this will ultimately depend on the particular case.

- Environmental grievances: Since some types of non-fuel extraction, such as open-pit mining, are associated with vastly negative externalities, including relocation of entire villages and major environmental disasters, there is no particular reason to believe that environmental grievances would be less serious when it comes to such cases as opposed to petroleum extraction.

For these reasons, mining can also be expected to trigger mobilization processes that protest against extractive activities as anticipated by Step 3. However, to the extent that the value involved is lower than in the case of oil, protests are likely to be more local and less organized than in regular rebel organizations fighting a civil war. If the state is less directly involved as well, the reaction to extraction could be more about staging protest that could rise to riots and protests rather than armed resistance. Indeed, Christensen's (2019) study of African mining is able to find evidence of a link from resources to protest activities, but not to armed civil conflict.

Finally, in terms of Step 4, it is unclear whether governments are more willing to accommodate resource-related grievances in cases of non-fuel minerals compared to oil and gas. Given that in the latter cases the stakes are oftentimes higher, distributional and other grievances are likely to be intense and widely held. If that is the case, however, the likelihood of repression may be higher since both extractors and the local communities are less prone to back down, which increases the risk of political violence. In contrast, since claims responding to mining can be expected to be more local and less far-reaching, such instances may invite more willingness by the extractors to find a grievance-reducing compromise. The extractors' reaction also hinges on whether this actor category is composed of primarily the state or private companies. Foreign companies based in developed countries may be more open to inclusive and non-violent bargains if they are exposed to pressure in favor of democratic and inclusive institutions, but as we have argued above, there is no systematic evidence showing that such commercial actors will succumb to the pressure.

Notes

1. However, since then there has been a convergence on "opportunities" rather than "greed" (see e.g. Collier et al. 2009).
2. Such a system of ethnic stratification can be conceptualized as "internal colonialism" where persistent structures of ethnopolitical dominance coincide with economic "ethnic division of labor," very much as in classical cases of colonialism (Hechter 1975, see also Scott 1972).
3. The sons-of-the-soil dynamic can also feature processes not driven by the state (see Fearon and Laitin 2011).
4. See the different resource characteristics introduced by Le Billon (2001, 2005).

References

Arellano-Yanguas, Javier. 2011. "Aggravating the Resource Curse: Decentralisation, Mining and Conflict in Peru." *Journal of Development Studies* 47: 617–638.

Asal, Victor, Michael Findley, James A. Piazza, and James Igoe Walsh. 2016. "Political Exclusion, Oil, and Ethnic Armed Conflict." *Journal of Conflict Resolution* 60: 1343–1367.

Aspinall, Edward. 2007. "The Construction of Grievance - Natural Resources and Identity in a Separatist Conflict." *Journal of Conflict Resolution* 51: 950–972.

Andrews, Tony, Jonathan Gamu, Philippe Le Billon, Chang Hoon Oh, David Reyes and Jioung Shin. 2018. *The Role of Host Governments in Enabling or Preventing Conflict Associated with Mining*. Report UNDP and CIRDI.

Ballard, Chris, and Glenn Banks. 2003. "Resource Wars: The Anthropology of Mining." *Annual Review of Anthropology* 32: 287–313.

Basedau, Matthias, and Jan Henryk Pierskalla. 2014. "How Ethnicity Conditions the Effect of Oil and Gas on Civil Conflict: A Spatial Analysis of Africa from 1990 to 2010." *Political Geography* 38: 1–11.

Basedau, Matthias, Annegret Mähler, and Miriam Shabafrouz. 2014. "Drilling Deeper: A Systematic, Context-Sensitive Investigation of Causal Mechanisms in the Oil– Conflict Link." *Journal of Development Studies* 50: 51–63.

Bezzola, Selina. 2020. "The consequences of Corporate Social Responsibilities for mining communities in Africa." Doctoral dissertation, SNF Zürich.

Berman, Nicolas, Mathieu Couttenier, Dominic Rohner, and Mathias Thoenig. 2017. "This Mine Is Mine! How Minerals Fuel Conflicts in Africa." *American Economic Review* 107: 1564–1610.

Brunnschweiler, Christa N., and Erwin H. Bulte. 2009. "Natural Resources and Violent Conflict: Resource Abundance, Dependence and the Onset of Civil Wars." *Oxford Economic Papers* 61 (4): 651–674.

Campbell, Bonnie. 2012. "Corporate Social Responsibility and Development in Africa: Redefining the Roles and Responsibilities of Public and Private Actors in the Mining Sector." *Resources Policy* 37: 138–143.

Cederman, Lars-Erik, and Kristian Skrede Gleditsch. 2009. "Introduction to Special Issue on 'Disaggregating Civil War'." *Journal of Conflict Resolution* 53: 487–95.

Cederman, Lars-Erik., Kristian Skrede Gleditsch, and Halvard Buhaug. 2013. *Inequality, Grievances and Civil War*. New York: Cambridge University Press.

Cederman, Lars-Erik., Kristian Skrede Gleditsch, and Julian Wucherpfennig. 2017. "Predicting the Decline of Ethnic Conflict: Was Gurr Right and for the Right Reasons?" *Journal of Peace Research* 54: 262–274.

Christensen, Darin. 2019. "Concession Stands: How Mining Investments Incite Protest in Africa." *International Organization* 73: 65–101.

Collier, Paul, and Anke Hoeffler. 1998. "On Economic Causes of Civil War." *Oxford Economic Papers* 50 (4): 563–573.

Collier, Paul, and Anke Hoeffler. 2004. "Greed and Grievance in Civil Wars." *Oxford Economic Papers* 56: 563–595.

Collier, Paul, Anke Hoeffler, and Dominic Rohner. 2009. "Beyond Greed and Grievance: Feasibility and Civil War." *Oxford Economic Papers* 61: 1–27.

Collier, Paul, and Nicholas Sambanis, eds. 2005. *Understanding Civil War: Evidence and Analysis*. Vol. 1 & 2. Washington, DC: The World Bank.

Conde, Marta, and Philippe Le Billon. 2017. "Why Do Some Communities Resist Mining Projects While Others Do Not?" *Extractive Industries and Society* 4: 681–697.

Cotet, Anca M., and Kevin K. Tsui. 2013. "Oil and Conflict: What Does the Cross Country Evidence Really Show?" *American Economic Journal: Macroeconomics* 5 (1): 49–80.

Dube, Oeindrila, and Juan F. Vargas. 2013. "Commodity Price Shocks and Civil Conflict: Evidence from Colombia." *Review of Economic Studies* 80: 1384–1421.

Emirbayer, Mustafa. 1997. "Manifesto for a Relational Sociology." *American Journal of Sociology* 103: 281–317.

Engels, Bettina. 2017. "Not All Glitter Is Gold: Mining Conflicts in Burkina Faso." In *Contested Extractivism, Society and the State: Struggles over Mining and Land*, ed. Bettina Engels and Kristina Dietz. London: Palgrave Macmillan

Fearon, James D., and David D. Laitin. 2003. "Ethnicity, Insurgency, and Civil War." *American Political Science Review* 97: 75–90.

Fearon, James D., and David D. Laitin. 2011. "Sons of the Soil, Migrants, and Civil War." *World Development* 39 (2): 199–211.

Franks, D. 2012. Social Impact Assessment of Resource Projects. International Mining for Development Centre: Mining for Development: Guide to Australian Practice.

Frederiksen, Thomas. 2018. "Corporate Social Responsibility, Risk and Development in the Mining Industry." *Resources Policy* 59: 495–505.

Frynas, Jedrzej George. 2005. "The False Developmental Promise of Corporate Social Responsibility: Evidence from Multinational Oil Companies." *International Affairs* 81: 581–598.

Gamson, William. 1992. *Talking Politics*. New York NY: Cambridge University Press.

Gurr, Ted Robert. 2000. "Ethnic Warfare on the Wane." *Foreign Affairs* 79: 52–64.

Haber, Stephen, and Victor Menaldo. 2011. "Do Natural Resources Fuel Authoritarianism? A Reappraisal of the Resource Curse." *American Political Science Review* 105 (01): 1–26.

Hechter, Michael. 1975. *Internal Colonialism: The Celtic Fringe in British National Development, 1536–1966*. London UK: Routledge.

Hechter, Michael. 2000. Containing Nationalism. Oxford: Oxford University Press.

Hilson, Christopher, J. 2006. "Mining and Civil Conflict: Revisiting Grievance at Bougainville, Minerals & Energy." Raw Material Report 21 (2): 23–35.

Humphreys, Macartan. 2005. "Natural Resources, Conflict, and Conflict Resolution." *Journal of Conflict Resolution* 49 (4): 508–537.

IFC. 2014. *Sustainable and Responsible Mining in Africa*. The World Bank Group: International Finance Corporation.

Karl, Terry L. 1997. *The Paradox of Plenty: Oil Booms and Petro-States*. Berkeley, CA: University of California Press.

Kell, Tim. 2010. *The Roots of the Acehnese Rebellion, 1989–1992*. Singapore: Equinox Publishing.

Kirsch, Stuart. 2014. *Mining Capitalism: The Relationship between Corporations and their Critics*. Los Angeles and San Francisco: University of California Press.
Koubi, Vally, Gabriele Spilker, Tobias Böhmelt, and Thomas Bernauer. 2014. Do Natural Resources Matter for Interstate and Intrastate Armed Conflict? *Journal of Peace Research* 51 (2): 227–243.
Kuhn, Annegret. 2018. "Explaining Ethnic Mobilization against Resource Extraction: How Collective Action Frames, Motives, and Opportunities Interact." *Studies in Conflict & Terrorism* 41: 388–407.
Larmer, Miles and Erik Kennes. 2019. "Katanga's Secessionism in the Democratic Republic of Congo." In Secessionism in African Politics: Aspiration, Grievance, Performance, Disenchantment, ed. Lotje de Vries, Pierre Englebert and Mareike Schomerus. Cham: Springer International Publishing.
Le Billon, Philippe. 2001. "The Political Ecology of War: Natural Resources and Armed Conflicts." *Political Geography* 20: 561–584.
Le Billon, Philippe. 2005. "Resources and Armed Conflicts." *The Adelphi Papers* 45: 29–49.
Lei, Yu-Hsiang, and Guy Michaels. 2014. "Do Giant Oilfield Discoveries Fuel Internal Armed Conflicts?" *Journal of Development Economics* 110: 139–157.
Lujala, Päivi. 2010. "The Spoils of Nature: Armed Civil Conflict and Rebel Access to Natural Resources." *Journal of Peace Research* 47 (1): 15–28.
Mähler, Annegret, and Jan H. Pierskalla. 2015. "Indigenous Identity, Natural Resources, and Contentious Politics in Bolivia: A Disaggregated Conflict Analysis, 2000–2011." *Comparative Political Studies* 48: 301–332.
Mitchell, Sara McLaughlin., and Cameron G. Thies. 2012. "Resource Curse in Reverse: How Civil Wars: Influence Natural Resource Production." *International Interactions* 38 (2): 218–242.
Murshed, S. Mansoob., and Scott Gates. 2005. "Spatial-Horizontal Inequality and the Maoist Insurgency in Nepal." *Review of Development Economics* 9: 121–134.
Okruhlik, Gwenn. 1999. "Rentier Wealth, Unruly Law, and the Rise of Opposition: The Political Economy of Oil States." *Comparative Politics* 31 (3): 295–315.
Østby, Gudrun, Ragnhild Nordås, and Jan Ketil Rød. 2009. "Regional Inequalities and Civil Conflict in Sub-Saharan Africa." *International Studies Quarterly* 53: 301–324.
Paine, Jack. 2016. "Rethinking the 'Resource Curse': How Oil Wealth Prevents Center-Seeking Civil Wars." *International Organization* 70: 727–761.
Roessler, Philip G. 2011. "The Enemy from Within. Personal Rule, Coups, and Civil Wars in Africa." *World Politics* 53: 300–346.
Ross, Michael L. 2001. "Does Oil Hinder Democracy?" *World Politics* 53 (3): 325–361.

Ross, Michael L. 2004. "What Do We Know about Natural Resources and Civil War?" *Journal of Peace Research* 41 (3): 337–356.

Ross, Michael L. 2006. "A Closer Look at Oil, Diamonds, and Civil War." *Annual Review of Political Science* 9: 965–300.

Ross, Michael L. 2007. "How mineral-rich states can reduce inequality." In *Escaping the resource curse*. Edited by Macartan Humphreys, Jeffrey D. Sachs and Joseph E. Stiglitz.

Ross, Michael L. 2015. "What Have We Learned About the Resource Curse?" *Annual Review of Political Science* 18: 239–259.

Ross, Michael L., Päivi Lujala, and Siri A. Rustad. 2012. "Horizontal Inequality, Decentralizing the Distribution of Natural Resources Revenues, and Peace." In *High- Value Natural Resources and Post-Conflict Peacebuilding*. Edited by Päivi Lujala and Siri A. Rustad.

Rustad, Siri Aas, and Helga Malmin Binningsbø. 2012. "A Price Worth Fighting for? Natural Resources and Conflict Recurrence." *Journal of Peace Research* 49 (4): 531–546.

Sambanis, Nicholas. 2004. "Using Case Studies to Expand Economic Models of Civil War." *Perspectives on Politics* 2: 259–279.

Scott, James C. 1972. "Patron-Client Politics and Political Change in Southeast Asia." *American Political Science Review* 66 (1): 91–113.

Sexton, Renard. 2020. "Unpacking the Local Resource Curse: How Externalities and Governance Shape Social Conflict." *Journal of Conflict Resolution* 64 (4): 640–673.

Sorens, Jason. 2011. "Mineral Production, Territory, and Ethnic Rebellion: The Role of Rebel Constituencies." *Journal of Peace Research* 48: 571–585.

Steinberg, Jessica. 2018. "Protecting the Capital? On African Geographies of Protest Escalation and Repression." *Political Geography* 62: 12–22.

Stewart, Frances, ed. 2009. *Horizontal Inequalities and Conflict: Understanding Group Violence in Multiethnic Societies*. Houndmills: Palgrave Macmillan.

Stewart, Frances. 2018. "Can horizontal inequalities be overcome?" Human Development Report. http://hdr.undp.org/en/content/can-horizontal-inequalities-be-overcome.

Stewart, Frances, Graham K. Brown, and Arnim Langer. 2009. "Major Findings and Conclusions on the Relationship between Horizontal Inequalities and Conflict." In *Horizontal Inequalities and Conflict: Understanding Group Violence in Multiethnic Societies*. Edited by Frances Stewart. Houndmills: Palgrave Macmillan.

Tilly, Charles. 1978. *From Mobilization to Revolution*. New York: McGraw-Hill.

Torvik, Ragnar. 2009. "Why Do Some Resource-Abundant Countries Succeed While Others Do Not?" *Oxford Review of Economic Policy* 25 (2): 241–256.

Valentino, Benjamin A. 2014. "Why We Kill: The Political Science of Political Violence against Civilians." *Annual Review of Political Science* 17: 89–103.

Van Der Ploeg, Frederick and Steven Poelhekke. 2017. "The Impact of Natural Resources: Survey of Recent Quantitative Evidence." *The Journal of Development Studies* 53: 205–216.

Vicente, Pedro C. 2010. "Does Oil Corrupt? Evidence From a Natural Experiment in West Africa." *Journal of Development Economics* 92: 28–38.

Watts, Michael. 2004. "Resource Curse? Governmentality, Oil and Power in the Niger Delta, Nigeria." *Geopolitics* 9: 50–80.

Weiner, Myron. 1978. *Sons of the Soil: Migration and Ethnic Conflict in India.* Princeton NJ: Princeton University Press.

PART II

Statistical Studies

CHAPTER 3

No Extraction Without Representation: The Ethno-Regional Oil Curse and Secessionist Conflict

Philipp Hunziker and Lars-Erik Cederman

In order to set the stage for the empirical chapters of this book, this chapter returns to the link between petroleum and political violence. A vast and influential literature argues that oil-producing countries face a

---

This chapter was previously published as an article, see Hunziker and Cederman. 2017. "No Extraction Without Representation: The Ethno-Regional Oil Curse and Secessionist Conflict." *Journal of Peace Research* 54(3): 365–81. We are grateful to the participants of the 'The Political Economy of Inequality and Conflict' workshop at the University of Konstanz and the brown-bag participants at PRIO for their extremely useful comments and suggestions on earlier drafts of this article. We would also like to thank Lukas Dick for his help with compiling the ACOR data. Any remaining errors are the authors' responsibility. This research was supported by the Swiss National Science Foundation under COST action IS1107, SERI project C12.0087.

P. Hunziker
Google, Zürich, Switzerland

L.-E. Cederman (✉)
International Conflict Research, ETH Zürich, Zürich, Switzerland
e-mail: lcederman@ethz.ch

© The Author(s), under exclusive license to Springer Nature Switzerland AG 2022
H. E. Ali and L.-E. Cederman (eds.), *Natural Resources, Inequality and Conflict*, https://doi.org/10.1007/978-3-030-73558-6_3

significantly larger risk of civil conflict than other states (Koubi et al. 2014; Ross 2015).[1] With the recent example of the Islamic State and its reliance on oil revenue to finance combat in Iraq and Syria, the relationship between oil and violence has also attracted significant attention from policymakers (World Bank 2011). In addition to its apparent effect on the outbreak of violence, oil has also been associated with autocratic regimes and weak economic growth, giving rise to the concept of an "oil curse" (Ross 2012).

Notwithstanding its status as "stylized fact," the oil-conflict link has recently come under attack. As we have shown in the previous chapter, critics rightly argue that the statistical evidence underlying much of the oil curse literature may be biased. These skeptics argue that oil production is not a random treatment, but an industrial activity subject to economic and political incentives. Consequently, correlational evidence of the oil-conflict link may be misleading. Indeed, once this inferential threat is addressed with more sophisticated research designs, the empirical support for a causal effect of oil on conflict becomes inconclusive (e.g. Brunnschweiler and Bulte 2009; Mitchell and Thies 2012; Cotet and Tsui 2013).

Despite these suggestive findings, the question of whether there is an oil curse remains open for several reasons. First, most causal identification strategies proposed in the literature are vulnerable to reverse causality. Second, research designs that focus on within-country variance or only on oil discoveries may help eliminating omitted variable bias, but discard so much information that they potentially conceal a positive effect. Third, focusing on empirics at the country level, the criticism of the oil curse literature has so far been largely detached from the debate about the theoretical underpinnings of the oil-conflict link.

This chapter addresses these challenges directly. First, we employ geospatial data on the location of sedimentary basins as a new spatially disaggregated instrument for petroleum production that offers a much more solid basis for causal inference than previous attempts to deal with endogeneity. Combined with newly introduced geocoded information on the exact location of productive oil and gas fields, this identification strategy enables us to reevaluate whether the oil curse is causal.

Second, beyond merely testing the existence of the oil-conflict link, we also argue that it is best explained as an *ethno-regional* oil curse. Petroleum extraction in regions inhabited by locally concentrated ethnic groups risks provoking secessionist violence, especially if locals see few of the benefits of oil production, while bearing most of its costs. This account differs from alternative explanations that locate the origins of the oil-conflict link at the individual or governmental levels.

Our empirical analysis confirms that petroleum extraction exerts a large and positive causal effect on the probability of violent conflict. Furthermore, in line with our ethno-regional argument, we find that the oil-conflict link originates in regions inhabited by territorially concentrated ethnic groups that seek secession. Moreover, this effect is particularly large for ethnic minorities that are politically excluded from the national executive. Finally, the results also show that studies that fail to correct for endogeneity tend to underestimate the effect of oil on conflict, especially at the sub-national level.

The remainder of this chapter is structured as follows. The next three sections review the literature, introduce our theoretical framework, and derive testable hypotheses. A subsequent section introduces the main datasets. We then test whether there is an oil curse, followed by an evaluation of our ethno-regional argument. Finally, the concluding section discusses the consequences of our analysis for theory and policy.

3.1 The Oil Curse and Its Critics

The claim that oil causes the outbreak of civil war is well established (for recent reviews, see Koubi et al. 2014; Ross 2015). Under the general heading of an "oil curse" (Ross 2012), this result is often cited in combination with the related findings that oil hinders democratization (e.g. Ross 2001) and economic growth (e.g. Sachs and Warner 1995).

As shown in Sect. 2.1 above, however, a growing number of scholars challenge this consensus while asserting that most statistical analyses in support of the oil curse make causal claims based on the incorrect premise that petroleum production is exogenous to societal outcomes (see, e.g., Brunnschweiler and Bulte 2009; Mitchell and Thies 2012; Cotet and Tsui 2013; Lei and Mitchaels 2014). They argue that whether, and to what extent a given country or region produces oil is not exogenously given, but determined by socio-political and economic factors.

Several mechanisms may cause such endogeneity. The most obvious one is the immediate negative effect that large-scale violence exerts on a country's ability to extract oil and gas. Unless accounted for, these effects may attenuate estimates of the oil-conflict link (Ross 2004). A second potential source of endogeneity is that oil-producing states may be structurally different in ways that affect their conflict propensity, but are difficult to observe or measure. In which direction this type of endogeneity biases estimates of the oil-conflict link depends on the underlying argument. Some authors argue that weak states are more likely to rely on an oversized oil industry because they are unable to establish competitive manufacturing and service sectors (Ross 2004, 338; Haber and Menaldo 2011, 2). Since weak and inefficient states are also more likely to experience violence, this mechanism would imply that previous studies have overstated the oil-conflict link. In contrast, Cotet and Tsui (2013, 50) and Torvik (2009, 245) suggest that fragile institutions may be associated with *less* oil production, because weak property rights disincentivize investments in extractive infrastructure. In this case, previous studies would have underestimated the gravity of the oil curse. Finally, another plausible source of endogeneity is long-term reverse causality. Specifically, the mere anticipation of conflict may deter prospective investors from financing oil exploration and extraction projects (Brunnschweiler and Bulte 2009, 654). This mechanism leads to an underestimation of the oil-conflict link, as particularly conflict-prone countries will systematically host less oil production.

A number of recent studies attempt to address endogeneity by reevaluating the oil-conflict link with more sophisticated causal identification strategies. First, some authors employ fixed effects panels, hoping to eliminate bias due to unobservable cross-country differences. Based on this strategy, Cotet and Tsui (2013) find no such effect. Similarly, Haber and Menaldo (2011) conclude that once unobserved cross-country differences are accounted for, there is no evidence for the claim that oil hinders democratization. Yet, fixed effects do not solve the issue of reverse causality. Moreover, removing all cross-country variance could produce false negatives, as differences between countries are an important source of explanatory power for analyzing political outcomes.

Another way to address endogeneity is to use an instrumental variable design. The merit of this approach depends on the quality of the instruments, which should be good predictors of oil production, exogenous to the outcome under investigation, without affecting the outcome through any other channel than oil. The latter two conditions are commonly known as the exclusion restriction. Yet, it is doubtful whether existing instruments meet these requirements. Instrumenting oil production through macroeconomic variables, Mitchell and Thies (2012) find no support for the oil-conflict link. However, it is debatable whether their instruments are good predictors of oil production, and these types of measures clearly do not meet the exclusion restriction.

As an alternative, other scholars use proven oil reserves as an instrument for resource dependence and oil production. Brunnschweiler and Bulte (2009) report that once instrumented, natural resource production no longer affects civil conflict. Similarly, Haber and Menaldo (2011) find no effect of oil production on regime type when using reserves as an instrument. While oil reserves certainly predict oil production, this variable is hardly exogenous to conflict. First, reverse causality may be an issue, as ongoing or anticipated conflict may not only deter oil production, but also oil exploration. Second, reserves are typically endogenous to structural economic or political factors, since the concept of "proven reserves" explicitly accounts for local socio-economic conditions.[2]

Finally, Cotet and Tsui (2013) and Lei and Michaels (2014) address endogeneity by relying on information about oil discoveries, rather than production. This method is appealing because assuming that exploration is taking place, discoveries are largely random, and thus approximate the ideal of an experimental 'random treatment'. Based on this approach, Cotet and Tsui (2013) find no evidence of an oil-conflict link, whereas Lei and Michaels (2014) report a positive effect for the case of *giant* fields. Yet, being limited to the analysis of newly discovered fields rather than the effects of total oil production, these studies arguably underestimate the true impact of petroleum on conflict.

3.2 If There is an Oil Curse, then Which One?

Since most skeptics question the very existence of the oil-conflict link, they say little about its underlying causal mechanisms. This theoretical deficit contrasts with the "embarrassment of mechanisms" (Humphreys, 2005) that characterizes most of the conventional literature. The question, then, is not only whether there is such a curse, but also which one.

Structuring our theoretical discussion according to levels of analysis, we start by considering the most influential explanations at the level of individual motivations and governmental structures, before discussing mechanisms located at the regional level. First, we summarize a set of mechanisms that highlight the motives of individuals under the heading of the *individualist oil curse*. Following the pioneering contributions by Collier and Hoeffler (1998), many scholars argue that natural resources trigger conflict by affecting the cost–benefit rationale of prospective rebels and warlords. Specifically, the expected revenue from trading valuable minerals and gemstones are assumed to motivate individuals to take up arms and challenge state authority. Moreover, this interpretation proposes that the financing of ongoing conflict by looting natural resource deposits and extorting resource extractors lowers the marginal costs of fighting (Collier and Hoeffler 2004, 565; see also Ross 2012, 151).

The main problem with these individualist interpretations of the resource-conflict link is that they are generally more convincing as accounts of conflict duration through rebel financing than as causes of conflict onset. While oil-fueled start-up funds are in principle possible, in most cases such a scenario is hardly feasible. In contrast to alluvial diamonds and drugs, the main problem pertains to lootability (Humphreys 2005). Indeed, oil extraction typically requires territorial control, or at least physical access. Most states and oil-extracting companies are capable of defending their installations. If rebels come to control petroleum production sites, they are already running successful campaigns, as illustrated by the Islamic State. As a rule, then, effective exploitation and marketing of oil require considerable resources that only a state or a state-like actor can field, thus casting doubt on the relevance of the individualist oil curse (Fearon 2005, 500).

At the country level, a class of mechanisms can be summarized as the *governmental oil curse*.

The most prominent explanation is based on the weak-state mechanism, which assumes that resource extraction does not affect the occurrence of rebellion directly, but prevents the state from prohibiting the rise of violent challengers in its periphery. Initially proposed by Fearon and Laitin (2003), this mechanism holds that the conflict-inducing effect of resource extraction runs via the latter's impact on government revenue. Freed from the need to generate tax-based revenue, oil-endowed states abstain from creating the type of intrusive institutions that are necessary for tax collection. Yet, the absence of a low-level administrative apparatus also prohibits the state from effectively policing its population, thus facilitating the organization of violent resistance against the state. An alternative account at the same level, sometimes referred to as the "honeypot effect," views the state as a lucrative target of enrichment, thus accounting for why greedy rebels would be motivated to topple the government (Fearon 2005; Le Billon 2005).

However, there are strong reasons to doubt the relevance of these country-level theories. While the perverting effects of petroleum on state-building appears plausible, such accounts overlook the obvious possibility that strategic governments should be able to deploy their often formidable oil revenues to defend against rebellious challenges (Colgan 2014, 7; Paine 2016). Regarding the argument of increased opportunity for capturing the state, this country-level mechanism also suffers from serious shortcomings. As explained by Ross (2012, 161), such a honeypot effect relies on unrealistic assumptions that fail to account for how collective action problems can be overcome.

Because of the theoretical weaknesses undermining both the individualist and the governmental oil curses, we shift our theoretical attention to the regional level. Our approach builds on previous ethno-regional explanations to develop a theoretical framework that accounts for when and why oil production leads to violent conflict. On this basis, we then derive a set of hypotheses that allow us to test not only whether the oil-conflict link exists, but also whether the ethno-regional approach provides more explanatory leverage than the alternative individualist and governmental versions of the oil curse.

The political economy of industrial oil and gas extraction has a number of properties that set it apart from other economic activities, making it particularly likely to evoke secessionist demands. First, whether oil extraction benefits the resident population in productive regions is almost entirely determined by policy. Unlike labor-intensive industries, such as plantation agriculture, oil extraction typically offers few employment opportunities for locals. However, because producers are relatively easily taxed, oil extraction typically generates large windfalls for the central government. Consequently, whether locals benefit from oil production is almost entirely a question of redistributive policy. As argued by proponents of the regional explanation of the oil-conflict link, this situation creates considerable incentives for locals to support secessionist movements. If oil-producing regions succeed in establishing an independent state, then the appropriation and redistribution of oil rents are relocated to the regional level, thus yielding a significant increase in per-capita payoffs to local residents (Collier and Hoeffler 2006; Sorens 2011; Ross 2012).

Absent strict regulation, oil production in populated areas is often associated with drastic negative externalities for the resident population. Numerous case studies document how oil production in developing countries may threaten local livelihoods through environmental pollution and large-scale land expropriation. For instance, Human Rights Watch (1999, 54) report oil spills and widespread pollution in the Niger Delta, Kell (2010, 37) discusses environmental and social externalities in Indonedisa's Aceh province, and Ramos (2012) documents the effects of oil production on fishing grounds in the Angolan Cabinda exclave. However, few central governments face incentives to address these externalities. While strict regulation benefits only a small part of the government's constituency, lax regulation provides the government with more funds to ensure its access to power. This dilemma creates additional incentives for locals to support groups advocating secessionism, simply as a means to ensure that local interests are represented in the regulation of oil extraction.[3]

The problems of rent redistribution and local externalities are particularly likely to spark violent secessionism if oil is extracted in the settlement area of territorially concentrated ethnic groups (Sorens 2011). This setting offers particularly fertile breeding grounds for local elites to mobilize support for secessionist goals by referencing petroleum-related grievances.

Territorially concentrated ethnic identities facilitate mobilization because they make promises over future oil-rent payoffs more credible. Clearly visible ethnic markers allow an unambiguous assessment of the future beneficiaries of independence, and thus attenuate the collective action problem associated with fighting for secession (e.g. Caselli and Coleman 2013). Further, ethnic differences between the "foreign" beneficiaries and the local victims of oil extraction will allow secessionist leaders to frame oil production as an issue of ethno-nationalist self-determination. Specifically, local elites may gather support for secession by framing grievances over unfair rent-distribution and the state's apparent indifference to local externalities as a problem of "internal colonialism" (Hechter 1975), whereby the "foreign" state is accused of illegitimately plundering locally-owned resources (see also Aspinall 2007). Finally, in regions inhabited by territorially concentrated ethnic groups, pre-existing intra-ethnic political and societal networks may be used to overcome the collective action problem inherent in political mobilization (Bates 1983).

In summary, these arguments imply the existence of an "ethno-regional oil curse": oil production in areas inhabited by locally concentrated ethnic groups is likely to cause widespread and easily mobilizable support for secessionism. Moreover, this mechanism is particularly relevant in regions inhabited by ethnic groups with limited control over government policy, which face the issues outlined above to their greatest extent.

Apart from its theoretical appeal, the ethno-regional account has also received tentative empirical support in recent years. Reanalyzing the relationship between oil production and center-seeking civil wars, Paine (2016) finds no evidence of an oil-conflict link once the positive impact of petroleum on governments' financial capabilities is taken into account. This finding runs counter to the weak-state and honeypot explanations of the oil curse. Furthermore, suggesting that the oil-conflict link may indeed operate at a regional level, Asal et al. (2016) and Morelli and Rohner (2015) find that oil-rich ethnic groups are particularly likely to engage in rebellion.

Despite these results, however, the empirical record of the ethno-regional explanation remains inconclusive. Most importantly, because the above-named studies do not account for endogeneity, it is questionable whether they permit strong theoretical conclusions. For instance, Paine's (2016) non-finding may be due to reverse causality since particularly vulnerable governments may be unable to maintain a large-scale petroleum industry. Another open question is whether the ethno-regional oil curse is limited to *secessionist* civil wars. While we expect this to be the case, Asal et al. (2016) and Morelli and Rohner (2015) do not distinguish between different types of conflict in their empirical analyses. Finally, it remains unclear whether the oil-conflict link is a function of political representation. Though these studies find that the oil-conflict effect is only statistically significant for groups without governmental representation, they do not test whether the oil-conflict effect is significantly different between politically included and excluded groups.

3.3 Observable Implications of the Ethno-Regional Oil Curse

In this section, we derive a number of observable implications from the ethno-regional account, and analyze how these differ from those yielded by the individualist and governmental explanations.

First, our theoretical discussion clearly implies that there *is* a causal oil-conflict link:

$H_{3.1}$: Oil extraction increases the risk of civil conflict.

Second, our theoretical framework implies that oil should be associated primarily with secessionist conflict. If locals support resistance against state rule due to the prospect of gaining exclusive access to local oil rents and being able to curb the externalities of oil extraction, then the more limited aim of secession is sufficient (Sorens 2011). In fact, even if assuming power over the central government were feasible, it implies that some fraction of local oil revenue would again have to be redistributed. In addition, the ethno-regional oil curse predominantly affects groups that are unlikely to succeed in center-seeking conflicts. Hence, we expect that

$H_{3.2}$: Oil extraction increases the risk of secessionist conflict.

Evaluating $H_{3.2}$ is important for two reasons. First, it serves as a critical test of our theory: if oil is *not* associated with secessionist, rather than center-seeking, civil wars, then the ethno-regional approach cannot explain the oil-conflict link. Second, this hypothesis evaluates the explanatory leverage of the ethno-regional argument in relation to other approaches. Specifically, evidence in favor of $H_{3.2}$ implies that the honeypot explanation for the oil-conflict link is insufficient.

Next, the ethno-regional argument implies that whether oil causes conflict depends on its evoking secessionist demands among the resident population in extractive regions. Whereas petroleum extraction in uninhabited areas neither threatens the livelihood of locals, nor evokes strong local ownership claims, in populated areas it should be associated with an increase in conflict risk. Thus, we postulate that

$H_{3.3}$: Only oil production in populated areas increases the risk of secessionist conflict.

Evaluating this hypothesis is important because it is inconsistent with the state-weakness and "honeypot" accounts. Since these alternative explanations rely on government revenue, rather than oil extraction, they imply that the local conditions of oil production should be inconsequential. Thus, $H_{3.2}$ suggests that there is an effect of oil on conflict that cannot be explained by these state-level mechanisms (cf. Lujala 2010).

Next, the ethno-regional mechanism implies that even if occurring in populated areas, oil extraction is more dangerous in some places than in others. Our theoretical argument suggests that territorially concentrated ethnic groups that lack governmental representation should be at a particularly high risk of reacting to oil extraction with secessionist demands. Hence, we expect that

$H_{3.4}$: Oil extraction has a particularly large effect on the risk of secessionist conflict in areas inhabited by locally concentrated ethnic groups that are excluded from central government.

Finally, demographic size also influences whether petroleum-producing ethnic groups engage in violent secessionism. Thus, we expect the ethno-regional oil curse to be particularly relevant for locally concentrated ethnic minorities. First, oil extraction in the territory of small, locally concentrated ethnic groups ensures that a significant proportion of group members is affected by the accompanying externalities, thus facilitating mobilization along ethnic lines. Second, demographic weight also has implications for the potential payoffs associated with independence. The smaller the size of a petroleum-producing group in relation to the rest of the country's population, the larger the potential increase in redistributive transfers if secession succeeds. Finally, limited demographic weight may also be relevant as very small minorities may feel that they are unable to defend their interests vis-à-vis larger ethnic groups even if they are presently represented in government. Thus, minorities may fear that even if the central government agrees to acceptable petroleum-related policies now, larger ethnic groups may easily renege on these promises in the future, thus creating an acute commitment problem (see e.g. Sorens 2011).

Given these considerations, we expect that

$H_{3.5}$: Oil extraction has a particularly large effect on the risk of secessionist conflict if it occurs in areas inhabited by an ethnic minority.

In order to distinguish our argument from alternative explanations, it is important to note that $H_{3.4}$ and $H_{3.5}$ are again incompatible with the state-weakness and honeypot mechanisms, as they postulate that the conditions under which oil is extracted determine whether it causes conflict. Moreover, evidence in support of $H_{3.4}$ and $H_{3.5}$ is also difficult to explain with individualist explanations, which imply that the relative demographic and political situation of the local populace in oil-extracting regions influences whether oil causes conflict. There is no reason to expect that opportunities for oil theft and extortion are affected by the ethnicity, relative demographic weight, or political representation of local residents. In contrast, these moderating factors are inherently regional, and evidence that they matter would support our argument that the oil-conflict link operates by causing widespread support for secessionist policies in oil-producing regions, rather than by affecting the incentive structure of prospective rebels.

3.4 Instrumenting and Measuring Oil: New Data

Addressing the endogeneity concerns discussed earlier, our identification strategy is to use information on the location and thickness of sedimentary basins to construct an instrumental variable (IV) for onshore oil and gas production. Sedimentary basins clearly meet the requirements for an IV design.

First, sedimentary basins are highly predictive of the location and extent of petroleum production, as they hold almost all of the world's recoverable oil and gas reserves (Hyne 2012, 17). The source of all oil and gas is organic matter that has been deposited in sedimentary material and then exposed to sufficiently high temperatures. These conditions are only given in particularly thick layers of sedimentary rock–called sedimentary basins–where geothermal energy is sufficiently high to trigger the formation of hydrocarbons. Second, the sediment instrument meets the exclusion restriction.

Unlike other potential instruments for oil production, sedimentary basins are absolutely exogenous to human activity. Moreover, there is little reason to believe that sedimentary rock affects conflict through any other channel than the presence of hydrocarbon deposits. One potential exception is the presence of mountainous terrain, which has been linked to the outbreak of civil conflict in various studies (see e.g. Fearon and Laitin 2003). However, it is straightforward to account for this possibility econometrically by adding a respective control.

A further advantage of the sediment-based IV design is that it allows causal inference at the sub-national level. Because geographically disaggregated information on the presence and thickness of sedimentary rock is available, we may construct corresponding IV for arbitrary sub-national units. Despite its advantages, the sediment instrument is also limited in that it is time-invariant, and thus does not allow distinguishing between the effects of long-term and recent petroleum extraction.

To identify regions featuring thick layers of sedimentary rock, we employ the CRUST 1.0 dataset by Laske et al. (2013). CRUST 1.0 is a raster map providing information on sediment thickness at a resolution of 1 decimal degree grid cells for the entire globe, as shown in Fig. 3.1. More detailed information for selected countries is shown in Fig. 3.2.

3 THE ETHNO-REGIONAL OIL CURSE AND SECESSIONIST CONFLICT   49

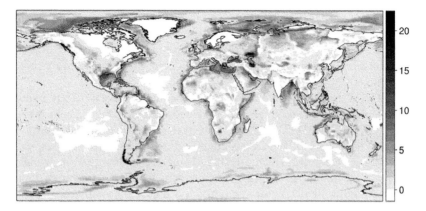

Fig. 3.1 Sedimentary thickness (in km) from the CRUST 1.0 dataset

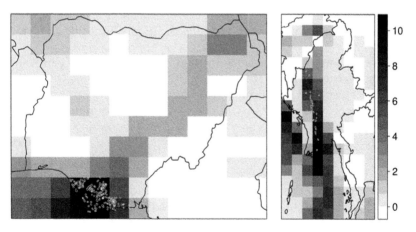

Fig. 3.2 Sedimentary thickness (in km) and ACOR fields (white/black dots) in Nigeria (left) and Burma (right)

Our theoretical argument implies that the location of oil extraction within countries affects whether and where conflict erupts. To test this claim, geocoded information on the location of oil production sites is indispensable. For this purpose, we introduce the new *ACOR* (Automatically Coded Oil Reserves) dataset, which provides precise geocoded information on the location of oil and gas fields. Specifically, the dataset records the shape, size and location of all known onshore oil and gas fields in 1982, and is based on an atlas by Mayer (1982).[4] To code these roughly 13,000 polygon features, we developed automatic vectorization software leveraging recent advances in computer vision and machine learning.

ACOR is not the first geocoded petroleum field dataset, but builds on the important work of Lujala, Rød and Thieme (2007), who introduced the PETRODATA dataset. The reason we collected new data is twofold. First, PETRODATA has limitations with respect to spatial precision. Lujala, Rød and Thieme (2007, 246ff) generalize petroleum field locations by buffering and aggregating them into large polygons. This approach is problematic for the empirical analyses conducted later in this chapter because it overestimates "petroleum producing" sub-national units. Second, PETRODATA does not permit approximating the intensity of petroleum production in any particular region. In contrast, being coded on a field-by-field basis, the ACOR data allow creating a rough estimate of total production by counting the number of fields in a given area.

Another dataset providing information on the location of petroleum fields is offered by Horn (2010).

While Horn's dataset encodes fields as points, and even provides estimates of their volume, its key shortcoming is that it is limited to *giant* fields. While giant oil fields do yield a majority of the world's oil production (65%, see Robelius 2007, 82ff), relying solely on the Horn data implies ignoring the vastly greater number of smaller fields. Furthermore, while giant fields are responsible for the majority of oil production in some regions, this is not the case for Africa and Asia, where in 2005, the majority of oil produced originated from other fields (ibid). Consequently, similar to PETRODATA, the Horn data do not permit measuring the actual extent of onshore oil production in a given region with high precision.[5]

The precision gains associated with using ACOR may be illustrated visually. Figure 3.3 maps discovered onshore oil and gas fields, as coded by ACOR and PETRODATA, for Burma in the year 1982.[6] Superimposed is the settlement area of Burma's majority Bamar ethnic group, as identified by the GeoEPR dataset by Wucherpfennig et al. (2011). Based on the ACOR data, it is evident that all Burmese oil production was located in regions inhabited by the Bamar at the time. In contrast,

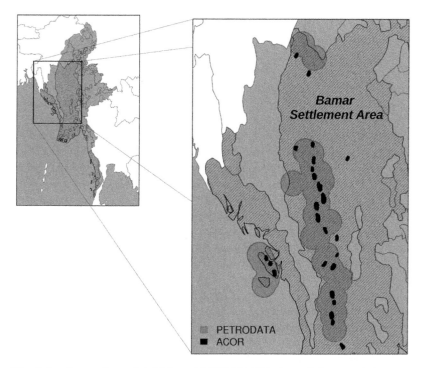

Fig. 3.3 Comparison of ACOR and PETRODATA data of discovered Burmese petroleum fields in 1982

the PETRODATA polygons also overlap with the settlement area of other ethnic groups.

Finally, the ACOR data allow demonstrating the close relationship between sedimentary basins and the location of petroleum deposits. Figure 3.2 displays the CRUST sediment thickness data together with the ACOR oil and gas field information for Nigeria and Burma. In both cases, visual inspection confirms the impressive predictive power of the sediment information.

3.5 Does Oil Cause Conflict?

This section evaluates the country-level evidence of the oil-conflict link using our newly proposed causal identification strategy. Specifically, we analyze whether the data support our expectations that there *is* a causal relationship between petroleum and civil war ($H_{3.1}$), that this relationship is limited to secessionist conflicts ($H_{3.2}$), and that it is due to oil production in populated areas ($H_{3.3}$). To do so, we pursue a cross-sectional research design, and estimate the effect of onshore oil production on whether countries experienced civil conflict in the 1990–2013 period. There are several reasons why we limit the analysis to this time frame.

First, we are only able to measure onshore oil production with reasonably high precision in the post-1982 period. The vast majority of today's oil reserves were discovered between 1950 and 1980 (Bentley et al. 2000, 170). Consequently, most regions producing oil today have been doing so since at least the early 1980s, and their output is thus approximated reasonably well by the 1982 ACOR data. Using the ACOR data for measuring production in the pre-1982 period, however, is likely associated with considerable measurement error, as we are bound to ascribe oil production to areas where no hydrocarbons were yet discovered. A similar caveat applies to the use of the time-variant PETRODATA or Horn datasets. Due to these datasets' aforementioned shortcomings, using them to expand the temporal scope of the study is only possible at the expense of measurement accuracy. The reason why we prefer to avoid these sources of measurement error—and thus pursue the temporally limited research design—is statistical efficiency. In IV designs, additional noise in the endogenous regressor translates directly into a less efficient estimate of the treatment parameter.[7] A second limiting factor is that geocoded data on settlement patterns–which we require to test the hypothesized importance of oil production in populated areas–is only available for the post-1990 period (CIESIN, 2010). In combination, these restrictions imply that we are only able to measure oil production–and especially oil production in populated areas–with relatively little measurement error for the years after 1990.[8]

We rely on a cross-sectional analysis of the data because both our treatment of interest–oil production–and the instrument–sediment volume– are measured in a time-invariant manner. Hence, while pursuing a panel design is feasible, doing so has few inferential benefits. Accordingly, as dependent variables, we employ dummies that indicate whether a country experienced at least one civil conflict onset during the 1991–2013 period.[9] These measures are constructed using the Uppsala Conflict Data Program's (UCDP) armed conflict dataset version 4-2014 (Pettersson and Wallensteen 2015), which also codes whether a given conflict involves territorial or governmental incompatibilities. We employ the latter distinction to measure secessionist and center-seeking conflicts, respectively. To measure onshore petroleum production, we use ACOR to calculate the logged number of onshore fields per country as a proxy (while adding a unit constant before logging). As an instrument for onshore production, we calculate the logged volume of sediment rock underneath each country's territory using the CRUST data.

Next, to evaluate $H_{3.3}$—stating that only oil production in populated areas should be associated with secessionist conflict—we introduce two new variables measuring the number of petroleum fields in populated and unpopulated areas for each country. In addition, we define two instruments capturing each country's total sediment volume in populated and unpopulated areas, respectively. We create these variables in two steps: First, we create a global raster map of populated areas in 1990 based on the GRUMP (version 1) settlement data by CIESIN (2010). A raster cell is coded as populated if the population density in its neighborhood exceeds a minimal threshold of 0.1 inhabitants per square kilometer. Second, the (un-) populated oil field and sediment volume variables are generated by intersecting the ACOR and CRUST data with the above-described raster map.

The IV design requires two types of control variables. First, it is necessary to control for logged country area, as sediment volume is an immediate function of surface area, and vast countries may be more prone to civil conflict simply because larger territories are more difficult to govern. Analogously, when distinguishing between petroleum fields in populated and unpopulated areas, we control for the total populated and unpopulated territory of each country. Further, as a cautionary measure, when analyzing the impact of oil in populated regions, we also control for each country's total logged population in 1991.

Second, as stated above, it is also necessary to control for mountainous terrain. We do so with a variable measuring fraction of each country's territory covered by mountainous terrain, as defined by UNEP-WCMC (2002). These controls are necessary for causal identification because they are causally antecedent to sedimentary volume, and omitting them carries the risk of wrongly attributing their effect on conflict to oil production. However, this does not apply to other commonly employed controls in the conflict literature. Income levels, for instance, are not causally antecedent to the presence of sedimentary rock, nor is there any reason to believe that sedimentary basins affect income levels through any other channel than hydrocarbon reserves.

Econometrically, we rely on standard 2SLS models to implement our IV design, and report Huber-White standard errors to account for heteroskedasticity. Angrist (2001) advocates this approach as the most consistent strategy for estimating treatment effects for binary outcomes. Further, to provide an inferential baseline, the IV results are complemented with estimates from uninstrumented linear probability models.

We now move to the discussion of the country-level results, summarized in Table 3.1, and visualized in Fig. 3.4. For each model specification, we present the results of an ordinary linear probability model next to the 2SLS estimated results. Further, for those IV models featuring only one endogenous regressor, we report first-stage estimates.

Columns 1 and 2 display the results for the relationship between oil and all types of civil conflict. First, we note that sediment volume is an exceptionally strong instrument for petroleum fields, as evidenced by its large, positive, and highly significant coefficient in the first stage regression. Further, comparing the F-statistic of the first-stage instrument against the critical value provided in Stock and Yogo (2005) clearly rejects the hypothesis that the instrument is weak.[10] Substantively, once instrumented, the effect of oil on conflict is positive, but only marginally significant ($p = 0.099$). Thus, though there is some evidence of a causal oil curse ($H_{3.1}$), it is associated with considerable uncertainty.

The source of this ambiguity is revealed once we distinguish between conflict types. In line with $H_{3.2}$, we find a strong effect of oil on *secessionist* conflict. The corresponding IV estimate, reported in Column 4, is positive and highly significant. Furthermore, the causal effect of oil on territorial conflict is large:

a country featuring a median level of oil fields would have had a 35 percentage point lower probability of experiencing territorial conflict had it not extracted any petroleum (see Panel B of Fig. 3.4).

Comparing the IV result with its uninstrumented counterpart in Column 3 shows that the positive relationship between petroleum and territorial conflict is only revealed once oil is instrumented. Because countries at risk of secessionist wars tend to see less oil production, we underestimate the strength of the oil-conflict link without proper causal identification. The presence of endogeneity is further confirmed by a Hausman-like test (Wooldridge 2002, 119), which rejects the null of exogenous second stage regressors at the 0.1% level.

Table 3.1 (Instrumented) petroleum and civil conflict, country-level, 1991–2013

	All Conflict		Territorial Conflict		Governmental Conflict		Territorial Conflict	
	(1) OLS	(2) 2SLS	(3) OLS	(4) 2SLS	(5) OLS	(6) 2SLS	(7) OLS	(8) 2SLS
Conflict								
Constant	−0.273 (0.149)	−0.029 (0.205)	−0.269* (0.134)	−0.004 (0.164)	−0.183 (0.135)	−0.054 (0.168)	−0.701*** (0.203)	−0.165 (0.325)
Fields (log)	0.002 (0.022)	0.095 (0.057)	0.008 (0.019)	0.108*** (0.031)	−0.000 (0.021)	0.049 (0.054)	0.033 (0.026)	0.154** (0.055)
Pop. Fields (log)								
Unpop. Fields (log)	0.078*** (0.021)	0.028 (0.034)	0.055** (0.019)	0.001 (0.023)	0.055** (0.020)	0.029 (0.030)	−0.092** (0.028)	−0.160* (0.074)
Area (log)							0.037 (0.032)	0.036 (0.039)
Pop. Area (log)							0.012 (0.012)	0.018 (0.017)
Unpop. Area (log)	0.191 (0.143)	0.154 (0.157)	0.060 (0.095)	0.020 (0.107)	0.150 (0.143)	0.131 (0.150)	0.023 (0.096)	0.023 (0.116)
Mountains							0.062 (0.034)	−0.014 (0.053)
Pop. (log)								
Oil & Gas								
Constant		−1.746** (0.641)		−1.746** (0.641)		−1.746** (0.641)		
Area (log)		0.224* (0.089)		0.224* (0.089)		0.224* (0.089)		

(continued)

Table 3.1 (continued)

	All Conflict		Territorial Conflict		Governmental Conflict		Territorial Conflict	
	(1) OLS	(2) 2SLS	(3) OLS	(4) 2SLS	(5) OLS	(6) 2SLS	(7) OLS	(8) 2SLS
Mountains		0.614		0.614		0.614		
		(0.407)		(0.407)		(0.407)		
Sed. Volume (log)		0.289***		0.289***		0.289***		
		(0.041)		(0.041)		(0.041)		
N	153	153	153	153	153	153	153	153
Exogeneity (p-val.)[1]		0.073		0.001		0.325		0.027
F-val.Instr. 1		50.712		50.712		50.712		33.521
F-val. Instr. 2								43.853
Stock Yogo CV²		16.380		16.380		16.380		16.380

***p < 0.001, **p < 0.01, *p < 0.05. Standard errors in parentheses. Huber-White robust standard errors reported.
[1] F-test of exogeneity of second-stage regressors.
[2] For a worst-case size of 10% for a 5% Wald test of the 2SLS estimates.

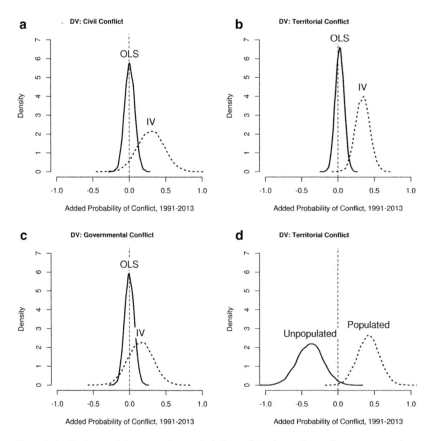

Fig. 3.4 Estimated increase in probability of civil conflict when moving from 0 to the median value of petroleum fields among producers. Panel D reports results for petroleum fields in populated areas. Density estimates reflect sampling variance. Based on Table I

Next, Column 6 reveals that there is little evidence of a causal relationship between oil and *governmental* conflict. Though the IV estimate is positive, it is associated with considerable uncertainty, and thus fails to attain statistical significance at conventional levels. Finally, as postulated by $H_{3.3}$, the results summarized in Column 8 suggest that only populated oil fields have a significantly positive effect on secessionist conflict. In fact, while the estimate associated with populated fields is 1.5 times larger than the respective coefficient for all types of oil fields reported in Column 4, the estimate for unpopulated fields is negative.[11] A possible interpretation of this result is that as long as oil production does not cause any grievances locally, it may help governments to prevent secessionist conflict elsewhere, either via repression or cooptation.

These results are highly robust to alternative specifications: We obtain substantively equivalent results when using a different IV method, adding various geographic controls, using petroleum measures based on PETRO-DATA or Horn, and employing panel data covering the entire period between 1950 and 2013.[12] Moreover, using the inferential procedures proposed by Conley, Hansen and Rossi (2012), we can additionally show that the positive causal link between onshore fields and territorial conflict remains intact even under moderately-sized violations of the exclusion restriction.

In summary, this section yields three important insights. First, focusing on secessionist conflict, there is strong evidence that the oil curse is causal. In contrast to the literature that rejects the oil-conflict link, we find that uninstrumented models tend to *underestimate* the true risks associated with oil production. Second, in support of $H_{3.2}$, the oil curse appears to be limited to *secessionist* conflicts. The null of no oil-effect can easily be rejected for territorial conflicts, but not for governmental conflicts. And third, in support of $H_{3.3}$, whether oil production increases the risk of secessionist violence depends on where it occurs. This result is clearly at odds with the governmental oil curse, which expects oil-rich states to experience conflict more frequently regardless of where oil extraction takes place. Indeed, we find that oil may even inhibit secessionist violence if extraction occurs in uninhabited regions.

3.6 Is There an Ethno-Regional Oil Curse?

After having established that there *is* evidence of an oil curse, we now assess whether it is indeed ethno-regional. To do so, we analyze data where the units of analysis are politically relevant and geographically concentrated ethnic groups. We identify these groups using the Ethnic Power Relations (EPR) (version 2014, Vogt et al. 2015) and GeoEPR (version 2014, Wucherpfennig et al. 2011) datasets. EPR enumerates politically relevant ethnic groups for all sovereign countries across the globe from 1946 to 2013, and GeoEPR geocodes corresponding settlement areas.

As in the country-level analysis, we focus on the period between 1991 and 2013. Group-level conflict is identified with the ACD2EPR dataset (version 2014, Wucherpfennig et al. 2012), which links the UCDP ACD (version 4-2014, Pettersson and Wallensteen 2015) conflict data to the EPR ethnic groups by coding whether the rebel organizations involved in these conflicts made ethnic claims, and recruited from a given group. The intensity of petroleum production within each group's territory is captured by the logged count of the ACOR fields within the groups' settlement areas (after adding a unit constant).

To instrument oil production, we again rely on the CRUST data to calculate the log of sediment volume per group settlement area, while controlling for group-level surface area and mountainous terrain. Finally, information on whether groups are represented in government (for testing $H_{3.4}$), as well as their demographic size (for testing $H_{3.5}$), is obtained directly from EPR.

We adopt the same econometric approach as in the previous section, with the key difference that we add country-level fixed effects, thus effectively removing all cross-country variation. This step ensures that we do not simply pick up a country-level effect, and addresses country-specific error dependence.

Table 3.2 displays the group-level results, presenting both OLS and 2SLS coefficients. Models 1 and 2 test whether the strong relationship between oil and territorial conflict found in the previous section is also detectable at the group-level. As anticipated, the 2SLS estimates indicate that the effect of group-level oil production on the probability of territorial conflict is positive and significant. Thus, the oil-conflict link is indeed ethno-regional: groups that host oil-production are more likely to engage in secessionist violence. Furthermore, there is strong evidence of endogeneity: comparing the results of Columns 1 and 2 show that the oil-conflict link is only identifiable with the IV design. Moreover, we can reject the null of exogenous second-stage regressors at the 1% level. Thus, petroleum production appears to be less likely in the territory of groups that are particularly conflict-prone, causing unadjusted research designs to underestimate the severity of the oil-conflict link.

Next, we reevaluate $H_{3.3}$ on the group-level, testing whether oil production in *populated* areas is particularly likely to cause secessionist conflict. For this purpose, we recalculate the (un-)populated petroleum field, sediment volume and surface area variables described in the previous

Table 3.2 (Instrumented) petroleum and territorial conflict, group-level, 1991–2013

	Territorial Conflict							
	(1) OLS	(2) IV 2SLS	(3) OLS	(4) IV 2SLS	(5) OLS	(6) IV 2SLS	(7) OLS	(8) IV 2SLS
Fields (log)	0.013 (0.017)	0.174** (0.059)						
Pop. Fields (log)			0.021 (0.020)	0.251** (0.085)	0.018 (0.022)	0.107 (0.057)	0.039 (0.024)	0.270** (0.082)
Unpop. Fields (log)			0.006 (0.023)	−0.096 (0.129)				
Pop. Fields × Exclusion					0.017 (0.025)	0.170** (0.058)		
Exclusion					0.094** (0.034)	0.005 (0.045)		
Pop. Fields × Rel. Size							−0.055 (0.042)	−0.360*** (0.105)
Rel. Size							−0.079 (0.106)	0.310* (0.143)
Area (log)	−0.015 (0.010)	−0.057** (0.018)						
Pop. Area (log)			−0.006 (0.016)	−0.036 (0.022)	0.004 (0.014)	−0.021 (0.017)	0.005 (0.015)	−0.026 (0.018)
Unpop. Area (log)			0.011 (0.009)	0.012 (0.015)				
Mountains	0.051 (0.055)	0.131* (0.066)	0.035 (0.056)	0.081 (0.070)	0.021 (0.055)	0.071 (0.069)	0.033 (0.056)	0.079 (0.068)
Abs. Pop. (log)			−0.033* (0.013)	−0.067** (0.022)	−0.024 (0.013)	−0.043* (0.019)	−0.026 (0.015)	−0.057* (0.022)

	(1) OLS	(2) IV 2SLS	(3) OLS	(4) IV 2SLS	(5) OLS	(6) IV 2SLS	(7) OLS	(8) IV 2SLS
				Territorial Conflict				
N	520	520	520	520	520	520	520	520
Exogeneity (p-val.)[1]		0.001		0.002		0.003		0.001
F-val. Instr. 1		32.232		32.727		43.227		37.559
F-val. Instr. 2				31.848		109.625		61.766
Stock Yogo CV[2]		16.380		16.380		16.380		16.380

***p < 0.001, **p < 0.01, *p < 0.05. Huber-White robust standard errors in parentheses. All models estimated with country FEs.
[1] F-test of exogeneity of second-stage regressors.
[2] For a worst-case size of 10% for a 5% Wald test of the 2SLS estimates.

section. Note that this analysis is only feasible because the GeoEPR settlement polygons often include unpopulated regions, as areas in-between population centers are often counted toward a nearby ethnic group. As expected, whereas the coefficient associated with (instrumented) populated fields is positive and significant, the estimate for (instrumented) unpopulated fields is negative (Column 4 of Table 3.2). However, an F-test reveals that we can only reject the null of equal effects at 10% level ($p = 0.059$). Thus, in contrast to the country-level results, here we only find limited evidence for $H_{3.3}$. This ambiguous finding may be due to many ethnic settlement regions' small size, and the resulting high correlation between the populated and unpopulated sediment volume estimates for these areas.

In a final step, we evaluate $H_{3.4}$ and $H_{3.5}$. Using suitably instrumented interaction terms, we test whether political exclusion and relative demographic size (measured in 1991) mediate the effect of oil on secessionist conflict. Moreover, given the above findings, we focus exclusively on petroleum fields in populated areas. Columns 5 and 6 report the results for political exclusion. In agreement with $H_{3.4}$, we find that oil is significantly more likely to cause secessionist violence for excluded groups. Panel A of Fig. 3.5 plots the effect of the populated fields within a group's territory on the probability of territorial conflict as a function of exclusion. While the effect for groups that are represented in government is only borderline significant ($p = 0.052$), the effect more than doubles in size and attains statistical significance ($p = 0.001$) for excluded groups.

Despite these promising results, there is an important caveat to this analysis. While ethnic groups' location and demographic size are convincingly exogenous to conflict, this is not necessarily the case for political exclusion. Importantly, if governments systematically exclude conflict-prone groups, we overestimate the conditioning effect of exclusion. However, recent research suggests that the opposite is the case. Wucherpfennig, Hunziker and Cederman (2016) show that governments tend to include threatening groups, which would imply that we underestimate its mediating role.

Finally, Columns 7 and 8 show the results obtained when conditioning on relative group size.

The point estimates of the 2SLS estimated model (Column 8) strongly support $H_{3.5}$: While the populated petroleum field estimate is positive and significant, the interaction parameter is negative and significant. Panel B

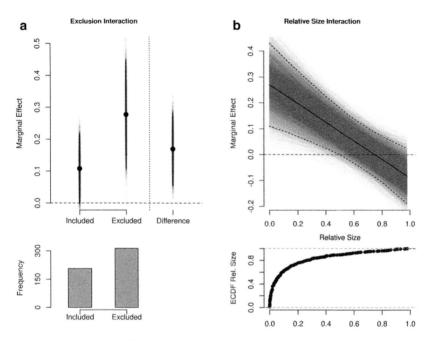

Fig. 3.5 Marginal effect of (logged) populated petroleum fields on the probability of group-level territorial conflict, conditional on exclusion (Panel A) and group size (Panel B). Black vertical lines (Panel A) and dashed lines (Panel B) indicate 95% confidence intervals. Based on Columns 6 and 8 of Table II

of Fig. 3.5 plots the effect of oil production in populated areas on the yearly probability of territorial conflict as a function of relative group-size. Visual inspection confirms that the oil-conflict link is associated primarily with ethnic minorities: we can only reject the null of no effect for groups with a relative size of less than 0.5.

How robust are these group-level findings? Further analyses show that adding geographic controls, using PETRODATA or Horn-based petroluem measures, and employing panel data covering the longer 1950–2013 time period all lead to equivalent results. Moreover, mirroring the country-level results, we can additionally show that the group-level link between onshore fields and territorial conflict also remains significant under moderately sized violations of the exclusion restriction.

In summary, this section yields four important results. First, there is a causal oil-conflict link at the ethno-regional level. Even at the subnational level, we find clear evidence in favor of a causal effect of oil and gas production on the likelihood of secessionist violence. Second, oil extraction appears to provoke secessionist violence only where local residents are immediately affected, and thus, local claims to resource ownership are particularly likely. As in the country-level analysis, there is no evidence of an oil-conflict link for petroleum production in unpopulated areas. Third, small and excluded ethnic groups are significantly more likely to react to petroleum extraction with violent secessionism. And finally, again, we find considerable evidence of endogeneity: conflict-prone ethnic groups host fewer productive petroleum fields than other groups, even in a within-country comparison.

3.7 Conclusion

Despite its prominence in theory and policy, the claim that oil abundance causes civil war continues to generate controversy. Major progress has been made, but there is still no consensus as regards the causal mechanisms driving the link, and some scholars even question its very existence. This chapter aims to overcome this fundamental ambiguity by addressing three outstanding difficulties that afflict the current literature.

First, we reaffirm the existence of a causal ethno-regional oil curse that depends on affected groups' political and economic grievances and material aspirations. In line with the theoretical expectations introduced in Chapter 2, oil production increases the risk of violent secessionist conflict if it occurs within the settlement area of politically and demographically marginalized ethnic groups. Petroleum extraction in other locations, however, appears to be largely inconsequential, or may sometimes even inhibit the outbreak of violence. In combination, these findings substantiate our theoretical argument, and are largely inconsistent with those explanations of the oil-conflict link that focus exclusively on governmental or individualist mechanisms.

Following up a major theme of this volume, the current chapter breaks new empirical ground by introducing an identification strategy that improves on existing attempts to handle endogeneity. Relying on sedimentary basins as an instrumental variable allows us to circumvent reverse causation and other sources of endogeneity. While showing that uninstrumented analyses have underestimated the effect of resource abundance, the sediments-based instrument lends strong support to our ethno-regional explanation.

Third, and finally, we introduce the new ACOR dataset that offers precise historical information on the location oil and gas fields.

These empirical advances still leave plenty of room for future progress in terms of data collection and integration. An important area of future research pertains to economic inequality, which we have chosen not to measure directly in this chapter, primarily because it is very difficult to separate household income from economic activities associated with the oil industry itself.

Pending such advances, the current chapter offers considerable evidence to suggest that conventional accounts of the oil-conflict link will have to be reassessed. In this light, attempts to prevent and resolve petroleum-related civil wars will need to pay more attention toward reducing political inequalities than conventional policy recommendations that merely attempt to strengthen state capacity or to buy off potential protesters. This calls for increased pressure to be put on oil-producing states by inducing them to redress, rather than repress, oil-related grievances. This message is all the more important as new oil fields come on line in peripheral areas of developing countries, especially in Sub-Saharan Africa.

Finally, it remains an open question whether the findings of this chapter can be generalized to cases that involve non-fuel minerals. This is the task of the remaining chapters of the book. Whereas the next chapter applies large-N data to this question, the remainder of the book is devoted to qualitative analysis of mining and its conflict potential in specific settings.

Notes

1. We use the terms 'oil' and 'petroleum' interchangeably to mean all liquid or gaseous hydrocarbon fuels.
2. The commonly adopted definition of the term "proven reserves" notes that deposits need to be deemed recoverable under "current economic conditions, operating methods and government regulations" (Society of Petroleum Engineers 2005, p. 10).
3. The argument that grievances over the local externalities of oil extraction may serve as a potential source of violence has also been made by other scholars, but without discussing the implications for secessionism (see e.g. Ross 2004; Humphreys 2005).

4. We rely on information from the year 1982 simply as a matter of data availability. Outside of Mayer's work, we were not able to find precise and globally consistent historical petroleum data.
5. Further estimations reveal that the ACOR-based field count is a surprisingly accurate proxy of contemporary oil production, surpassing variables based on PETRODATA or Horn's data.
6. The Horn data do not include any onshore fields in Burma.
7. Additional results provide a formal proof of this statement.
8. Restricting the sample to the post-1990 period may even have inferential benefits. In an exploratory analysis, Ross (2012, ch. 5) finds that the oil-conflict link may have only become relevant after the end of the Cold War. If this is the case, including pre-1990 data in the analysis will make us underestimate the contemporary conflict-inducing effect of oil.
9. We follow standard practices and code an onset if a given conflict exceeds the 25 battle death threshold after at least two calendar years of inactivity.
10. Since we find no evidence of a weak instrument problem in any of the analyses presented in this article, we refrain from discussing the respective F-statistics below. In those analyses involving several instruments, we report the conditional F-statistic proposed by Sanderson and Windmeijer (2016).
11. An F-test rejects the hypothesis that the two effects are of equal size at the 1% level.
12. Inspired by previous findings in the resource curse literature (especially Collier and Hoeffler 1998), we also test whether the relationship between oil production and conflict risk is non-monotonic. However, we find little evidence of non-monotonicity.

References

Angrist, Joshua D. 2001. "Estimation of Limited Dependent Variable Models with Dummy Endogenous Regressors." *Journal of Business and Economic Statistics* 19 (1): 2–28.

Asal, Victor, Michael Findley, James A. Piazza, and James Igoe Walsh. 2016. "Political Exclusion, Oil, and Ethnic Armed Conflict." *Journal of Conflict Resolution* 60 (8): 1343–1367.

Aspinall, Edward. 2007. "The Construction of Grievance." *Journal of Conflict Resolution* 51 (6): 950–972.

Bates, Robert. 1983. "Modernization, Ethnic Competition, and the Rationality of Politics in Contemporary Africa." In *State versus Ethnic Claims: African Policy Dilemmas*. Edited by David Rothchild and Victor A. Olunsorola. Boulder, CO: Westview, 152–171.

Bentley, Roger W., R.H. Booth, J.D. Burton, M.L. Coleman, B.W. Sellwood, and G.R. Whitfield. 2000. "Perspectives on the Future of Oil." *Energy, Exploration and Exploitation* 18 (2): 147–206.
Brunnschweiler, Christa N., and Erwin H. Bulte. 2009. "Natural Resources and Violent Conflict: Resource Abundance, Dependence and the Onset of Civil Wars." *Oxford Economic Papers* 61 (4): 651–674.
Caselli, Francesco, and Wilbur J. Coleman. 2013. "On the Theory of Ethnic Conflict." *Journal of the European Economic Association* 11 (1): 161–192.
CIESIN. 2010. "Global Rural-Urban Mapping Project (GRUMP)." v1. Center for International Earth Science Information Network, Columbia University. http://sedac.ciesin.columbia.edu/data.
Colgan, Jeff D. 2014. "Oil, Domestic Conflict, and Opportunities for Democratization." *Journal of Peace Research* 52 (1): 3–16.
Collier, Paul, and Anke Hoeffler. 1998. "On Economic Causes of Civil War." *Oxford Economic Papers* 50 (4): 563–573.
Collier, Paul, and Anke Hoeffler. 2004. "Greed and Grievance in Civil War." *Oxford Economic Papers* 56 (4): 563–595.
Collier, Paul, and Anke Hoeffler. 2006. The Political Economy of Secession. In *Negotiating Self-Determination*, ed. Hurst Hannum and Eileen Babbitt, 37–59. Oxford: Lexington.
Conley, Timothy G., Christian B. Hansen, and Peter E. Rossi. 2012. "Plausibly Exogenous." *Review of Economics and Statistics* 94 (1): 260–272.
Cotet, Anca M., and Kevin K. Tsui. 2013. "Oil and Conflict: What Does the Cross Country Evidence Really Show?" *American Economic Journal: Macroeconomics* 5 (1): 49–80.
Fearon, James, and David D. Laitin. 2003. "Ethnicity, Insurgency, and Civil War." *American Political Science Review* 97 (1): 75–90.
Fearon, James. 2005. "Primary Commodity Exports and Civil War." *Journal of Conflict Resolution* 49 (4): 483–507.
Haber, Stephen, and Victor Menaldo. 2011. "Do Natural Resources Fuel Authoritarianism? A Reappraisal of the Resource Curse." *American Political Science Review* 105 (01): 1–26.
Hechter, Michael. 1975. *Internal Colonialism: The Celtic Fringe in British National Development, 1536–1966*. London: Routledge.
Horn, Myron. 2010. "Giant Oil and Gas Fields of the World. American Association of Petroleum." Geologists Datapages http://www.datapages.com/Partners/AAPGGISPublicationsCommittee/GISOpenFiles/HornGiantFields.aspx.
Human Rights Watch. 1999. *The Price of Oil: Corporate Responsibility and Human Rights Violations in Nigeria's Oil Producing Communities*. New York: Human Rights Watch.

Humphreys, Macartan. 2005. "Natural Resources, Conflict, and Conflict Resolution." *Journal of Conflict Resolution* 49 (4): 508–537.
Hyne, Norman J. 2012. *Nontechnical Guide to Petroleum Geology, Exploration, Drilling, and Production.* Tulsa, OK: PennWell Books.
Kell, Tim. 2010. *The Roots of the Acehnese Rebellion, 1989–1992.* Singapore: Equinox Publishing.
Koubi, Vally, Gabriele Spilker, Tobias Böhmelt, and Thomas Bernauer. 2014. "Do Natural Resources Matter for Interstate and Intrastate Armed Conflict?" *Journal of Peace Research* 51 (2): 227–243.
Laske, Gabi, Guy Masters, Zhitu Ma and Mike Pasyanos. 2013. "Update on CRUST 1.0 – A 1-degree Global Model of Earth's Crust." *Geophysical Research Abstracts*, 15, Abstract EGU2013-265. http://igppweb.ucsd.edu/~gabi/rem.html.
Le Billon, Philippe. 2005. *Fuelling War: Natural Resources and Armed Conflicts.* New York: Routledge.
Lei, Yu-Hsiang and Guy Michaels. 2014. "Do Giant Oilfield Discoveries Fuel Internal Armed Conflicts?" *Journal of Development Economics* 110 (September): 139–157.
Lujala, Päivi. 2010. "The Spoils of Nature: Armed Civil Conflict and Rebel Access to Natural Resources." *Journal of Peace Research* 47 (1): 15–28.
Lujala, Päivi., Jan K. Rød, and Nadja Thieme. 2007. "Fighting over Oil: Introducing a New Dataset." *Conflict Management and Peace Science* 24 (3): 239–256.
Mayer, Ferdinand. 1982. *Petro-Atlas: Erdöl und Erdgas.* Braunschweig: Westermann.
Mitchell, Sara McLaughlin and Cameron G Thies. 2012. "Resource Curse in Reverse: How Civil Wars: Influence Natural Resource Production." *International Interactions* 38(2): 218–242.
Morelli, Massimo, and Dominic Rohner. 2015. "Resource Concentration and Civil Wars." *Journal of Development Economics* 117 (November): 32–47.
Paine, Jack. 2016. "Rethinking the Conflict 'Resource Curse': How Oil Wealth Prevents Center-Seeking Civil Wars." *International Organization* 70 (4): 727–761.
Pettersson, Thérèse, and Peter Wallensteen. 2015. "Armed conflicts, 1946–2014." *Journal of Peace Research* 52 (4): 536–550.
Ramos, Maria L. 2012. "Angola's Oil Industry Operations." The Open Society Initiative for Southern Africa Report. http://www.osisa.org/sites/default/files/angola_oil_english_final_less_photos.pdf.
Robelius, Fredrik. 2007. *Giant Oil Fields - The Highway to Oil: Giant Oil Fields and their Importance for Future Oil Production.* Uppsala: Uppsala University.
Ross, Michael. 2001. "Does Oil Hinder Democracy?" *World Politics* 53 (3): 325–361.

Ross, Michael. 2004. "What Do We Know about Natural Resources and Civil War?" *Journal of Peace Research* 41 (3): 337–356.

Ross, Michael. 2012. *The Oil Curse: How Petroleum Wealth Shapes the Development of Nations*. Princeton, NJ: Princeton University Press.

Ross, Michael. 2015. "What Have We Learned about the Resource Curse?" *Annual Review of Political Science* 18 (May): 239–259.

Sachs, Jeffrey D. and Andrew M. Warner. 1995. "Natural Resource Abundance and Economic Growth." Working Paper 5398. Cambridge, MA: National Bureau of Economic Research.

Sanderson, Eleanor, and Frank Windmeijer. 2016. "A Weak Instrument F-test in Linear IV Models with Multiple Endogenous Variables." *Journal of Econometrics* 190 (2): 212–221.

Society of Petroleum Engineers. 2005. "Glossary of Terms Used in Petroleum Reserves/Resources Definitions." http://www.spe.org/industry/docs/Glo ssaryPetroleumReserves-ResourcesDefinitions_2005.pdf.

Sorens, Jason. 2011. "Mineral Production, Territory, and Ethnic Rebellion: The Role of Rebel Constituencies." *Journal of Peace Research* 48 (5): 571–585.

Stock, James H. and Motohiro Yogo. 2005. "Testing for Weak Instruments in Linear IV Regression." In *Identification and Inference for Econometric Models: Essays in Honor of Thomas J. Rothenberg*. Edited by James H. Stock and Donald W.K. Andrews. Cambridge: Cambridge University Press, 80–108.

Torvik, Ragnar. 2009. "Why Do Some Resource-Abundant Countries Succeed While Others Do Not?" *Oxford Review of Economic Policy* 25 (2): 241–256.

UNEP-WCMC. 2002. *Mountain Watch*. Cambridge: UNEP-WCMC.

Vogt, Manuel, Nils-Christian. Bormann, Seraina Rüegger, Lars-Erik. Cederman, Philipp Hunziker, and Luc Girardin. 2015. "Integrating Data on Ethnicity, Geography, and Conflict: The Ethnic Power Relations Data Set Family." *Journal of Conflict Resolution* 59 (7): 1327–1342.

Wooldridge, Jeffrey M. 2002. *Econometric Analysis of Cross Section and Panel Data*. Cambridge, MA: MIT Press.

World Bank. 2011. "World Development Report 2011: Conflict, Security, and Development." Report.Washington, DC: World Bank.

Wucherpfennig, Julian, Nils B. Weidmann, Luc Girardin, Lars-Erik Cederman and Andreas Wimmer. 2011. "Politically Relevant Ethnic Groups across Space and Time: Introducing the GeoEPR Dataset." *Conflict Management and Peace Science* 28 (5): 423–437.

Wucherpfennig, Julian, Nils Metternich, Lars-Erik. Cederman, and Kristian Skrede Gleditsch. 2012. "Ethnicity, the State and the Duration of Civil War." *World Politics* 64 (1): 79–115.

Wucherpfennig, Julian, Philipp Hunziker, and Lars-Erik Cederman. 2016. "Who Inherits the State? Colonial Rule and Post-Colonial Conflict." *American Journal of Political Science* 60 (4): 882–898.

CHAPTER 4

Digging Deeper: On the Role of Grievances in African Mining Conflicts

Yannick Pengl and Lars-Erik Cederman

The previous chapter showed that the link between petroleum extraction and political violence appears to operate primarily through ethnic inequalities in a way that is compatible with the general grievance logic that was introduced in Chapter 2. Given the theme of this book, the question that this chapter addresses is to what extent this finding can be generalized to cases involving the extraction of non-fuel minerals.

A previous version of this paper was presented at the Annual Convention of the American Political Science Association, Washington, August 29-September 1, 2019. We thank Alex Downes for comments on that version. We are also grateful to Selina Bezzola and Ravi Bhavnani for their helpful comments on an even earlier version.

Y. Pengl · L.-E. Cederman (✉)
International Conflict Research, ETH Zürich, Zürich, Switzerland
e-mail: lcederman@ethz.ch

© The Author(s), under exclusive license to Springer Nature Switzerland AG 2022
H. E. Ali and L.-E. Cederman (Eds.), *Natural Resources, Inequality and Conflict*, https://doi.org/10.1007/978-3-030-73558-6_4

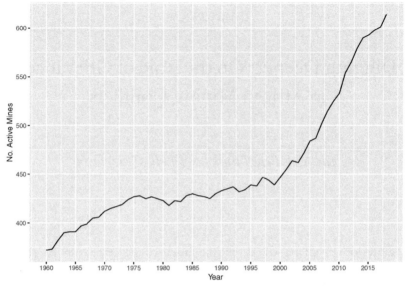

Fig. 4.1 The African mining boom

This is a particularly urgent question because, as we have argued in Chapter 1, a veritable mining boom has swept through large parts the world since the turn of the century (Le Billon 2012). Extractive operations have entered production at a rate unparalleled in recent history both in Latin America (Bebbington and Bury 2013) and Africa (Chuhan-Pole et al. 2017). Figure 4.1 illustrates a steep increase in the number of operating mines on the African continent, the empirical focus of this chapter. Driven by the industry's rapidly increasing demands for precious metals, not the least in China, this impressive wave of foreign direct investment has done much to accelerate development in previously underdeveloped regions. Yet, as shown in the case of oil, there is a dark side to these positive developments. As minerals are extracted at a rapid pace, new problems emerge that may block, and even reverse, the benefits of mining (see, e.g., Koubi et al. 2014).

Covering mostly sub-Saharan Africa, most of the contemporary scholarship in this area assumes that the resource curse derives from mobilization opportunities relating to incomplete information (Christensen 2019) and greed-related factors driven by "rapacity" and rebel finance (Berman et al. 2017). Yet, despite being based on sophisticated difference-in-differences research designs applied to extensive datasets, these findings still leave open the possibility that grievance-related factors may be at play. First, most of this research has tended to rely on relatively time-limited samples, which risk obscuring the influence of longer-term mobilization responding to structural inequalities. Second, as a rule, these studies are to some extent "color-blind" in that they do not conceptualize and measure inequality along ethnic lines. Third, this recent scholarship tends to rely on conflict data that risk blurring the distinction between theoretically relevant event types.

This chapter attempts to overcome all three limitations. First, while also exploiting within-case variation over time, we rely on datasets that span over several decades of history rather than shorter periods. Second, the empirical analysis of this chapter captures the extent to which ethno-political exclusion conditions the effect of differences in resource extraction over time. Third, and finally, the conflict data used here allow us to narrow down the focus to theoretically meaningful categories, for instance pertaining to the targets of violence and the motivations driving it in a way that is more specific than in the existing literature.

Based on these modifications, we find strong support for the grievance logic postulated in Chapter 2 of this book. To test this logic, we analyze whether homelands of ethnically excluded groups see systematically different, potentially more dangerous forms of violent mobilization in response to mineral extraction than what recent research suggests. The empirical strategy relies on grid cells and ethnic settlement areas as units of analysis, with spatial information on conflict events drawn from the SCAD dataset (Salehyan et al. 2012) and data on ethnic rebellion from ACD2EPR. Our analysis of conflict events at the grid cell-level indicates that mining projects in politically excluded ethnic settlement areas provoke different forms of contestation than is the case in politically represented areas. Mining conflict in excluded regions is more likely to be explicitly cast in ethnic terms and is often directed against the national government. As such, the potential for further escalation beyond the local level seems large. The group-level analysis suggests that, perhaps as a consequence of more confrontational events at the local level, mining operations in the homelands of politically excluded groups increase the risk of full-blown ethnic rebellion.

The chapter is structured as follows. The next section provides an overview of the relevant literature, followed by a section that derives the main hypotheses. Then we present the group-based and cell-based empirical analysis including data, methods, and results, before summarizing and discussing the results in a final section.

4.1 Minerals and Political Strife in the Literature

In Chapter 2, we offer a general introduction to the literature on the link between mineral resources and political violence. Here we merely recapitulate the most important aspects that are directly relevant to the current chapter. The contemporary scholarly debate over whether, and to what extent, mineral resources affect political violence largely dates back to two influential articles by Collier and Hoeffler (1998) and Fearon and Laitin (2003). While Collier and Hoeffler argue that revenues from natural resource extraction give rebels an incentive to launch "greedy" rebellions, Fearon and Laitin stress a conflict driving logic based on "opportunities" flowing from weak state capacity. Collier and Hoeffler's and Fearon and Laitin's contributions have sparked a quickly growing strand of quantitative literature further investigating the presence, magnitude, and causes of this "resource curse" (for recent reviews, see Koubi et al. 2014; Ross 2015).

This resource-conflict literature has developed along two main lines. First, to identify the underlying causal mechanisms, there has been a trend toward more disaggregated data and analyses, both in terms of moving from the analysis of natural resources to more specific groups of commodities and by replacing country-level aggregates with sub-national metrics of resource production and violence. Second, scholars have exhibited a growing concern with endogeneity and causal identification.

Disaggregation has turned out to be a very successful strategy for unpacking the resource curse, especially regarding the role of oil and gas extraction. By measuring the location of oil production sites, Ross (2006) and Lujala (2010) are able to show that only onshore oil production appears to affect conflict risk, contradicting Fearon and Laitin's state capacity explanation, and suggesting that the underlying mechanism operates through a more local channel. Some scholars have outlined an active role played by grievances (see, e.g., Murshed and Gates 2005; Østby et al. 2009). Much of this scholarship rests on Stewart's (2008) notion of "horizontal inequalities," among culturally or ethnically defined groups, as opposed to "vertical inequalities," which compare individuals. Stewart, Brown, and Langer (2008, 294–295) argue that natural resources tend to augment the effect of such ethnic differences on conflict. More recently, Asal et al. (2015) and Hunziker and Cederman (2017), the latter included as Chapter 3 of this volume, present results suggesting that oil affects civil conflict primarily by triggering violent ethno-nationalist secessionism.

On the non-fuel side, however, results have been less conclusive. Inspired by popular accounts of "conflict diamonds," several authors analyze the relationship of diamond mines with civil war with mixed results (see, e.g., Lujala et al. 2005; Ross 2006). Analyzing data on the level of ethnic groups, Sorens (2010) finds some support that non-fuel mineral resource production increases the risk of secessionism. Similarly, using a grid cell-level approach and focusing on Africa, Berman et al. (2017) show that an increase in a commodity's global market price leads to a greater number of conflict-related events in areas where it is being mined. This finding is in line with Collier and Hoeffler's (1998) opportunity-focused explanation for the resource curse. Pursuing a similar approach, Christensen (2019) analyzes political violence in Africa by comparing local levels of political violence before and after non-fuel mines have gone into production. In contrast to Berman et al. (2017), he finds that mining increases the likelihood of protests and riots, but *not* civil-war related events.

All in all, the literature on mining has been less inclined to highlight explanations based on inequalities and grievances. While considering such a pathway in theory, Berman et al. (2017) focus their empirical investigation on issues relating to the feasibility of fighting rather than grievances. Going even further, Christensen (2019) explicitly rules out such explanations in favor of his own uncertainty-based interpretation.

In parallel to the trend toward more fine-grained analyses, a growing number of scholars have argued that many of the initial resource-curse findings may be the result of spurious inference (see, e.g., Brunnschweiler and Bulte 2009; Mitchell and Thies 2012; Cotet and Tsui 2013; Lei and Michaels 2014). As discussed in Chapter 2, there are several reasons to believe that whether, and to what degree a given country or region exhibits mineral resource production is not determined exogenously, but the result of sociopolitical and economic factors. One such confounding variable is the quality of political institutions. Some authors argue that countries featuring poor institutions are more likely to rely an oversized mining sector because they are unable to establish competitive manufacturing and service industries (Ross 2004; Haber and Menaldo 2011). Since weak, inefficient states are also more likely to experience violence, this mechanism would imply that previous studies have overstated the resource-conflict link. Others suggest that weak institutions may be associated with fewer mining projects, as weak property rights disincentivize investments in extractive infrastructure (Cotet and Tsui 2013; Torvik 2009). In this case, previous studies would have underestimated the gravity of the resource curse. Another potential threat to inference arises due to reverse causality. In particular, the mere prospect of political violence may deter investments in extractive infrastructure. In this case, correlational analyses would underestimate the risks associated with mining, as the most dangerous locations never actually see mineral resource production.

Several strategies have been proposed to address these endogeneity problems. For example, the previous chapter instruments for oil extraction based on geological variables. While this approach works relatively straightforwardly in the case of petroleum deposits, unfortunately, it is less directly applicable to non-fuel minerals.[1]

A more common approach is to dismiss between-unit variance and focus solely on how resource extraction and political violence covary over time. This design eliminates bias caused by unmeasured time-invariant confounders such as political institutions (e.g., Cotet and Tsui 2013; Haber and Menaldo 2011). This is also the strategy Christensen (2019) relies upon in his study of mineral resource production in Africa. In particular, following the standard generalized difference-in-differences setup, he shows that areas with newly opened mines exhibit elevated levels of political protest, while featuring pre-treatment trends of protest comparable to non-mining areas. Berman et al. (2017) take a slightly different approach, using fluctuations in world commodity prices as an exogenous source of variation in the market value of local African mineral resource deposits. Hence, Berman et al. (2017) and Christensen (2019) compare levels of violence within a geographic unit over time, investigating whether conflict-related events are more frequent when local resources become available or more valuable.

Despite making important progress, we argue that these studies suffer from three main limitations. First, the time series are in both cases limited to the period between 1997 and 2010. Yet, relying on short-term changes in production or prices as an identification strategy makes it difficult to analyze effects that only materialize over long time periods. For instance, both Christensen (2019) and Berman et al. (2017) report that economic inequality does not increase the effect of mining on the likelihood of political violence. It is possible, however, that grievances over unfair rent allocation only translate into violence after sustained periods of mineral resource production. Second, while the two studies take inequality and grievances into account, they do not do so systematically along ethnic lines. Third, and finally, their reliance on the ACLED dataset (Raleigh et al. 2010) limits their ability to break up the results into events categories that reveal the extent to which the state was targeted and whether the motivation was related to ethnic grievances.

To address these shortcomings, we turn to alternative empirical data and analysis that address these concerns.

4.2 How Do Ethnic Grievances Affect Mining Conflict?

At this point, we return to the grievance-related mechanisms that we introduced in Chapter 2 in order to show how mineral resource extraction could trigger civil conflict. Extractive activities impact the affected population in various ways, including by potentially deepening already existing horizontal inequalities among ethnic groups. According to our argument, those affected by resource extraction may harbor grievances that derive from unfair distribution, exposure to non-local, potentially better paid labor, marginalization of the groups' political influence, and finally, negative externalities resulting from environmental pollution or other disruptions of the local population's livelihood or lifestyle.

As illustrated by the previous chapter, the aforementioned grievance-based scenarios are primarily inspired by a series of prominent ethno-regional conflicts involving petroleum or gas, the latter being the case in the Acehnese civil war. In these cases, the high cost of extraction calls for major state involvement, which has far-reaching consequences for the grievance repertoire shown above. In particular, it can be expected that extraction has repercussions that go well beyond environmental grievances.

To what extent can we generalize from this mostly petroleum-focused account to other types of natural resources, such as non-fuel minerals?

What is at stake is not merely the type of resource, but also the political context at hand. Chapter 2 contends that there are good reasons to believe that similar grievances will emerge in connection with mining operations, at least to the extent that they are of reasonably large scale. It is not difficult to find evidence of mobilization around distributional claims, especially if the local population suffers from underdevelopment (e.g., Bebbington et al. 2008). In terms of migration, it is well known that many mining companies rely on foreign workers rather than the local population. In fact, Weiner (1978) introduced his notion of sons-of-the-soil partly in connection with mining operations in South Asia, which attracted an influx of mining workers into peripheral regions of India. When it comes to political grievances, however, we expect less disruption than state-led petroleum projects, which are known to trigger a major surge in state capacity. Yet, even in connection with mining, the threat to their political status constitutes an incentive for local elites to mobilize political support against central rule by appealing to the community's right to "control its own destiny" (see, e.g., Ballard and Banks 2003, 297). Sometimes, political grievances emanate from the extractor's repressive activities that may even include violent suppression of protest and targeted killings of activists (Ibid.). Furthermore, local politicians and community leaders may well be affected by mining even in cases where private companies are involved, for example through an increase in corruption (see, e.g., Knutsen et al. 2017). Finally, since many types of mining are associated with major environmental damage, environmental grievances are in principle as likely as in the case of petroleum extraction (see, e.g., Bebbington and Williams 2008).

Based on this reasoning, we introduce our first empirical hypothesis postulating a direct effect exerted by non-fuel extraction:

Hypothesis 4.1. *Mining increases the probability of ethnic civil conflict.*

It seems unlikely, however, that mining operations spur similar grievances and mobilization processes across the board. Instead, we expect national-level ethnic politics to moderate the relationship between resource extraction and ethnic conflict. According to this logic, mining-related grievances are particularly likely to be expressed in sustained mobilization against the state where they activate or reinforce pre-existing frustration over exclusion from political power. So far, we have considered explanations relating to grievance formation, but other stages of the conflict process have to be activated before political violence emerges. In particular, according to Step 3 introduced in the theoretical framework of Chapter 2, grievances need to be transformed into mobilized and armed resistance, which is an effort that requires considerable resources and organization (see, e.g., Tilly 1978).[2]

We see three main reasons why mining may be more dangerous in areas populated by politically excluded ethnic groups. First, national governments are less likely to effectively respond to mining-related grievances in politically excluded areas. Political accountability often does not extend beyond African governments' ethnic core constituencies and pressure to accommodate demands from excluded groups is accordingly low. In addition, governments often lack access to elite networks in excluded areas making it harder to correctly anticipate and address grievances related to mining operations (Kasara 2007; Roessler 2016). Second, political exclusion provides opportunities to—correctly or incorrectly—attribute responsibility for any type of unwanted change brought about by mineral extraction to national governments. Even where private extractors are the main players, ethnically excluded groups can more plausibly blame governments for distributional, migration-related, political, and environmental grievances or, at least, accuse them of insufficient assistance. Third, pre-existing political inequalities turn economic policy issues into questions of inter-group fairness and ethnic discrimination. While local residents' initial discontent may be rooted in the distribution of revenues or environmental externalities, political exclusion increases the likelihood that these issues are perceived and framed as part of a larger pattern of ethnic discrimination.

As a result of these processes, we expect mining to have stronger conflict-inducing effects in politically excluded ethnic homelands. This leads to our second empirical hypothesis:

Hypothesis 4.2. *Mining increases the probability of ethnic civil conflict in areas inhabited by excluded ethnic groups.*

4.3 Data, Methods and Results

Our empirical analysis proceeds in two steps. First, we follow recent research and analyze the impact of mining on local-level conflict events at the cell level. Second, we aggregate data on African mining activities to the level of ethnic settlement areas and run models with group-level ethnic conflict onset as the dependent variable. We use the commercial Deposit Database provided by MinEx Consulting (MinEx 2018) to construct our main independent variables. The MinEx data aims to capture all African mining deposits and provides information on discovery dates, years of extraction activity, main metals, deposit size, approximate value, and geographic location. For the present purpose, we focus on the (logged) number of active mines within a spatial unit as the main independent variable and analyze how within-unit changes in mining activity over time affects different forms of (ethnic) conflict.

4.3.1 Cell-Based Analysis of Conflict Events

We draw on the Social Conflict Analysis Database (SCAD) to identify conflict events below the threshold of organized ethnic rebellion against the state (Salehyan et al. 2012). SCAD codes low-intensity events of social conflict in Africa as well as the actors, targets, and issues involved, from 1989 onward. Our preference for SCAD over alternative event datasets like UCDP GED (Sundberg and Melander 2013) and ACLED (Raleigh et al. 2010) is based on several reasons. The UCDP GED dataset only covers violence conducted by organized armed actors and in the context of a broader conflict that has surpassed the conventional intensity threshold of 25 battle-related deaths. As a result, UCDP GED misses many theoretically interesting cases of violent or peaceful mobilization like protests, riots, strikes, or violence by armed groups unrelated to large-scale conflicts. ACLED, on the other hand, only starts in 1997 and thus covers eight years less than SCAD. Longer time series are especially important for analyses exploiting temporal variation within units and for effects that may not immediately materialize in the first year after a new mine has opened. Even more important for our purposes, SCAD provides more detail on individual conflict events allowing, for example, to identify the degree of organization, whether or not protests or violence explicitly target the government, and the political issues driving peaceful or violent mobilization (Salehyan et al. 2012). This enables us to disaggregate

SCAD events to categories more closely reflecting the grievance-related mechanisms at the heart of this volume than generic protest or conflict events.

To construct our dataset, we aggregate all active mines and SCAD conflict events to spatial cells with an average area of 500 sqkm. We construct these units as Voronoi polygons nested within African country borders. Voronoi cells offer several advantages over frequently used rectangular grids. First, they result in more compact shapes than conventional grids. Second, the distribution of cell sizes has less outliers than is the case with regular raster cells. Third, they are constructed to perfectly align with country borders which makes them more suitable for analyses that employ country or country-year fixed effects. After constructing our spatial units via Voronoi tessellation, we code, for each cell and year, whether at least one conflict occurred. We also code separate dummies for different event types. More specifically, we (i) distinguish organized events (demonstrations, riots, strikes, anti-government violence, extra-government violence) from spontaneous demonstrations and riots, (ii) identify events that explicitly target the national government, and (iii) differentiate between different issues that were "mentioned as the source of tension/disorder" (Salehyan et al. 2012). We estimate linear probability models with a conflict event dummy multiplied by 100 as the dependent variable. All models include cell fixed effects to account for all time-invariant heterogeneity across cells and thus identify effects from within-cell temporal variation only. In addition, we include country-year fixed effects controlling for temporal shocks affecting all cells within the same country. We cluster standard errors at the grid cell level and, at first, only include the logged mine count as main predictor. In a second set of specifications, we add an interaction term with a political exclusion dummy, coding all cells whose centroid falls within an excluded groups' settlement area as 1.

Fig 4.2 Results from cell-level analysis of conflict event data Table 4.1 summarizes the results from the baseline models without interactions. Model 1 in Table 4.1 indicates that doubling the number of mines in a cell increases the likelihood of conflict by about one percentage point. This general effect is somewhat larger and more precisely estimated for spontaneous riots and demonstrations (Model 2) than for organized conflict events (Model 3). Models 4–6 restrict the focus to events that explicitly target the central government. Again, there is a positive and significant general effect of active mines on conflict events but the disaggregation

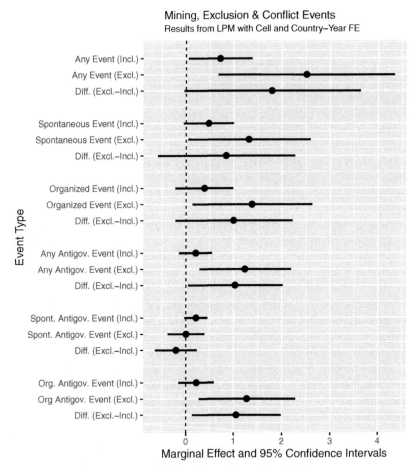

Fig. 4.2 Results from cell-level analysis of conflict event data

according to the degree of organization yields smaller, only marginally significant estimates. These initial results are broadly in line with Christensen (2019) who finds that African mining increases local protests and riots but not more organized rebel activities. The smaller effects on antigovernment events may be interpreted as consistent with his argument that contentious events in mining regions result from unmet expectations

Table 4.1 Mining and conflict events

	100 × Event Dummy					
	All Events			Anti-government Events		
	Any (1)	Spontaneous (2)	Organized (3)	Any (4)	Spontaneous (5)	Organized (6)
Active Mines (log)	1.035***	0.625***	0.560*	0.387**	0.174	0.407*
	(0.352)	(0.238)	(0.307)	(0.177)	(0.109)	(0.211)
Grid Cell FE	yes	yes	yes	yes	yes	yes
Country Year FE	yes	yes	yes	yes	yes	yes
Sample Mean DV	0.362	0.156	0.109	0.194	0.087	0.086
Observations	1,680,056	1,680,056	1,680,056	1,680,056	1,680,056	1,680,056
Adjusted R^2	0.265	0.263	0.333	0.288	0.238	0.321

Standard errors clustered on cell in parentheses
Significance: *$p < 0.1$; **$p < 0.05$; ***$p < 0.01$

of economic improvement and may target mining companies and/or local governments first.

Table 4.2 reports findings from our interactive specifications. Figure 4.2 plots the associated marginal effects in included and excluded areas as well as the difference between these estimates (i.e., the interaction term coefficient). The mining coefficient in Model 1 shows a large and significant conflict-enhancing effect of new or additional mines in politically represented ethnic homelands. The exclusion interaction is substantively large but only marginally significant. Models 2 and 3 in Table 4.2 show that the conflict effect in included ethnic settlement areas is, if anything, driven by spontaneous riots, strikes, and protests. Shifting the focus to explicitly anti-government events reveals a strikingly different pattern. Mining does not affect such events in included homelands but has a large and significant effect in politically excluded areas (Model 4). This interaction is entirely driven by more organized forms of anti-government mobilization (Models 5 and 6). In line with our theoretical argument, mining-related conflict is amplified by political ethnic inequality. Mineral extraction in politically excluded settlement areas leads to more organized challenges directed at the central government.

Table 4.3 disaggregates events according to the issues motivating mobilization: (1) "economy/jobs," (2) "food, water, subsistence," (3) "economic resources/assets," (4) "environmental degradation," and (5) "ethnic discrimination, ethnic issues" (Salehyan et al. 2012). Increasing

Table 4.2 Mining, exclusion and conflict events

	100 × Event Dummy					
	All Events			Anti-government Events		
	Any (1)	Spontaneous (2)	Organized (3)	Any (4)	Spontaneous (5)	Organized (6)
Active Mines (log)	0.716**	0.475*	0.382	0.203	0.210*	0.219
	(0.341)	(0.269)	(0.310)	(0.178)	(0.123)	(0.191)
Excluded	0.054	0.039	−0.003	0.016	0.015	0.002
	(0.040)	(0.024)	(0.019)	(0.027)	(0.016)	(0.018)
Mines × Excl.	1.793*	0.843	0.999	1.032**	−0.206	1.058**
	(0.935)	(0.729)	(0.622)	(0.503)	(0.222)	(0.472)
Grid Cell FE	yes	Yes	yes	yes	yes	yes
Country Year FE	yes	Yes	yes	yes	yes	yes
Sample Mean DV	0.362	0.156	0.109	0.194	0.087	0.086
Observations	1,680,056	1,680,056	1,680,056	1,680,056	1,680,056	1,680,056
Adjusted R^2	0.265	0.263	0.333	0.288	0.238	0.321

Standard errors clustered on cell in parentheses
Significance: *$p < 0.1$; ** $p < 0.05$; *** $p < 0.01$

Table 4.3 Mining and conflict issues

	100 × Event Dummy				
	Economy (1)	Subsistence (2)	Resources (3)	Environment (4)	Ethnicity (5)
Active Mines (log)	0.168	−0.229	0.286*	0.012	0.256**
	(0.163)	(0.194)	(0.167)	(0.017)	(0.118)
Grid Cell FE	yes	yes	yes	yes	yes
Country Year FE	yes	Yes	yes	yes	yes
Sample Mean DV	0.067	0.03	0.056	0.003	0.059
Observations	1,680,056	1,680,056	1,680,056	1,680,056	1,680,056
Adjusted R^2	0.265	0.116	0.058	0.029	0.057

Standard errors clustered on cell in parentheses
Significance: *$p < 0.1$; ** $p < 0.05$; *** $p < 0.01$

mining activity is associated with substantively large and statistically significant increases in conflicts motivated by resource-related (Model 3) and ethnic issues (Model 5). Mobilization over environmental degradation does not increase as a result of increasing mining activities (Model 4). These findings are harder to square with conventional accounts stressing opportunities for rebellion, economic expectations, or environmental degradation. The interaction models presented in Table 4.4 and Fig. 4.3 show that the mining effect on ethnically motivated conflict events only holds in politically excluded areas (Model 5). Mobilization in included regions is, if anything, about the distribution of economic resources. This heterogeneity in conflict drivers supports our expectation that political exclusion has the potential to turn mining-related grievances into ethnic ones, perhaps explaining the more sustained and explicitly anti-government forms of mobilization shown above.

In sum then, mineral extraction does increase conflict risk at the local level but the forms of mining-related mobilization systematically vary between politically excluded and included ethnic settlement areas. The space for compromise is likely to be smaller where central governments lack incentives and capacity to effectively accommodate mining-related grievances and where local groups' anti-government mobilization is

Table 4.4 Mining, exclusion and conflict issues

	100 × Event Dummy				
	Economy (1)	Subsistence (2)	Resources (3)	Environment (4)	Ethnicity (5)
Active Mines (log)	0.145	−0.207	0.307*	0.019	−0.080
	(0.195)	(0.207)	(0.173)	(0.025)	(0.127)
Excluded	0.022	0.013	−0.008	0.012**	−0.031
	(0.015)	(0.011)	(0.018)	(0.005)	(0.020)
Mines × Excl.	0.131	−0.123	−0.121	−0.039	1.887**
	(0.587)	(0.311)	(0.224)	(0.044)	(0.887)
Grid Cell FE	yes	yes	yes	yes	yes
Country Year FE	yes	yes	yes	yes	yes
Sample Mean DV	0.067	0.03	0.056	0.003	0.059
Observations	1,680,056	1,680,056	1,680,056	1,680,056	1,680,056
Adjusted R^2	0.245	0.116	0.058	0.029	0.057

Standard errors clustered on cell in parentheses
Significance: *$p < 0.1$; **$p < 0.05$; *** $p < 0.01$

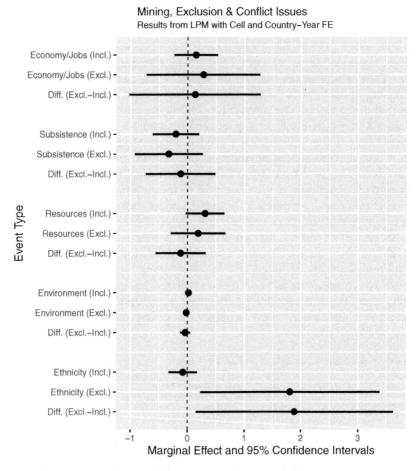

Fig. 4.3 Results from cell-level analysis of conflict event data

explicitly framed in ethnic terms. As a result, mining conflict in excluded areas can be more plausibly expected to escalate beyond single events at the very local level. In the second part of our empirical analysis, we therefore analyze whether resource extraction in excluded areas leads to full-blown ethnic rebellion against the state.

4.3.2 Group-Level Analysis of Ethnic Conflict Onset

To investigate whether mining activity predicts ethnic conflict onset at the group level, we use politically relevant ethnic group years from the Ethnic Power Relations (EPR) dataset as the unit of analysis (Vogt et al. 2015). The sample is restricted to African ethnic groups that have a settlement area polygon coded in the GeoEPR dataset (Wucherpfennig et al. 2011). Our approach uses the GeoEPR polygons to spatially aggregate the MinEx mines to ethnic group years. More specifically, we count, for each year between 1960 and 2017, the number of active mines within each politically relevant groups' settlement area. The main independent variable in our onset models is one plus the natural log of the number of mines. Conflict onset is taken from the ACD2EPR dataset that links UCDP conflict actors to EPR ethnic groups (Vogt et al. 2015).

We again estimate simple linear probability models with a conflict onset dummy multiplied by 100 as the dependent variable. We first run naive models that only include a standard set of control variables from the ethnic conflict literature as well as country and year fixed effects. As a result, these models exploit both within-group variation over time and cross-sectional variation between ethnic groups residing in the same country. We then augment these specifications with ethnic group and country-year fixed effects to approximate a difference-in-differences setup that flexibly controls for country-specific temporal shocks. In these models, all effects are identified from temporal variation in mining and conflict within ethnic homelands. In all models, we cluster standard errors at the ethnic group level to account for serial correlation. Expecting grievance-related mechanisms to be particularly relevant in areas mainly inhabited by politically unrepresented ethnic groups (H2), we interact our group-level mining activity variable with a political exclusion dummy from the core EPR dataset (Vogt et al. 2015).

Table 4.5 summarizes our findings. Columns 1 and 2 show coefficients from the models that still exploit cross-group variation within countries. The mining coefficient in Column 1 is positive, significant, and substantively large. A doubling in the number of active mines (+100%) is associated with an increase in the probability of ethnic conflict onset of 0.5 percentage points. This amounts to almost a doubling of conflict risk compared to the sample mean of 0.68 conflict onsets per 100 ethnic group years. Results in Column 2 show that the association between

Table 4.5 Group-level specifications

	100 × Conflict Onset				
	(1)	(2)	(3)	(4)	(5)
No. of Active Mines (log)	0.504**	0.217	0.332	−0.210	−6.286*
	(0.221)	(0.203)	(0.510)	(0.494)	(3.311)
Excluded	1.209***	0.613**	2.131***	1.459**	1.741***
	(0.314)	(0.299)	(0.689)	(0.649)	(0.670)
Mines × Excl.		0.992**		1.505**	1.306*
		(0.400)		(0.746)	(0.760)
Mines × Capital Dist.					0.912
					(0.565)
Mines × Ruggedness					0.020*
					(0.011)
Country FE	yes	yes	-	-	-
Year FE	yes	Yes	-	-	-
Ethnic Group FE	no	no	yes	yes	yes
Country Year FE	no	no	yes	yes	yes
Controls	yes	yes	no	no	no
Observations	9,725	9,725	9,811	9,811	9,025
Adjusted R^2	0.029	0.031	0.212	0.213	0.215

OLS linear probability models with onset dummy multiplied by 100 as dependent variable. The sample mean of the dependent variable is 0.73 conflict onsets per 100 group years. Control variables include ethnic groups' demographic size, their settlement areas' size, mean elevation, ruggedness, and capital distance, as well as recent downgrades from power and cubic polynomials for peace duration. Standard errors clustered at the ethnic group level in parentheses. Significance codes: *$p < 0.1$; ** $p < 0.05$; *** $p < 0.01$

mining and conflict only reaches significance in settlement areas of politically excluded ethnic groups. The marginal effect of mining in politically excluded ethnic settlement areas is substantively even larger than in the model without interaction term (see Fig. 4.4).

Columns 3–5 show results from our within-group specifications. Model 3 indicates that there is no significant unconditional effect of increasing mining activities on a given group's probability to engage in ethnic rebellion. Model 4 again interacts our mining variable with the political exclusion dummy. The coefficient of the interaction term is positive and statistically significant indicating that increasing mining activity has a significantly stronger effect on conflict risk in politically excluded settlement areas compared to their included counterparts. The marginal effect of a 100% increase in the number of mines in politically excluded

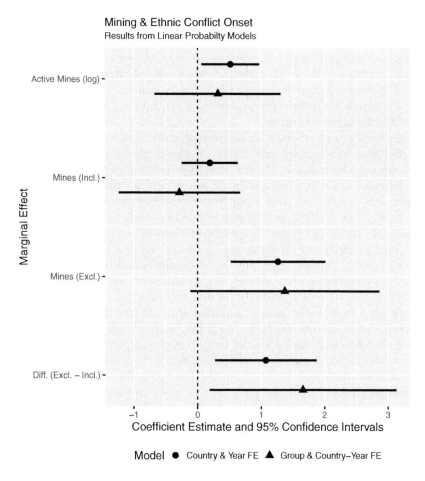

Fig. 4.4 Results from group-level analysis of ethnic conflict onset data (Based on Models 1–4 in Table 1)

areas is 1.38 percentage points which amounts to an 78% increase from the average conflict risk among politically excluded ethnic groups. This marginal effect is significant at the 10% level (last row in Fig. 4.4).

Omitted variables correlating with political exclusion and conflict risk pose a challenge to interpreting these interactive effects as causal. To address this problem, we further interact the logged mine count with the log of group polygons' centroid distance to their respective national capital as well as mean terrain ruggedness. These variables appear as the most obvious proxies for the feasibility of rebellion that may at the same time correlate with ethnic exclusion. Model 5 indicates that the inclusion of these additional interactions minimally reduces size and precision of the Mines × Exclusion term, but the basic pattern from the previous specifications remains intact.

In sum, our group-level analysis suggests that mining activity is associated with an increased probability of ethnic rebellion but only when extraction takes place in the homelands of politically excluded groups. Effects are somewhat stronger in the naive models relying not only on temporal but also on cross-group variation within countries. While the more rigorous within-group models minimize the risk of omitted variable bias, they throw out potentially informative variation between groups.

Taken together, these findings suggest that mining may increase the risk of social conflict, especially in politically excluded areas where it leads to more organized, explicitly anti-government, and ethnically motivated forms of mobilization. In short, mining conflicts appear more dangerous in excluded than in included areas. Where the local population is excluded from national-level political representation, ethnic elites and their followers have an easier time to blame the central government for mining-related grievances and externalities. This may lead to more organized challenges to the state and less space for compromise and accommodation. The analysis of the most salient issues behind instances of social conflict reveals that in excluded areas, mining-related grievances tend to be expressed and mobilized through an ethnic lens.

Even though economic expectations and environmental degradation may matter in many cases, political exclusion turns these issues into ethnic issues for which the discriminatory central government can be blamed. The prospects for compromise and accommodation seem lower than in the case of purely economically driven mobilization. Perceiving and framing mining-related grievances in ethnic terms and actively mobilizing against the government as main culprit implies a higher risk of escalation of mining-related unrest in politically excluded than in included ethnic homelands. In this sense, some of the findings of our conflict event analysis may reflect the early stages of what may turn into large-scale ethnic rebellion, the group-level outcome analyzed above.

4.4 Conclusion

By introducing new data and analysis, this chapter reinterprets the role of grievances in African mining conflicts. While the recent quantitative literature on non-fuel resources and political violence casts doubt on the grievance logic in this part of the world, we believe that this non-finding reflects empirical limitations rather than the absence of such an effect. In response, our investigation extends the relevant time series, focuses explicitly on ethno-political inequality, and uses data that introduce more precision in the assessment of conflict events. Based on these modifications, we find solid evidence that resource-related rebellion is more likely where ethnic groups are excluded. This finding offers considerable support in favor of the theoretical framework introduced in Chapter 2.

While disaggregating theoretically meaningful event categories, this chapter has not been able to fully unpack the precise nature of the causal mechanisms driving the overall findings. There is thus plenty of room for further research efforts in this area. Future quantitative studies could rely on individual-level survey data from, for example, the Afrobarometer to more directly test for the relevance of the different grievance mechanisms postulated in Chapter 2. Furthermore, in analogy to Chapter 3, it may be possible to exploit variation on geological variables to construct a new statistical instrument, but as noted above, this research strategy is arguably more difficult to implement for minerals than for hydrocarbons as done in Chapter 3. Finally, it should be noted that the analysis reported here spans over a large number of cases during a comparatively long period of time. Thus, it is also useful to trace the process linking mining to conflict in greater detail focusing on specific cases. Indeed, this is the task of the remaining chapters of this volume.

Notes

1. The problem is that the linearity assumption does not hold for mining, since the mapping between geological fundamentals and mineral resource production is both highly non-linear and complex.
2. It is likely, however, that mass-held grievances facilitate mobilizational activities (Cederman et al. 2013).

References

Asal, Victor, Michael Findley, James A. Piazza, and James Igoe Walsh. 2015. "Political Exclusion, Oil, and Ethnic Armed Conflict." *Journal of Conflict Resolution* 60 (8): 1–25.

Ballard, Chris, and Glenn Banks. 2003. "Resource Wars: The Anthropology of Mining." *Annual Review of Anthropology* 32: 287–313.

Bebbington, Andrew, and Jeffrey Bury. 2013. *Subterranean Struggles: New Dynamics of Mining, Oil, and Gas in Latin America*. Austin, TX: University of Texas Press.

Bebbington, Andrew, and Mark Williams. 2008. "Water and Mining Conflicts in Peru." *Mountain Resources and Development* 28 (3): 190–195.

Bebbington, Anthony, Denise Humphreys Bebbington, Jeffrey Bury Bury, Jeannet Lingan Lingan, Juan Pablo Munoz, and Martin Scurrah. 2008. "Mining and Social Movements: Struggles Over Livelihood and Rural Territorial Development in the Andes." *World Development* 36 (12): 2888–2905.

Berman, Nicolas, Mathieu Couttenier, Dominic Rohner, and Mathias Thoenig. 2017. "This Mine Is Mine! How Minerals Fuel Conflicts in Africa." *American Economic Review* 107 (6): 1564–1610.

Brunnschweiler, Christa N., and Erwin H. Bulte. 2009. "Natural Resources and Violent Conflict: Resource Abundance, Dependence and the Onset of Civil Wars." *Oxford Economic Papers* 61 (4): 651–674.

Cederman, Lars-Erik., Kristian Skrede Gleditsch, and Halvard Buhaug. 2013. *Inequality, Grievances, and Civil War*. Cambridge: Cambridge University Press.

Christensen, Darin. 2019. "Concession Stands: How Mining Investments Incite Protest in Africa." *International Organization* 73: 65–101.

Chuhan-Pole, Punam, Andrew L Dabalen and Bryan Christopher Land. 2017. *Mining in Africa: Are Local Communities Better Off?* The World Bank.

Collier, Paul, and Anke Hoeffler. 1998. "On Economic Causes of Civil War." *Oxford Economic Papers* 50 (4): 563–573.

Cotet, Anca M., and Kevin K. Tsui. 2013. "Oil and Conflict: What Does the Cross Country Evidence Really Show?" *American Economic Journal: Macroeconomics* 5 (1): 49–80.

Fearon, James D., and David D. Laitin. 2003. "Ethnicity, Insurgency, and Civil War." *American Political Science Review* 97 (1): 75–90.

Haber, Stephen, and Victor Menaldo. 2011. "Do Natural Resources Fuel Authoritarianism? A Reappraisal of the Resource Curse." *American Political Science Review* 105 (01): 1–26.

Hartford, Jason, Greg Lewis, Kevin Leyton-Brown, and Matt Taddy. 2017. "Deep iv: A Flexible Approach for Counterfactual Prediction." In *International Conference on Machine Learning*, 1414–1423.

Hunziker, Philipp, and Lars-Erik. Cederman. 2017. "No Extraction Without Representation: The Ethno-regional Oil Curse and Secessionist Conflict." *Journal of Peace Research* 54 (3): 365–381.

Kasara, Kimuli. 2007. "Tax Me If You Can: Ethnic Geography, Democracy, and the Taxation of Agriculture in Africa." *American Political Science Review* 101 (1): 159–172.

Knutsen, Carl Henrik, Andreas Kotsadam, Eivind Hammersmark Olsen, and Tore Wig. 2017. "Mining and Local Corruption in Africa." *American Journal of Political Science* 61 (2): 320–334.

Koubi, Vally, Gabriele Spilker, Tobias B̈ohmelt, and Thomas Bernauer. 2014. "Do Natural Resources Matter for Interstate and Intrastate Armed Conflict?" *Journal of Peace Research* 51 (2): 227–243.

Le Billon, Philippe. 2012. *Wars of Plunder: Conflicts, Profits and the Politics of Resources*. New York: Columbia University Press.

Lei, Yu-Hsiang, and Guy Michaels. 2014. Do Giant Oilfield Discoveries Fuel Internal Armed Conflicts? *Journal of Development Economics* 110: 139–157.

Lujala, Päivi. 2010. "The Spoils of Nature: Armed Civil Conflict and Rebel Access to Natural Resources." *Journal of Peace Research* 47 (1): 15–28.

Lujala, Päivi., Nils Petter Gleditsch, and Elisabeth Gilmore. 2005. "A Diamond Curse? Civil War and a Lootable Resource." *Journal of Conflict Resolution* 49 (4): 538–562.

MinEx. 2018. *Africa Deposit Database*. Melbourne: MinEx Consulting.

Mitchell, Sara McLaughlin., and Cameron G. Thies. 2012. "Resource Curse in Reverse: How Civil Wars: Influence Natural Resource Production." *International Interactions* 38 (2): 218–242.

Murshed, S. Mansoob., and Scott Gates. 2005. "Spatial-Horizontal Inequality and the Maoist Insurgency in Nepal." *Review of Development Economics* 9 (1): 121–134.

Østby, Gudrun, Ragnhild Nordås, and Jan Ketil Rød. 2009. "Regional Inequalities and Civil Conflict in Sub-Saharan Africa." *International Studies Quarterly* 53: 301–324.

Raleigh, Clionadh, Andrew Linke, Havard Hegre, and Joakim Karlsen. 2010. "Introducing ACLED: An Armed Conflict Location and Event Dataset." *Journal of Peace Research* 47 (5): 651–660.

Roessler, Philip. 2016. *Ethnic Politics and State Power in Africa: The Logic of the Coup-Civil War Trap*. Cambridge: Cambridge University Press.

Ross, Michael. 2004. "What Do We Know about Natural Resources and Civil War?" *Journal of Peace Research* 41 (3): 337–356.

Ross, Michael. 2006. "A Closer Look at Oil, Diamonds, and Civil War." *Annual Review of Political Science* 9: 265–300.

Ross, Michael L. 2015. "What Have We Learned about the Resource Curse?" *Annual Review of Political Science* 18: 239–259.

Salehyan, Idean, Cullen S. Hendrix, Jesse Hamner, Christina Case, Christopher Linebarger, Emily Stull, and Jennifer Williams. 2012. "Social Conflict in Africa: A New Database." *International Interactions* 38 (4): 503–511.

Sorens, Jason. 2010. "The Politics and Economics of Official Ethnic Discrimination: A Global Statistical Analysis, 1950–2003." *International Studies Quarterly* 54 (3): 535–558.

Stewart, Frances. 2008. Horizontal Inequalities and Conflict: An Introduction and some Hypotheses. In *Horizontal Inequalities and Conflict. Understanding Group Violence in Multiethnic Societies*, 3–23. New York: Palgrave Macmillan.

Stewart, Frances, Graham K. Brown, and Arnim Langer. 2008. "Major Findings and Conclusions on the Relationship Between Horizontal Inequalities and Conflict." In *Horizontal Inequalities and Conflict: Understanding Group Violence in Multiethnic Societies*, edited by Frances Stewart. Houndmills: Palgrave Macmillan.

Sundberg, Ralph, and Erik Melander. 2013. "Introducing the UCDP Georeferenced Event Dataset." *Journal of Peace Research* 50 (4): 523–532.

Tilly, Charles. 1978. *From Mobilization to Revolution*. London: Addison-Wesley.

Torvik, Ragnar. 2009. "Why Do Some Resource-Abundant Countries Succeed While Others Do Not?" *Oxford Review of Economic Policy* 25 (2): 241–256.

Vogt, Manuel, Nils-Christian. Bormann, Seraina Rüegger, Lars-Erik. Cederman, Philipp M. Hunziker, and Luc Girardin. 2015. "Integrating Data on Ethnicity, Geography, and Conflict: The Ethnic Power Relations Dataset Family." *Journal of Conflict Resolution* 59 (7): 1327–1342.

Weiner, Myron. 1978. *Sons of the Soil: Migration and Ethnic Conflict in India*. Princeton: Princeton University Press.

Wucherpfennig, Julian, Nils B. Weidmann, Luc Girardin, Lars-Erik. Cederman, and Andreas Wimmer. 2011. "Politically Relevant Ethnic Groups Across Space and Time: Introducing the GeoEPR Dataset." *Conflict Management and Peace Science* 28 (5): 423–437.

PART III

Case Studies

CHAPTER 5

Ethnic Mobilization and Collective Grievances in the Copper Mining Areas of Zambia

Robby Kapesa, John Bwalya, and Owen Sichone

In the early 1920s, when commercial copper production began on the colonial Northern Rhodesian, now Zambian, Copperbelt, perceived lack of economic benefits and opportunities from copper mining provoked significant expressions of ethnic grievance from the Lamba people— the area's indigenous group. However, these grievances were quickly subsumed under a more nationalistic trade union and political party-based anti-colonial struggle that tended to be pan-ethnic (Perrings 1977). Notably, very early in the life of the new mining towns new loyalties to trade union, church groups, voluntary urban clubs and political parties replaced ethnic associations (Mitchell 1956). Since then, the Copperbelt developed into a cosmopolitan melting pot where professional and other voluntary associations supplanted and dampened ethnic-based articulation of grievances on mining benefits.

Following privatization of the mines in the early 2000s, three large-scale copper mines were developed in Solwezi in North-Western Zambia:

R. Kapesa · J. Bwalya (✉) · O. Sichone
Copperbelt University, Kitwe, Zambia
e-mail: johnb.bwalya@cbu.ac.zm

© The Author(s), under exclusive license to Springer Nature Switzerland AG 2022
H. E. Ali and L.-E. Cederman (eds.), *Natural Resources, Inequality and Conflict*, https://doi.org/10.1007/978-3-030-73558-6_5

First Quantum Minerals (FQM) in Kansanshi, which began production in 2005 followed by Barrick (Formerly Equinox) in Lumwana, since 2009, and most recently FQM in Kalumbila, since 2015. In these regions, traditional chiefs act as gatekeepers of the natural resources, are holders of customary land rights and donate, sell or otherwise make available huge tracts of land for mining development, which means they play a critical role in unskilled labor recruitment for the mines. These gatekeepers expected more mining investment to create jobs and other mining-induced economic benefits for the local population (Kapesa 2019). However, even with all the three mines in the production phase, this expectation remains utopian, prompting the locals to air out grievances about their perceived lack of benefits from the mineral resources (Kabemba and Lange 2018).

The rapid mining-induced transformation of Solwezi attracted a large number of foreign nationals and Zambians from other parts of the country, akin to the development of the Copperbelt towns in the 1940s to 1960s. In 2019, Solwezi's population reached 324,194 from 203,797 in 2000, a growth rate of 59% (CSO 2019). This population boom has heightened competition between the locals and migrants for the limited job opportunities and contracts in the mines and reduced the local peoples' chances of securing positions even as unskilled laborers. Moreover, instead of procuring locally available goods and services, the mining companies disregard legislative positions and seek these goods and services from abroad (Kapesa 2019). With practices like these, mining corporations further contribute to the frustration of the local people, who as a result perceive themselves as the losers in the resource economy. In response, they have accused the multinational mining companies operating in the area, the national government as well as ordinary Zambians from other parts of the country (mostly the Bemba-speaking migrants) of benefiting from the mineral resources at their expense. The risk of ethnic-based violence can thereby be increased by such mining activities which is what this chapter tries to explore.

The role of copper mining in North-Western Zambia's ethnic power relations and mobilization demonstrate the complexity of the linkages between natural resources and conflict. While most scholars have focused on how oil and other high-value minerals, such as gold, alluvial diamond and gemstones, influence the risk of civil conflict in resource-rich countries, less attention has been given to ethnic grievances resulting through the extraction of low-value resources, for which the copper boom in

North-Western Zambia is a good example. We show how such grievances have encouraged ethnic mobilization, as well as tensions and clashes in the extraction area. Even though mining increased the levels of violence, it is important to emphasize that the boom in the copper region did not lead to secessionist conflict or armed conflict at the national level. Instead mining-induced grievances remained at the local level and were not used by the elites of affected communities to either topple the legitimate government from power or gain tight control of it (which would fit much better with the popular image of resource conflicts in Africa).

While the copper mining boom might have produced ethnic conflicts through unfair distribution of resource rents, the observed violence cannot entirely be attributed to such a government failure. There are multiple factors associated with mining that can lead to local grievances and thereby elevate the levels of violence for which we present empirical evidence below. Acknowledging these multiple factors means that informed policy aimed at managing and reducing these challenges requires a deep understanding of the mechanisms that link mineral resources to conflict so that violence can be reduced or even avoided in the future.

In this chapter, we draw on micro-level evidence from the emerging mining areas of Solwezi in North-Western Zambia to test whether copper mining provokes significant grievances and whether they engender significant ethnic mobilization and conflict. Specifically, the chapter builds on the second step outlined in Chapter 2 of this volume based on which resource-related grievances could be categorized into distributive, migration-induced, political and environmental grievances. Empirically, the chapter focuses on a single exploratory case study and theoretically focuses on the global inequality-conflict nexus between low-value natural resources and civil conflict, which includes ethnic mobilization, tension and clashes.

The chapter is structured as follows: In order to explain the surroundings of our case study, we first discuss the ethnic power relations in Zambia. Building on that, we present the research design and methods, followed by a section that presents empirical findings from fieldwork conducted in the mining areas of North-Western Zambia. The final section concludes by discussing the observed links between collective grievances, horizontal inequalities and the workings of global mining corporations.

5.1 ETHNIC POWER RELATIONS IN ZAMBIA

In order to understand how ethnicity conditions mining-induced violence in Zambia, we first have to look at the ethnic makeup of the country. For the purpose of simplification, this chapter divides Zambian's population of 16 million into five ethnolinguistic groups: Bemba, Nyanja, Tonga, Lozi and Kaonde-Lunda-Luvale (North-Westerners).[1] This list resonates well with the ethnic power relations (EPR) dataset's list of the politically relevant ethnic groups in Zambia (see Vogt et al. 2015).[2] Five-group categories like these were, in the colonial era, associated with a statutory intervention to create regional languages for use in education and government radio broadcasts and resulted in enclave geographic territories for each of these groups within the country. In the contemporary Zambian state, the Bemba-speaking population is associated with the Copperbelt, Northern, Luapula, Muchinga and some parts of Central provinces, while the Nyanja-speakers are associated with Eastern and Lusaka provinces. The Tonga-speakers are linked to Southern and some rural parts of Lusaka and Central provinces, while the Lozi-speakers are connected to Western province. The North-Westerners are, as the names already implies, associated with North-Western province (Fig. 5.1). At the national level, the Bemba represents the largest group (approximately 43% of the national population), the Nyanja and Tonga-speakers follow with roughly 30% and 12% shares in the national population, respectively. The Lozi (8%) and North-Westerners (5%) trail, respectively (Posner 2003).

Although the Kaonde, Lunda and Luvale are associated with North-Western Zambia and are at the national level referred to as North-Westerners, the Solwezi region is associated with the Kaonde, Lunda and Lamba (CSO 2011). However, the Lunda and Lamba are often viewed as migrants to the region since the Lunda are associated with the Mwinilunga-region within the North-Western province and the Lamba with the Copperbelt province. The three mines which we looked at for this study are in the Kaonde area (both the Kansanshi and Lumwana mines) and in the Lunda territory (the Kalumbia mine).[3]

A further complexity to the political and ethnic makeup of the region comes through different Chiefs who can be the head of parts or even major segments of an ethnic group. In Solwezi, the Lunda are led by Chief Musele, while the Kaonde are headed by Chiefs Kapijimpanga, Mujimanzovu and Mumena in the east and Mukumbi and Matebo in the west and the Lamba are under Chiefs, Mulonga, Kalilele, Chikola and

5 ZAMBIA CASE STUDY 101

North-Western Province of Zambia

Solwezi-District in North-Western Zambia

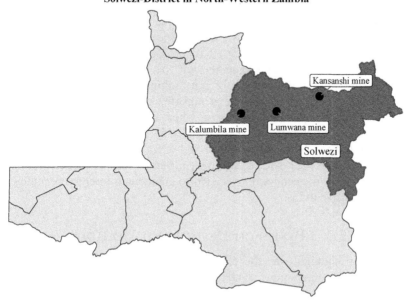

Fig. 5.1 Map of North-Western province and Solwezi district. *Source* Disaster Management and Mitigation Unit (DMMU) Zambia

Musaka. While it is possible that a territory can be entirely dominated by members of one ethnic group, the pragmatism with which the groups practice a mixture of *uxorilocality* and *virilocality* within a mostly matrilineal system does not guarantee this (Papstein 1989).[4] Thus, it would be a gross oversimplification to suggest, for example, that the Kaonde chiefs rule exclusively over the Kaonde, while the Lunda chiefs over the Lunda as they both settle and mix freely with members of the other ethnic groups largely for purposes of marriage and fulfillment of other economic, social and cultural functions.

Even though ethnicity remains the predominant dimension of social identity in the context of traditional rulers and customary law, there are always many other identities to navigate. A recent survey conducted among Zambian university students revealed that when parents are from different ethnic groups the children automatically take the father's surname and ethnic identity irrespective of the children's cultural capital, competencies or even loyalty (Roberts and Silwamba 2017). This shows that in Zambia, like in many other countries within the sub-Saharan African region, ethnicity is ascribed whereas political association is voluntary (Posner 2005).

Zambians generally show strong cultural attachments to their home districts which is why a lack of economic development in a particular area can often be interpreted as economic marginalization of the group associated with that region. Likewise, geographically concentrated resources such as copper are now considered to belong to the ethnic groups in whose area they are found even though the mining sector in Zambia is dominated and controlled by foreign multinational mining companies (Kapesa 2019). Members of these groups thus claim exclusive ownership, access and rights over those resources which are however not backed by either law or Zambian custom (see GRZ 2015). Instead they constitute an invention of the Chiefs, party officials and other local leaders who seek to control access to the resources and their material benefits since the 1990s liberalization of the economy which led to augmented foreign investment in the extractive industry.

5.2 Research Design and Methods

In order to highlight why this ethnic and political makeup matters when it comes to resource-induced grievances and violence, this chapter relies on an embedded explorative case study design (see Creswell 2009) in which we look at three mining communities of the Solwezi region inside North-Western Zambia (Kansanshi, Lumwana and Kalumbila) between March 2015 and February 2019. The case study aims to establish whether the booming copper mining in the area provoked perceptions of marginalization among the local population, whether such perceptions generated significant levels of collective grievances, and if in turn such grievances engendered ethnic mobilization, tension and clashes in the mining communities (see Step 3 in Chapter 2).

For this purpose, we collected data through three different approaches: In-depth interviews, focus group discussions and document analysis.

5.2.1 In-Depth Interviews

First, we conducted sixty in-depth interviews in the three mining communities of Solwezi. All participants were purposively selected based primarily on their first-hand experiences with copper mining and its effects on the local economy and livelihoods. Additionally, we interviewed three out of the five chiefs hosting the large-scale mines.[5] We also interviewed local civil society groups dealing with mining and other related activities in the three communities. These comprise the North-Western Council of Elders (NWCE), Musele Chamber of Commerce (MCC) and Musele Taskforce (MT). Furthermore, we interviewed members of the school authorities in each of the three mining communities. We only selected school managers from primary schools who had received support from their respective mines. In addition, we held interviews with three government officials based in Solwezi: from the Ministries of Mines, Agriculture and Lands. We selected these officials because they were actively involved in the resettlement and compensation of the affected households, and land expropriation. We also interviewed three Human Resource mine officials from the respective communities.

We further interviewed 45 local community members (local Kaonde and Lunda, and migrants—15 from each mining community), where interviews were conducted with traditional leaders (headmen/women), youths, jobseekers, retrenched miners and migrants. For headmen/women, we selected nine individuals (three from each mining community). For ease of reach and more direct contact with the mines, we only contacted those within five kilometers radius from their respective mining concessions. Furthermore, we talked to 15 youths (five from each community)[6] and interviewed nine (three from each community) retrenched mineworkers.[7] Finally, we interviewed 12 migrants (four from each mining community) where we only considered people as migrants who had moved to Solwezi at least six months before we conducted the interviews.[8]

With consent of participants, interviews were recorded and, on average, lasted about 45 minutes. Interviews gathered demographic data, ethnicity, education qualification attained, the period of residence in Solwezi, their place of birth, occupation and employment status, among others. Rather than requesting participants to reveal their actual names, we assigned them random codes (e.g., PN1 = Participant Number 1, PN2 = Participant Number 2 and so on). The second part of the interview sought participants' perception of how mining had affected their livelihoods, their economic benefits as well as the opportunities created and the challenges associated with it. We also asked them about who they thought benefits most from the mineral resources and prompted them to discuss their personal view as well as the local population's understanding of the benefits associated with copper mining.

The resulting data was analyzed using qualitative content analysis technique (Yin 2013). First, we transcribed interview conversations and discussions. To avoid wordiness and cloudiness of the information (Creswell 2009), naturalized transcription was applied (Bucholtz 2000). Before beginning the detailed data analysis, we counterchecked the transcripts for errors, clustered important themes as coding units, and created dimensions and relations between them in order to uncover patterns and test categories against the full range of data (Creswell 2009). This methodological step brought out important inferences from the data which, to a great extent, aided our interpretation process. Finally, the relevant literature on resource conflict and ethnic mobilization helped us contextualize the findings from the North-Western Zambian case (e.g., McNeish 2018; Rudel 2018). The underlying logic was to compare and contrast the findings obtained to other related cases in the literature.

5.2.2 Focus Group Discussions

We conducted nine focus groups discussions (three from each mining community—male only, female only and mixed gender participants). There were seven participants in each single gender focus groups, while each mixed gender group featured eights participants (four males and four females). The selection of participants was based on demographic characteristics such as male, female and youth, as well as proximity to their respective mining concession, their length of residence in the local community and employment status.

On average, each focus group discussion lasted 1 hour 30 minutes. On highly contentious issues, the participants were asked to vote in order to break the tie and get a group position on a point of discussion. We analyzed the information collected in the same manner as the interview data. The aim was to validate the main issues participants raised during personal interviews.

5.2.3 Document Analysis

Both public and non-public institutional reports provided evidence on the contribution of the copper mining sector to the national economy and living standards of the local population regarding specifically the mining areas of Solwezi in North-Western Zambia as well as of Zambia, in general. To do this, we relied on the Statistician (CSO 2019); Zambia's 2018 Demographic and health Survey (ZDHS 2019); and the 9th Zambia Extractive Industry Transparency Initiative report (ZEITI 2018). Due to data availability issues we restricted our analysis to the financial year 2016. We analyzed and presented the data collected using descriptive statistics, mostly percentages and frequencies.

5.3 Empirical Findings

This section presents empirical evidence analyzing the effects of the copper mining sector in Solwezi on the local economy. It further shows how copper mining provoked perceptions of inequality and marginalization among the local population, whether such perceptions facilitated collective grievances and whether, in turn, the grievances encouraged ethnic mobilization, tension and clashes, particularly in communities adjacent to the mines (the local community).

5.3.1 Effects of the Copper Mining Boom on Local Economy and Livelihoods

Table 5.1 indicates Zambia's 2016 total copper production in metric tons, disaggregated between Solwezi in North-Western, the country's

Table 5.1 Total copper production and contribution of the Solwezi mines, 2016

Mine		Total copper production (Mt)	% of national production
Solwezi mines	Kansanshi	246,794	31.9
	Lumwana	122,971	15.9
	Kalumbila	139,600	18.0
	Sub-Total	509,365	65.8
Others		264,925	34.2
Grand Total		774,290	100.0

Source Calculated from ZEITI (2018)

new mining frontier, and the Copperbelt, the country's traditional copper mining hub. Comparatively, the three Solwezi mines, Kansanshi, Lumwana and Kalumbila, accounted for 65.8% of the total copper produced, surpassing the Copperbelt by a great margin (32.6%), hence transforming Solwezi and North-Western Zambia, in general, into the country's "New Copperbelt." This development brought to the fore unrealistic local expectations of massive mining-induced economic benefits and opportunities. The major question then is whether the booming copper mining in Solwezi created sufficient economic benefits and opportunities to meet local expectations and demands.

Being capital-intensive and lacking strong linkages with the local economy, the main benefits from mining in Zambia lie in its contributions to export earnings and government revenues. Generally, however, even these are a source of tension since the government has been granting the multinational companies huge amounts in value-added taxes (VAT) refunds, and which has been suspected of transfer pricing and tax avoidance operations. In 2016, the mining sector contributed 2.0%, 10.5%, 26.4% and 72.8% to the country's GDP, total employment, government revenues and export earnings, respectively. Seen from these figures, the sector's contributions to the GDP (at constant prices) and paid employment were unreasonably low, much to the frustrations of many Zambians, especially those in the new mining areas of Solwezi who anticipated the mining boom to drastically improve their livelihoods (see Kapesa 2019).

Table 5.2 shows the contribution of the mining sector to Zambia's export earnings in 2016. Approximately, 68% of the sector's total contribution came from copper mining alone. Overall, the mining sector

Table 5.2 Contribution to export earnings by metal exports, 2016

	Total export value (US$ Million)	% of total revenue
Metal exports	4,738.2	72.8
Copper	4,399.1	67.6
Cobalt	112.9	1.7
Gold	191.2	2.9
Gemstones	28.4	0.4
Manganese concentrates	6.6	0.1
Zambia exports (f.o.b)	6,504.7	100.0

Source Calculated from CSO (2019) and ZEITI (2018)

provided the government with US$ 1.1 billion in revenue, of which the three mines in Solwezi accounted for US$ 462.0 million. Comparatively, the total contribution (43.1%) of the Solwezi mines to the government revenues failed to match with the quantity of copper produced (65.8%). Based on this gap, some migrant participants we interviewed suspected the mines of engaging in tax avoidance activities.[9] In contrast, some members of the local community we interviewed disputed the claim that the Solwezi mines were not paying their fair share of taxes. They believed the mines were paying "huge" amounts to the central government in taxes, and as such, they expected the government to use part of the tax revenue to improve the local economy and livelihoods.[10] While these opinions demonstrate the wide gap between local perceptions and the contributions of the local mines to the government revenues, they also illustrate the secrecy shrouding the mining activities in the area.

The central government received most of the mining revenues.[11] District councils and the communities located in mining areas received a smaller part of the rent. The district councils received a combined total of approximately 0.9% of the total mining revenues in property rates and annual business fees, while the local community received 2.7% as social payments under the heading of corporate social responsibility (CSR). Solwezi Municipal Council received the highest amount (US$ 2.9 million) in property rates, while the Chingola, Chililabombwe and Luanshya Municipal Councils on the Copperbelt received US$ 1.20 million, US$ 1.15 million and US$ 0.9 million, respectively. Generally, the government maintained a semi-decentralized fiscal system, in which district councils and the local community participated. Local participants demanded a fully decentralized fiscal system in which the local community could receive and disburse parts of the mining revenue that the central government collected beyond being a mere recipient of social payments (CSR).[12]

Table 5.3 indicates mining companies' spending on education and health facilities, infrastructure and sports as part of CSR activities. Of the total US$28.1 that the mines spent on CSR activities, the Solwezi mines spent a combined total of US$ 13.0 million. This shows that the local community only received about 0.3% in CSR activities of the total national metal export value generated in 2016. With this small budget, the mines could not execute meaningful CSR projects to meet local expectations, which provoked a sense of economic exclusion among the locals which were however directed against the central government (see Chief's statement at the beginning of the chapter).

Table 5.4 shows employment figures in the mining sector and the contribution of the Solwezi mines toward those figures in 2016. Given the towering expectations for jobs among the local population, these figures were "a drop in an ocean," especially when compared to a workforce of over 70,000 recorded in the 1990s prior to the privatization of the mines in the early 2000s (see ZCCM 2000). Generally, the Solwezi mines maintained a lean workforce, mostly of semi- and skilled workers over the entire period of the study. Although the mines had maintained a smaller number of expatriate workers most of the managerial and technical positions were filled by expatriate workers, while a majority of Zambian

Table 5.3 Corporate social responsibility spending in the mining sector, 2016

Mine		Spending on (US$ Million)					
		Education	Health	Infrastructure	Sports	Others	Total
Solwezi Mines	Kansanshi	0.5	0.01	5.0	0.4	1.0	6.9
	Lumwana	0.4	0.4	0.1	–	0.2	1.1
	Kalumbila	0.1	0.3	0.4	–	4.0	4.9
	Sub-Total	1.1	0.6	5.6	0.4	5.2	13.0
Others		1.9	12.1	–	0.4	0.7	15.1
Grand Total		3.0	12.8	5.6	0.8	5.9	28.1

Source Calculated from ZEITI (2018)

Table 5.4 Employment figures in the mining sector and contributions of Solwezi mines, 2016

Mine	Direct domestic employees	Share in national total (%)	Direct foreign employees	% of industry employment
Solwezi—Kansanshi	2,723	9.0	141	15.8
Mines—Lumwana	1,575	5.2	59	6.6
Kalumbila	2,076	6.8	150	16.9
Sub-Total	**6,374**	**21.0**	**350**	**39.3**
Others	**24,046**	**79.0**	**540**	**60.7**
Grand Total	30,420	100.0	890	100.0

Source Drawn from CSO (2019) and ZEITI (2018)

workers were left foraging for low-wage semi- and unskilled jobs (see Kapesa 2019).

5.3.2 Perceptions of Lack of Benefits from Mineral Resources: Collective Grievances

Our evidence shows that the failure of the copper mining sector to live up to local expectations and demands in terms of its contributions to the local economy and livelihoods in Solwezi in North-Western Zambia provoked a sense of economic marginalization and frustration among the local population. This affected particularly those in the communities adjacent to the mines who directly shoulder the brunt of mining negative externalities such as massive in-migration, environmental pollution, land expropriation, and forced displacement and resettlement. The perceived lack of benefits from the mineral resources triggered all four types of collective grievances that were referred to in Chapter 2. These distributive, migration-induced, political and environmental grievances in turn engendered ethnic mobilization and tensions, which we will demonstrate below.

5.3.3 Distributive Grievances

Local participants claimed the mining revenues generated from Solwezi in North-Western Zambia were transferred to other parts of the country, while the local people in the mining communities continued to live in abject poverty. A local Lunda in Kalumbila complained that "[d]espite Solwezi district currently being the country's economic backbone, the North-Western, where it belongs, still remains Zambia's most economically marginalized province."[13] Local civil society groups monitoring the socioeconomic consequences of mining development in Solwezi also cast blame on the government for lack of economic development and benefits from the mineral resources. Their representatives demanded:

> The Government must retain a large portion of the mining revenue collected from Solwezi, in Solwezi to facilitate infrastructure development. When you look at the state of infrastructure in the area, it needs urgent attention. Look at the roads, schools and hospital; they are all in dire need of urgent attention. In fact, Kalumbila has no proper roads, schools and hospitals. Why should it be like that when the Government is collecting huge taxes from the mines operating from the area [Solwezi]?[14]

Traditional authorities also blamed the central government for not using the mining revenues to support and improve the living standards of the local people, particularly in the mining communities. A senior Kaonde Chief openly complained: "We are not benefiting from our mineral resources."[15] The traditional leader accused the central government of transferring all the mineral wealth generated from Solwezi to other parts of the country, at the expense of the mining communities whose natural environment had been polluted and whose land had been expropriated by the mines. Epitomizing this sense of economic marginalization and inequality, another senior Kaonde chief in Lumwana opined:

> What comes out of Solwezi [mining revenue] does not match with what comes in [economic development]. Solwezi currently contributes over 75% resources [as mining revenue] to the national treasury, of which less than 2% comes back to support economic development in the area.[16]

Focus group participants believed that the Solwezi mines were paying huge amounts of money in taxes to the central government, which the government unjustly transferred to other parts of the country, particularly in the Bemba-Nyanja areas from where the majority of the cabinet ministers, including the president, originate. As did the local civil society groups, the focus group participants demanded that the mining revenues which the government collected should be divided into two portions and that the local community should receive the larger share because they were the ones that directly shouldered the brunt of the negative externalities associated with mining. None of the participants commented on the revenues deriving from property rates, ground rents and annual business fees that the Solwezi Municipal Council and the local community received as social payments. When the issue was brought to their attention during the discussion, they trivialized it and claimed most mining revenues went to the central government that needed to be shared.[17]

The area's Member of Parliament (MP) launched an official complaint in parliament, arguing that "[d]espite Kansanshi, Kalumbila and Lumwana in Solwezi paying huge amounts in taxes to government, there is no meaningful development in my constituency and North-Western Province as a whole" (GRZ 2016). At home, the MP was highly eulogized for the stance taken and for being the mouthpiece of the local people. Supporting his stance, an ordinary Kaonde in Lumwana wondered, "[w]hy should the government use the mineral revenue generated from Solwezi to develop infrastructure in other ethno-regions?"[18] According to the local population, the existing mineral wealth distribution mechanisms that allowed the central government to collect and disburse the mining revenues favored outsiders at the expense of the locals because the mechanisms did not prioritize the welfare of the local people in the distribution of such revenues.

Regarding CSR spending, participants claimed the investment was inadequate and rarely met local expectations. In Lumwana, for example, it was reported that the community needed a secondary school and a clinic, but the mine constructed additional classroom blocks at Kakaindu Primary School and boreholes around the community.[19] The nearest school was at Manyama Day-Secondary School, a distance of more than 5 km, where the teacher–pupil ratio stood at 1 to 120.[20] Equally at Kisasa community in Kalumbila, the community wanted a secondary school and a hospital because the nearest secondary school (Jiundu) and the main hospital (Solwezi) are located too far away (20 km and 140 km, respectively). Instead, the mine built an additional classroom block and three teachers' houses at Kisasa Primary School and a ward at Kisasa clinic.[21] At Kansanshi, it was alleged that the mine initially constructed bore holes for its own use (to monitor the extent of underground water levels and pollution around the mine) but later paraded them as part of its CSR contribution to the community.[22] These conditions demonstrated the extent of underdevelopment and lack of government support which the mining communities had to endure even in the face of the copper mining boom. At the same time, it also confirmed the opacity surrounding the execution of CSR activities in the area, which in turn jeopardized the relevance of the CSR projects.

At the community level, the distribution of the mining-induced economic benefits was seen as skewed in favor of the local elite, particularly traditional chiefs, who directly negotiated with the multinational companies on behalf of their subjects. Several meetings "prior to our resettlement were held behind our back between the chief and the company [FQML]," revealed one of the resettled persons at Kalumbila.[23] At Lumwana, it was also reported that although the three chiefs were defending the interests of their subjects, they prioritized the employment of their relatives and friends at the mine.[24] Although affected households at Kansanshi had not received adequate compensation according to international standards for their land and property, they had been directly involved in the resettlement process. The mine also managed its labor directly, its contracted companies notwithstanding, which disenchanted the Kaonde Chief (Kapijimpanga) in whose district the mine is located. Like his counterparts at Lumwana, he too wanted to manage the recruitment of unskilled labor on behalf of the mine.

5.3.4 Migration-Induced Grievances

One of the issues that featured prominently in our interviews as well as in the focus group discussions was the lack of fairness regarding the distribution of mining-related jobs and business contracts between the locals and the migrants. Local participants expressed frustration that the mines were favoring outsiders, in particular the Bemba-speaking migrants, for unskilled jobs that originally were meant for the local population. One of the unemployed local Kaonde in Lumwana put it like this:

> The presence of the Bemba (speakers) in the area from the Copperbelt, who are more qualified academically and with better experience in mining and other related activities, makes it extremely difficult for us [local Kaonde] to find a job at the mine [Lumwana].[25]

Local participants also severely underestimated their own chances and those of the entire local population of getting a job or promotion at their respective mines. A local Lunda in Kalumbila put it simply: "The Bemba migrants have taken all our jobs."[26] His Kaonde counterpart in

Lumwana claimed that "[t]he Bemba migrants are in majority among the Zambian workers at Lumwana."[27] The mine reported, "[w]e [are] willing to recruit anyone with the necessary qualifications and skills regardless of gender, ethnicity and race, but priority is always given to the locals [the Lunda]."[28] Accordingly, the three mines indicated that most of their semi-skilled and unskilled laborers were local, that is from the Kaonde for Kansanshi and Lumwana, and Lunda for Kalumbila.[29]

Efforts to get labor details at all the three mines in order to segregate labor figures according to the five ethno-linguistic groups, especially unskilled laborers with Zambian origin, proved futile. It even seemed that the mines did not possess this information, since after all, they did not employ their labor based on ethnicity. In the absence of this information, however, we observed that the local Kaonde and Lunda dominated the rank-and-file of unskilled labor at the Lumwana and Kalumbila mines, especially those directly under the mine payroll. This is because they were employed through chiefs, who used ethnicity as the main criterion to determine who is "local" and who is not. Those who could use a national identity card (NRC) in order to prove that they were born in Solwezi and could speak the vernacular (Kaonde for Lumwana and Lunda for Kalumbila) fluently were able to enlist their names in the community database, from which the respective mines drew their unskilled labor. Being in the production phase, all the three mines had hired a combined total of about 3,000 unskilled workers directly on their payroll, and slightly over 4,000 indirectly through their contracted companies (see Zambia Chamber of Mine 2016).

Who the companies hired in terms of ethnicity and region depended on many factors. For example, contractors employed more from where the company's headquarters was based. Whereas mines domiciled in the Copperbelt had more Bemba-speaking dwellers among its workers, Solwezi companies had more Kaonde and Lunda employees. Local participants, however, demanded that semi-skilled and unskilled jobs, whether offered by contracted companies or the mines directly, should be restricted to the local population, whose mineral resources the mines were exploiting. In contrast, migrant participants insisted that all Zambians should be allowed to access formal jobs from any part of the country as they hitherto had been, without discrimination based on ethnicity or region.

5.3.5 Political Grievances

One of the main reasons why the mining revenues alleged transferred to other ethno-regions was repeatedly cited as the lack of proportional representation for the Kaonde-Lunda-Luvale group (North-Westerners) in government. Local interviewees reported they had no one to speak for them in government. The evidence, however, shows that the Kaonde-Lunda-Luvale had been consistently and proportionally represented in government (e.g., in the police service, national assembly and cabinet) since the country's independence in 1964 (see also Kapesa 2019). Yet, despite this, a local Lunda in Kalumbila alleged that "[t]he Bemba migrants have political connections [which we do not have] to help them get mine jobs, even unskilled jobs meant for us [the local Lunda]."[30] A Kaonde miner in Lumwana also recounted:

> When the mine started, the company owners were listening to our traditional chiefs, but now they listen more from senior politicians. To get a job in the mine you need to be connected to senior politicians [cabinet ministers], whom unfortunately, we [the Kaonde] lack, but our friends the Bemba have.[31]

First of all, there appear to be clear differences in terms of perceptions of inequalities and marginalizations between the Bemba and Nyanja-speaking participants on the one hand, and the Tonga-Lozi-North-Westerners participants on the other: As local Kaonde and Lunda participants, Tonga- and Lozi-speaking participants claimed that cabinet ministers helped the Bemba- and Nyanja-speaking migrants to secure mine jobs and business contracts. The Bemba- and Nyanja-speaking participants on the other hand insisted it was their prior experience and professional qualifications acquired from the mines in the Copperbelt that actually made them more attractive than the locals on the job market, especially as semi- and skilled mineworkers.

5.3.6 Environmental Grievances

Apart from distributional, migration-based and political grievances, this case study also found evidence relating to the fourth grievance type of our theoretical framework which looks at environmental grievances. The importance of these grievances has in this case even been acknowledged by the government which, in response to environmental concerns, enacted the Environmental Management Act (EMA) No. 12 of 2011 (see GRZ 2011). The Act repealed the outdated Environmental Protection and Pollution Control Act (EPPCA) and re-named the Environmental Council of Zambia (ECZ), the country's principal regulatory body, as the Zambia Environmental Management Agency (ZEMA). Notably, the EMA empowers both ZEMA and members of the general public to sue any companies, including mines, operating in Zambia that flouts environmental regulations, among many other improvements. Despite this, however, it was reported that the three Solwezi mines rarely faced litigation for their deliberate negative impacts on the environment. Poor civil society networks, ZEMA's limited funding, political interference and inadequate qualified personnel exacerbated the problem. It was noticed that despite witnessing sustained copper mining boom, the North-Western had no ZEMA presence. In fact, the whole northern region of the country consisting of Copperbelt, Northern, Muchinga, Luapula and North-Western provinces, was being monitored by the Ndola office.[32] This centralization seriously handicapped ZEMA's operations, which in turn created an enabling environmental within which the mines flouted environmental regulations with impunity.

In predominantly rural regions, such as Solwezi in North-Western Zambia, where over 98% of land is still under customary tenure, individuals own land as long as they cultivate it or build a house or other valuable structure on it (see GRZ 1995). Traditionally, no one person owns customary land in Zambia which means that the land belongs to all community members as a group (see Chileshe 2005). That is not to say that in rural Zambia an individual land ownership does not exist but that it is always subject to the common interest of the entire community. The government, however, enacted a law in 1995 (The Land Act No. 29 of 1995) to recognize the title of individuals holding land under customary tenure (see GRZ 1995) which, aimed to attract and protect foreign investment, permits the conversion of tenure over such lands from customary to leasehold tenure. As a result, the affected community members in Solwezi can no longer claim ownership of the customary land that had been turned into private mining concessions, which has led participants in all the three mining communities to report massive land expropriation and mining-induced environmental damage. They cited various pollutions that include dust, noise and vehicle emissions. Vibrations from heavy earth moving equipment were also pointed out as the major threat to the built environment which has created huge cracks in several houses, churches and schools built along major roads. This generated discontent among the local people who deemed themselves economically marginalized. A local participant bemoaned that "despite directly shouldering the brunt of mining negative externalities in pollution, land expropriation and damage to our built environment, we [the locals] have remained sidelined from accessing the mining-induced economic benefits [jobs and contracts]."[33] The participant further reported that mining development in Solwezi had threatened land-based livelihood activities such as cropping, livestock, and harvesting and processing of environmental products.[34] Specifically, local participants indicated that mining development in the area had led to the conversion of most of the village's public goods, such as forests and water bodies, into private properties in the form of mining concessions on which the locals were not allowed to trespass. Other interviewees stated that the mining development had curtailed the local population's open access to the important natural resources such as trees for charcoal burning, caterpillars, wild edible vegetables and fruits, as well as mushroom for their consumption, and thatch grass and poles for constructing houses.[35] The loss provoked collective disenchantment among the locals whose livelihoods are intimately connected to the land and its resources (see also Kapesa et al. 2015).

In Kalumbila, the members of the local community interviewed accused the mine of expropriating the Kalumbila forest and polluting the Kisola River, where the mine had constructed a dam, thereby negatively impacting the many local livelihoods which depend upon them.[36] In Lumwana, the members of the local community accused the mine of fencing-off the entire mining concession, including areas that were not being used, which curtailed local population's access to the important environmental services and products upon which they depend.[37] And in Kansanshi, some of the locals interviewed accused the mine of expropriating the nearby forest and polluting underground water.[38]

Overall, the mining-induced environmental challenges in North-Western Zambia have generated significant levels of grievances among the local population which has in turn heightened ethnic competition for the scarce environmental services and products on the residual commons. Furthermore, the grievances have engendered sharp tension and clashes between neighboring communities, as well as between locals and migrants.

5.3.7 Ethnic Mobilization, Tension and Clashes in the Copper Mining Communities

We now turn from the articulation of grievances to mobilization processes (see Step 3 in the theoretical framework in Chapter 2). In March 2015, a violent protest at Kisasa in Kalumbila erupted and expanded to the surrounding mining communities. Many Zambians were shocked as the Bemba-speaking migrants became targets for violence and animosity because they were accused of getting mine jobs and business contracts meant for the local population. The violence lasted for several hours, and many Bemba-speaking migrants were injured as a result. Initial police response came late and failed to contain the violence. With reinforcement from nearby police stations, police managed to apprehend eighteen perpetrators, all of whom were local Lunda with strong links with the traditional authority.[39] The arrests sent shock waves through the community, which helped to temporarily quell the violence. In the following few days, the traditional authority and the local population put pressure on the police and the government to release the suspects. However, their release would not occur until the suspects had spent close to a week in police custody. Their case was also closed shortly after their release.

Participants described the move by the police to release the suspects and terminate the case as politically induced. They accused senior government officials of interfering into police operations in order to use the incidence to gain the much-needed political support for the ruling Patriotic Front party and its candidates in the region for the general elections in 2016. The North-Western region including Solwezi had been an opposition party, the United Party for National Development stronghold since 2011. In the January 2015 presidential by-election, the PF lost in all the 15 constituencies to the UPND (ECZ, 2015). Some local participants even accused the ruling PF party to manipulate this incidence in order to change its political fortunes in the area.[40] For the locals, the move by the police vindicated them and justified their actions.[41] As a result, demands for increased local stake in the mineral wealth and the associated economic benefits have gained local attention and approval.

The Kalumbila mine denounced the violence and accused Musele Traditional Authority of instigating it in order to restrict mine jobs and other mining-induced economic opportunities to the local population, a move of which the company, the government and the general public strongly disproved (Zambia Daily Mail 2015). Even after the restoration of peace and with a significant improvement of ethnic relations a few months after the event, tension between the local Lunda population and the Bemba-speaking migrants continued to foment. A Lunda at Kisasa vowed: "The Bemba will never be our brothers because they are after our jobs"[42] and in other mining communities, tension between the locals (the Kaonde) and the Bemba-speaking migrants continued to escalate: In Lumwana, a local Kaonde declared, "[t]he Bemba should go back home [the Copperbelt] before we start killing them."[43] His colleague in Kyawama asserted that "[a]s long as the Bemba migrants continue to take away our jobs, we [the Kaonde] will continue to attack them."[44] Inquired if the Bemba migrants were being attacked, the participant affirmed with an emphatic yes: "We sort them out."[45] These examples demonstrate just how distressingly tense the local-Bemba migrant relations in the mining communities of Kansanshi, Lumwana and Kalumbila had become.

Domestically, the copper mining boom has exacerbated inter-ethnic group tensions and clashes. The three Kaonde chiefs, whose land overlaps with the Lumwana mining concession, had early on treated the mine as a community property. For them, the local community meant the Kaonde population within the three chiefdoms with which the mining concession overlap. The rest were treated as "foreigners," who therefore had no right to partake in the mining-induced economic benefits. As a local Lunda recounted: "Whenever we [the Lunda] seek for jobs at Lumwana, we are told [by the Kaonde] your jobs are at Kalumbila; the jobs at Lumwana are for us [the Kaonde]."[46]

At Kalumbila, the picture was similar. During the mine's construction phase, the traditional authority had a chance, albeit a brief one, to recruit unskilled laborers on behalf of the mine. The authority ensured that all jobseekers were subjected to oral interviews in Lunda. The idea was to recruit only the local people, who could fluently speak Lunda as semi-skilled and unskilled laborers for the mine. Although this intervention was generally meant to eliminate Zambians from other provinces from the job market, locally, it was used to discriminate against the Kaonde, who were previously accused of discriminating against the Lunda in a similar manner at Lumwana: "The Kaonde have been omitted in the [Kalumbila] database because we [the Lunda] were also left out at Lumwana," alleged a local Lunda in Kalumbila.[47]

5.4 Discussion

We have found evidence that all four types of grievances, that is distributive, migration-induced, political and environmental grievances, are present in the local communities' response to mining. These four grievance dimensions reinforce the underlying factors that cause and shape ethnic mobilization, tension and clashes in the emerging mining areas of Solwezi in North-Western Zambia. These themes, however, should be seen as neither ubiquitous nor mutually exclusive. At Kansanshi, for example, it was the non-existence of formal arrangement between the mine and the local community concerning recruitment of unskilled labor and the general lack of unskilled job opportunities at the mine that provoked a sense of unfairness in the distribution of jobs. This facilitated distributive grievances among the locals which in turn generated other types of grievances. At both Kalumbila and Lumwana mines it was the presence of large influx of the Bemba-speaking migrants that provoked migration-induced grievances among the locals, which in turn facilitated other types of grievances. Overall, resource-related concerns driven by profit-seeking and grievances constantly reinforced each other to cause and shape ethnic mobilization, tension and clashes. Next, we go back to the theoretical framework introduced in Chapter 2 in order to best explain these findings and to put them into context.

Although the issues that participants raised and those we observed in the mining areas of Solwezi in North-Western Zambia provide support for the plausibility of all four steps introduced in Chapter 2, our contribution focused in particular on Step 2 by looking at collective grievances among the locals in the mining areas of North-Western Zambia. Our observations correspond closely to the four grievance types that were introduced in Step 2. This suggest that the boom in copper mining can provoke collective grievances among the local population, particularly in the mining areas, which in turn could engender conflict.

In line with Chapter 4 of this volume, which uses an Africa-wide sample, the participants in the North-Western Zambian case highlighted concerns relating to the distribution of political influence and wealth. Participants in the mining areas of Solwezi emphasized the notion that they were excluded and "forgotten" by the central government, which was captured by the Bemba- and Nyanja-speaking elites. They claimed that the government had transferred most of the mining revenues to other regions. Although this sense of injustice referred mainly to the province, interviewees also applied it to the chiefdom. Extending beyond the distribution of local jobs, the grievances also concerned cabinet, diplomatic and civil service leadership positions that local elites felt had been denied to them. Based on this evidence, we have found that the strong influence of traditional chiefs and the blurred presence of the state led to increased local (*mis*)perceptions of political and economic marginalization in Solwezi. However, despite this finding, the common assumption in the civil conflict and ethnic mobilization literature that ethnic coalitions at the elite level can be easily translated to the grassroot level (Cederman et al. 2010, 2011; Wimmer 2002), what Sisk and Stefes (2005, 298) termed "ethnic bridging," could not be confirmed by our evidence. We found that ethnic cooperation at the elite level, which is dominated by chiefs, politicians and civil society group leaders, rarely extended to the grassroots level.

For unranked societies, where no one ethnic group monopolizes access to the state power, Vogt (2019 shows that increased ethnic competition for the limited resources exacerbates ethnic mobilization and conflict. Inadequate job opportunities and massive labor in-migration increase the risk of ethnic mobilization and conflict in ethnically plural mining regions (Banks 2013). Furthermore, groups that lose in this competition over limited resources and opportunities "share both common grievances and a common identity", which in turn makes ethnic mobilization and conflict more likely, particularly for multiethnic, resource-rich areas (Fjelde and Østby 2014). Still Chapters 3 and 4 of this volume have shown that exclusion and competition along ethnic lines could provoke ethnic mobilization and conflict in resource-rich societies. The evidence from the North-Western Zambian case provides strong support to all these observations and suggests that inadequate mining-induced economic benefits and opportunities and massive in-migration could make emerging copper mining areas more prone to ethnic mobilization, tension and conflict.

Rational theorists provide a different theoretical framework through which the evidence from the North-Western Zambian case can be interrogated. Rather than the collective injustice-related grievances at the grassroots level, they point to "the silent force of greed" at the elite level as the main cause of violent conflict (Collier 2000; Collier and Hoeffler 2004; Fearon and Laitin 2003). They have argued that elite-level "greed," rather than the grievance of the *masses*, makes the outbreak of violent conflict in resource-rich societies more likely. The evidence presented above shows that local elites indeed prioritized their personal gratification at the expense of the community welfare, which predisposes the mining areas to intra-group conflict. However, we have found that elite authority and influence last as long as the elites' actions and behaviors conform to expected norms (they should put the interests of their subjects first). Once they deviated and began to pursue their own benefits, they attracted local animosity that ultimately threatened their authority. This may put a limit to the explanatory power of the "greed hypothesis," at least in the context of the North-Western Zambian case. The grassroots rarely acted on greed-driven elite orders. Instead, the local populations often had their own grievance-related motivation to mobilize.

The picture emerging from more recent case studies that explore the within-country social consequences of resource extraction is that both the abundance and scarcity of natural resource wealth can induce civil violence (Ross 2015; Manzano and Gutiérrez 2019), and the robustness of this link seems to depend on the economic and socio-political conditions specific to the extraction areas (McNeish 2018). Conflict is more likely in areas where mining activities coincide with relative deprivation of the local ethnic groups (Koubi et al. 2014). Resource extraction within an ethnically plural region can also provoke separatist or territorial conflict (Sorens 2011). Further, the political status of ethnic groups living in source areas contributes to determining whether resource extraction leads to conflict (Banks 2013; Rudel 2018). Broadly, local political and economic grievances can play an important role in explaining whether natural resource extraction will provoke violence (Ross 2006; Manzano and Gutiérrez 2019).

Overall, this chapter has shown that contrary to the notion that only fuel and other high-value minerals can provoke conflict, the exploitation of low-value minerals such as copper can influence the risk of civil conflict through newly created and pre-existing inequalities, particularly in ethnically plural resource-rich areas. However, despite this finding, the often applied assumption in the literature, which states that ordinary people as a rule perceive inequalities in the society correctly, was not confirmed. The evidence from the North-Western Zambian case shows the interviewees in the emerging copper mining areas often misperceived inequalities and their position in the economic and political power distribution. Indeed, it is likely that these misperceptions contribute to making resource extraction conflict prone.

Finally, the unfulfilled expectations of improved livelihoods and meaningful economic development that the local population embraced at the beginning of the mining development have provoked collective grievances among the locals in the three mining communities under scrutiny. However, these grievances have been misdirected. Contrary to the common perception among the local population, the biggest beneficiaries of the mineral wealth in North-Western Zambia were, and still are, not the Bemba-speaking migrants, but the foreign mining and other related conglomerates (Dobler and Kesselring 2019). They expropriate huge tracts of land without having to offer any significant compensation, while forcefully displacing legal occupants, cutting down on labor, engaging in tax avoidance activities, executing pitiable CSR projects in areas where they operate and illegally outsourcing labor, goods and services from outside the country (Kapesa 2019). It is the combination of these issues and the fact that copper mining involves multiple stakeholders, some of which with ulterior motives, that make copper a "political resource" and copper mining conflict prone.

5.5 Conclusion

This chapter has shown that while mining can bring economic development to previously economically marginalized areas, it can in addition promote massive labor in-migration as well as fierce competition over the mining-induced economic benefits and opportunities. These findings show that copper mining may increase intra- and inter-regional inequalities, which could provoke collective grievances among the local losers, and thereby encourage ethnic mobilization and clashes in the mining areas. Seeking to hide their private benefits from the mines, chiefs have resorted to blaming migrant workers and the villagers by seeing their exclusion from the job market as their only means of benefiting from the mining investments on their lands. Thus, this chapter has illustrated that in a similar way to high-value resources, even mineral extraction of a lower value can lead to conflict. The grievance approach applied in this chapter shows, how ethnic divisions can be strengthened by resource extraction. Policymaking should therefore consider the ethnic makeup surrounding the extraction site as well as the different grievance mechanisms in order to reduce or even prevent future violent events.

NOTES

1. Other classification feature 20 ethnic groups (CSO 2019). The conventional literature, however, divides this population into 73 ethnic groups (or to give them their correct colonial nomenclature—tribes) (Posner 2003). This diversity is grossly exaggerated and takes the colonial era list of tribes at face value. In practice, about 98% of Zambians could be categorized into seven socio-cultural or ethno-linguistic groups: *Bemba*, *Nyanja-Chewa*, *Tonga-Ila*, *Lozi-Luyana*, *North-Westerners*, *Mambwe-Namwanga*, and *Tumbuka*. The North-Westerners could be further divided into three fairly small ethnic or linguistic groups: Kaonde, Lunda and Luvale. Likewise, the rest of the groups consist of several smaller ethnic groups with similar language, economic life and customs. In the absence of the colonial tribal map, overlapping linguistic groups were quite fluid and had not yet acquired today's rigid contemporary boundaries.
2. With this simplification, the Mambwe-Namwanga group becomes part of the Bemba-speaking although they are culturally not cognate groups, while the Tumbuka becomes part of the Nyanja even though they too are neighbors with quite different histories.
3. See Fig. 5.2.
4. *Virilocality* is where the groom pays bride wealth and the bride moves to his home and becomes part of that family, while *uxorilocality* is where the groom moves to the bride's home and becomes part of her family.
5. Only the chiefs actively involved in mining were interviewed, one from each of the three mining communities.
6. For Lumwana and Kalumbila, we only considered youths enlisted in the community database since January 2015, of which five were selected from each community. Community database was an initiative of traditional leadership to influence mines to employ from the enlisted subjects. For Kansanshi, we interviewed only those youths enlisted in the company employment waiting list.
7. These had lost their jobs within a six-month period prior to the date of the interview.
8. Where we had no official registers for the targeted population, convenience (availability of potential participants, time and place) guided our participant selection process. We, for example, positioned ourselves in strategic locations within our study site, such as in migrants' landing points, mining communities, public market, miners' residential areas, and in proximity to working sites. Suitable times varied but included when miners were knocking-off, when migrants were arriving and during company-community meetings.

9. PN40, Interviews, Kansanshi, Solwezi, 24 February 2018; PN41, Interviews, Kalumbila, Solwezi, 25 February 2018.
10. PN49, Interviews, Kalumbila, Solwezi, 16 June 2018.
11. The revenues consisted of mineral royalty, import Value Added Tax (VAT), pay-as-you-earn, company income tax, withholding taxes, import/custom duty, dividends and environmental protection fund.
12. PN10, Interviews, Kansanshi, Solwezi, 10 December 2015.
13. PN49, 16 June 2018.
14. PN10, 10 December 2015.
15. PN11, Interviews, Kansanshi, Solwezi, 22 November 2015.
16. PN55, Interviews, Lumwana, Solwezi, 22 February 2019.
17. Focus Group discussion, Kansanshi 21 January 2018; Focus Group discussion, Lumwana 24 January 2018; Focus Group discussion, Kalumbila, 28 January 2018.
18. PN45, Interviews, Lumwana, Solwezi, 14 April 2018.
19. PN42, Interviews, Lumwana, Solwezi, 26 February 2018.
20. PN43, Interviews, Lumwana, Solwezi, 26 February 2018.
21. PN59, Interviews, Kalumbila, Solwezi, 27 February 2019.
22. PN52, Interviews, Kansanshi, Solwezi, 17 February 2019.
23. PN5, Interviews, Kalumbila, Solwezi, 18 June 2015.
24. PN42, 26 February 2018.
25. PN16, Interview, Kansanshi, Solwezi, 24 June 2016.
26. PN20, Interview, Kalumbila, Solwezi, 20 September 2016.
27. PN18, Interview, Kalumbila, Solwezi, 20 September 2016.
28. PN29, 12 December 2017.
29. PN29, Interviews, Kalumbila, Solwezi, 12 December 2017; PN32, Interviews, Lumwana, Solwezi, 14 December 2017; PN36, Interviews, Kansanshi, Solwezi, 18 December 2017.
30. PN14, Interviews, Kansanshi, Solwezi, 24 January 2016.
31. PN12, Interviews, Lumwana, Solwezi, 5 January 2016.
32. ZEMA has only two offices in Zambia. The main services that the Agency provides include: Enforcement of regulations and standards on all aspects of the environment. Advising government on the formulation of policies, standards and regulations related to environmental management. Accordingly, the Ndola office carries out all ZEMA activities in the Northern part of the country, while the Lusaka covers the remaining region.
33. PN58, Interviews, Kalumbila, Solwezi, 26 February 2019.
34. Ibid.
35. PN48, Interviews, Kalumbila, Solwezi, 8 June 2018.
36. PN58, 26 February 2019; PN48, 8 June 2018.
37. PN12, 5 January 2016; PN45, 14 April 2018.
38. PN52, 17 February 2019; PN14, 24 January 2016.

39. PN1, Interviews, Kansanshi, Solwezi, 12 April 2015 (see also Zambia Daily Mail 31 March 2015).
40. PN20, 20 September 2016; PN18, 20 September 2016; PN58, 26 February 2019.
41. Ibid.
42. PN53, Interviews, Kalumbila, Solwezi, 19 February 2019.
43. PN57, Interviews, Lumwana, Solwezi, 25 February 2019.
44. PN52, 17 February 2019.
45. Ibid.
46. PN51, Interviews, Lumwana, Solwezi, 18 June 2018.
47. PN2, Interviews, Kalumbila, Solwezi, 12 April 2015.

REFERENCES

Banks, Glenn A. 2013. "Little by Little, Inch by Inch: Project Expansion Assessments in the Papua New Guinea Mining Industry." *Resource Policy* 38 (4): 688–695.
Bucholtz, Mary. 2000. "The Politics of Transcription." *Journal of Pragmatics* 32: 1439–1465.
Cederman, Lars-Erik., Andreas Wimmer, and Brian Min. 2010. "Why Do Ethnic Groups Rebel? New Data and Analysis." *World Politics* 62 (1): 87–119.
Cederman, Lars-Eric., Nils B. Weidmann, and Gleditsch Kristian. 2011. "Horizontal Inequalities and Ethnic-Nationalist Civil War: A Global Comparison." *American Political Science Review* 105 (3): 478–495.
Central Statistical Office (CSO). 2011. *2010 Census of Population and Housing for Zambia*. Lusaka: Central Statistical Office.
Central Statistical Office (CSO). 2019. "Zambia 2020 Census of Population and Housing Is Upon Us!" *The Statistician* June 8.
Chileshe, Roy. 2005. *Land Tenure and Rural Livelihoods in Zambia: Case studies of Kamena and St Joseph*. Unpublished Doctoral Thesis. University of the Western Cape.
Collier, Paul. 2000. "Doing well out of War: An Economic Perspective." In *Greed and Grievance: Economic Agendas in Civil Wars*, edited by Mats Berdal, and David M. Malone. Boulder, CO: Lynne Rienner/International Peace Academy.
Collier, Paul, and Anke Hoeffler. 2004. "Greed and Grievance in the Civil War." *Oxford Economic Paper* 56 (4): 563–595.
Creswell, John W. 2009. *Research Design: Qualitative, Quantitative, and Mixed Method Approaches*. Thousand Oaks, CA: Sage.
Dobler, Gregor, and Rita Kesselring. 2019. "Swiss Extractivism: Switzerland's Role in Zambia's Copper Sector." *Journal of Modern African Studies* 57 (2): 223–245.

Fearon, James D., and David D. Laitin. 2003. "Ethnicity, Insurgency, and Civil War." *American Political Review* 97 (1): 75–90.
Fjelde, Hanne, and Gudrun Østby. 2014. "Socioeconomic Inequality and Communal Conflict: A Disaggregated Analysis of Sub-Saharan Africa, 1990–2008." *International Interactions* 40 (5): 737–762.
Government of the Republic of Zambia (GRZ). 2015. *Mines and Minerals Development Act No. 11 of 2015*. Lusaka: Government Printers.
Government of the Republic of Zambia (GRZ). 2016. *Parliamentary Debate*, 28 October 2016. Lusaka: Government Printers.
GRZ. 1995. *The Lands Act* (No. 29). Lusaka: Government Printers.
GRZ. 2011. *The Environmental Management Act* (No. 12). Lusaka: Government Printers.
Kabemba, Claude, and Edward Lange. 2018. "Living in a Parallel Universe: First Quantum Mine versus Communities in Zambia." *Resource Insight* 1: 1–20.
Kapesa, Robby. 2019. "Local Perceptions of Horizontal Inequalities, Collective Grievances and Ethnic Mobilization in the Emerging Mining Areas of North-Western Zambia" (Doctoral Thesis). Kitwe: The Copperbelt University.
Kapesa, Robby, Jacob Mwitwa, and Chikumbi Donald. 2015. "Social Conflict in the Context of the Development of New Mining Concessions in Zambia." *Southern African Peace and Security Studies* 4 (2): 41–62.
Koubi, Vally, Gabriele Spilker, Tobias Böhmelt, and Thomas Bernauer. 2014. "Do Natural Resources Matter for Interstate and Intrastate Armed Conflict?" *Journal of Peace Research* 51 (2): 227–243.
Manzano, Osmel, and Juan David Gutiérrez. 2019. "The Subnational Resource Curse: Theory and Evidence." *The Extractive Industries and Society* 6: 261–266.
McNeish, John Andrew. 2018. "Resource Extraction and Conflict in Latin America." *Colombia International* 93: 3–16.
Mitchell, Clyde J. 1956. *The Kalela Dance*. Manchester: Manchester University Press.
Papstein, R. 1989. "From Ethnic Identity to Tribalism: The Upper Zambezi Region of Zambia, 1830–1981." In *The Creation of Tribalism in Southern Africa*, edited by Leroy Vail. Berkeley and Los Angeles: University of California Press.
Perrings, Charles. 1977. "Consciousness, Conflict and Proletarianization: An Assessment of the 1935 Mineworkers' Strike on the Northern Rhodesia Copperbelt." *Journal of Southern African Studies* 4 (1): 31–51.
Posner, Daniel N. 2003. "The Colonial Origins of Ethnic Cleavages: The Case of Linguistic Divisions in Zambia." *Comparative Politics* 35 (2): 127–146.
Posner, Daniel N. 2005. *Institutions and Ethnic Politics in Africa*. Cambridge: Cambridge University Press.

Roberts, Derek, and Simusa Silwamba. 2017. "Ethnicity, Politics and Zambian Youth." *Journal of Academy of Social Sciences* 12 (3–4): 189–201.
Ross, Michael. 2006. "A Closer Look at Oil, Diamond, and Civil War." *Annual Review of Political Science* 9 (1): 265–300.
Ross, Michael. 2015. "What Have We Learnt about the Resource Curse?: *Annual Political Review* 18: 239–259.
Rudel, Thomas K. 2018. "The Extractive Imperative in Populous Indigenous Territories: The Shuar, Copper Mining, and Environmental Justice in the Ecuadorian Amazon." *Human Ecology* 46: 727–734.
Sisk, Timothy D., and Christoph Stefes. 2005. "Power Sharing as an Interim Step in Peacebuilding: Lessons from South Africa." In *Sustainable Peace: Power and Democracy after the Civil War*, edited by Phillip G. Roeder, and Donald Rothchild. Ithaca, NY: Cornell University Press.
Sorens, Jason. 2011. "Mineral Production, Territory, and Ethnic Rebellion: The Role of Rebel Constituencies." *Journal of Peace Research* 48 (5): 571–585.
United Nations Development Programme (UNDP). 2016. *Zambia Human Development Report 2016*. Lusaka: UNDP.
Vogt, Manuel. 2019. *Mobilization and Conflict in Multiethnic States*. Oxford: Oxford University Press.
Vogt, Manuel, Nils-Christian. Bormann, Seraina Ruëgger, Lars-Erik. Cederman, Philipp Hunziker, and Luc Girardin. 2015. "Integrating Data on Ethnicity, Geography, and Conflict: The Ethnic Power Relations Dataset Family." *Journal of Conflict Resolution* 59 (7): 1327–1342.
Wimmer, Andreas. 2002. *Nationalist Exclusion and Ethnic Conflict*. Cambridge: Cambridge University Press.
Yin, Robert K. 2013. *Case Study Research: Design and Methods*. Thousand Oaks, CA: Sage Publication.
Zambia Chamber of Mines. 2016. *Employment in the Mining Industry*. Kitwe: Chamber of Mines
Zambia Consolidated Copper Mines Limited (ZCCM). 2000. *Annual report-2000*. Lusaka: ZCCM.
Zambia Daily Mail. 2015. "Kalumbila Mine Clashes: Police Arrest, Charge 18." 31 March 2015, p. 1. Lusaka: Zambia Daily Mail.
Zambia Demographic and Health Survey (ZDHS). 2019. *Demographic and Health Survey 2018: Key Indicators Report*. Lusaka: ZDHS.
Zambia Extractive Industry Transparency Initiative (ZEITI). 2018. *The Ninth Report, 2016*. Lusaka: ZEITI.

CHAPTER 6

Resource Extraction and Conflict in India

Madhushree Sekher, Mansi Awasthi, Subhankar Nayak, and Rajesh Kumar

6.1 Introduction

Natural resources have for a long time been at the center of multiple domestic and international conflicts. Whereas the literature has investigated primarily the conflict inducing effects of oil and gas, newer research has also started to look at so-called non-fuel minerals which, as a result of the 'Commodity Super Cycle', have witnessed an increase in demand as well as higher prices. While these resources are also linked to conflict, it is still an open debate under which conditions they materialize and what can be done to avoid their occurrence in future. In order to advance our knowledge in this regard, this chapter examines resource-rich areas within India where mining activities have led to resentments on the side of the local community and in some cases even to violent events.

Despite its natural wealth, there are a staggering number of poor people in the resource-abundant regions of the country. Not only have few people been able to gain economically from the extraction, they have additionally witnessed large-scale displacements as mining companies take

M. Sekher (✉) · M. Awasthi · S. Nayak · R. Kumar
Tata Institute of Social Sciences, Mumbai, India

© The Author(s), under exclusive license to Springer Nature Switzerland AG 2022
H. E. Ali and L.-E. Cederman (Eds.), *Natural Resources, Inequality and Conflict*, https://doi.org/10.1007/978-3-030-73558-6_6

over pieces of land previously inhabited by the locals. According to the estimations of Padel and Das (2010), mining activities have caused the displacement of about three million people in India since 1951. This is, especially problematic since the resource-rich regions also hold the country's green forests, which are the home to large tribal population. These communities, often referred to as 'Adivasis' meaning the original and autochthonous inhabitants of the region, are among the poorest and most marginalized groups in the country. Since, most of the displacements caused by mining activities affect them, they struggle both in terms of losing access to their livelihoods as well as due to a change of lifestyles brought about by the eviction from what was perceived to be their 'own land'.

With the rise in mining activities and the large-scale displacement that comes with it, there is rising discontent among the Adivasis living in these resource-rich areas which has led to protest and even violent acts. Those grievances can also create fertile ground for opportunistic extremist groups. The Naxalites, a Communists guerrilla insurgency group that stated in 1967 as an uprising of poor sharecroppers against local landlords in the Indian state of West Bengal, are thereby the most important example. The danger of this particular group is made evident by looking at the last two decades of recorded data, where there have been 483 incidents of killings in which 360 civilians, 222 security forces, 299 insurgents and 7 unspecified lost their lives between March 2000 and August 2020[1] in the regions affected by Naxal insurgency.

With the new mining boom and the local grievances that have emerged as a result, they were able to take advantage of such grievances in their fight against the state forces, leading to the formation of new violent insurgencies in response to mining-related displacements.

In order to further understand the links between natural resources extraction and local grievances, this chapter examines the Niyamgiri hill region in Odisha and the interactions between tribal communities and a private mining company. Based on the extraction of bauxite, it is one of the biggest land conflicts in the country affecting 20,000 people and covering about 150 hectares of land. Conflicts like this can erupt when industrial projects are proposed on land that communities have inhabited for centuries, thereby putting their livelihoods and lifestyles connected to adjacent forests at risk. Such land use practices are based on customary rights that the local communities have over the land and its forest. Governmental decision to allow extraction to take place can infringe upon these rights, thereby preventing communities' access to the forest needed for basic living requirements.

This chapter, thus, highlights the conflict risks in resource-rich areas in India, where mining-induced grievances of indigenous communities are one of the many causes of conflict. Thereby, we focus on three of the four steps introduced in Chapter 2: first, we explain how new mining activity in so far untouched areas can lead to the articulation of local grievances as affected communities fear losing access to their lands. Second, we show how such grievances can lead to local mobilization amongst the local community and how this can lead to violent conflict. Lastly, we show how the actions of the state can significantly alter the resource-conflict nexus: on one hand, we show how the actions of the Supreme Court of India preserved local rights by scrapping the petition filed by a state-owned mining company, the Odisha Mining Corporation (OMC), to consider the possibility of bauxite mining atop the Niyamgiri hills. As a result, the OMC lost its mining bid in the Niyamgiri hills following the Supreme Court judgement which went against the interest of the Vedanta Aluminium Ltd's efforts to expand the operations of its aluminium plant in this area (the Langhigar Alumina Refinery). Despite this apparent victory for the local indigenous communities, the conflict between communal property rights and mining interests remains a major source of contention. In the present case of Odisha, locals residents continue to fight the ecological degradation of previous extraction in the area, especially as they fear that similar mining projects will be allowed in future.

On the other hand, the state government of Odisha is alienating the local population in its drive to make the state a core investment destination by creating an industrial 'land bank', which makes both private and common lands available to industries. The state government has offered various sops like these in order to attract investment in the mineral-rich state. A land bank of 100 thousand acres has already been acquired to offer land to private investors without them having to wrangle with local issues in the land acquisition process. In its rush to attract investment, the government is, however, again ignoring the people's dependency on these lands and undermining community rights, thereby restricting local's access to forest and land resources where they have traditionally harvested crops needed to sustain their livelihoods. Given the fact that 54.28 percent[2] of the population in Odisha is already landless, further reduction of available forest lands would create additional negative effects:

the contribution of commons to household income plays a significant role in the livelihood of the landless rural poor, for whom income generation opportunities from private land are negligible. This could explain why land conflicts across the state have risen as a result of the newly created 'land banks'[3] made available by the state. About 717 land conflicts related to mining sector are reported which have affected 6,720,051 people and involving 2,386,127 hectares of land area in the state (Worsdell et al. 2020).

6.2 Engines of Growth or Catalysts for Resentments: The India Case

Natural resources have been at the heart of the Indian growth story. Increasing industrialization and the rapid economic growth, which accompanies it, have intensified the mining activities in the country. Paradoxically, many of the mineral-rich states are also amongst the poorest in which a large proportion of the population is still untouched by India's increasing economic prosperity.

Between 2014 and 2015 India's total mineral production[4] was worth more than INR 10,000 crores (approximately USD 13,40,000) with Odisha (32.2 percent), Rajasthan (18.4 percent), Chhattisgarh (14.5 percent), Jharkhand (7.7 percent), gaining most from royalties.[5] Still, if we compare these states with the country's Human Development Index, it becomes evident that despite this apparent wealth they still underperform significantly (Suryanarayan, 2011): of the 50 major mining districts, 60 percent are among India's most backward districts[6] and 25 percent rank in the top 50 most backward districts (Chandra 2015).

These numbers highlight an 'inclusive growth paradox': given the fact that the mining gains are not distributed equally, there have been multiple local movements, which have emerged in order to press for the internalization of local externalities into the economic evaluation of such a development process (Shiva 1991; Gadgil and Guha 1992). In context of such a limited resource base, local movements have initiated a new political struggle for safeguarding the interests and survival of local communities, including the poor and the marginalized, comprising of indigenous people, women and poor peasants.

The largest externality of mining activities have so far come in the form of large-scale displacement of local inhabitants—mostly Adivasis who live in the forest and mountainous areas designated for extraction. The Adivasis have for centuries helped conserve and manage forests as they are dependent on them for their livelihood. When they are relocated from their native lands for the pursuit of mining, they are rarely rehabilitated in a fair way. In the absence of economic and political resources of their own, these Adivasis are neglected by the state institutions and the mining companies, as they find it difficult to negotiate their legitimate claims. It is this grievance that has been the catalyst for the mobilization of local tribal groups. Many parts of the country with extensive mining activities have now started to witness collective mobilization as an expression of their resistance to mining on land and forests over which they stake their historical claims (Worsdell et al. 2020).

6.3 Tribal Societies in India and Their Rights Concerning Forest Lands

Before the advent of the British East India Company, the tribes had a history of common ownership of land and forest resources which meant that inequalities within tribal societies were rather small compared to their non-tribal counterparts. During the colonial period, non-tribals started encroaching on tribal lands after the Permanent Settlement Act 1793 when land became a saleable property whereby vast amount of land was passed to non-tribals. The British administration made itself the proprietor of forest land which was a substantial change since the preceding political regime had not attempted anything similar. Post Sepoy Mutiny of 1857 during which forests and forest dwelling communities provided rebels with a safe hiding place, the British withdrew access to forest resources from the local communities, and the tribals were declared encroachers on the land on which they had lived for centuries. This change as well as further restrictions and control over forests during the colonial era were designed to push the indigenous population into the labour markets which ultimately backfired as it gave rise to intense rebellions (Mathur 2004; Stokes 1978; Simhadra 1979; Gough 1974).

Through their policies, the British tried to bring the tribals into mainstream culture for which they appointed revenue collectors, forest officials and local people to collect data pertaining to the tribal people. In order to legitimize government control, an Imperial Forest Department (1864) was created which made forestry a scientific operation thus making it inaccessible to forest dwellers. In 1865, 1878 and 1927, a series of acts were passed to provide the British with further access to the forests. When rebellions broke out as a result, they declared the areas as 'disturbed' which led to the introduction of several protective measures for the tribal areas. Simultaneously, the British also started the process of identifying the tribal communities and, as a step to address unrests, gradually granted autonomy and protections against forcible displacement from their lands.

In the aftermath of this process, the British introduced different policies such as the Wilkinson Rules (1839), the Chota Nagpur Tenures Act (1869) and the Santhal Parganas Act (1855). These acts created a legal framework for the protection of the land belonging to the tribal communities following recurrent rebellion in the tribal areas. This meant that the areas were removed from general administration and placed in a special category whereby the Deputy Commissioners were entrusted with the administration of the tribal people and the areas inhabited by them. Later, the tribal questions attracted the Simon Commission[7] as they considered these tribes to be politically less advanced. The commission felt that educating the tribes was essential for which special funds were required.

After independence, a number of laws were passed designed to further support the indigenous communities. This included provisions under the Indian Constitution in Schedule V & VI (for scheduled areas inhabited by tribal population), the Fourth and Fifth Five Year Plan (1969–1974 and 1974–1978), the National Forest Policy of 1988, the Panchayat[8] Extension to Scheduled Area (PESA), the Forest Right Act (RFA) of 2006 and the Land Acquisition, Rehabilitation and Resettlement Act of 2013.

The latter is, especially important for this study: this law concerns the rights of forest dwelling communities to land and other resources, denied to them over decades as a result of the continuation of colonial forest laws in India. It is said that this act redresses the historical injustices upon the tribal communities as it provides them with a legal right to protect their forests. Some of the basic features of this act mention the type of rights, eligibility criteria as well as the exact process of recognition of those rights, especially when it comes to resettlements and wildlife conservation.

Another important milestone was the passage of the FRA, which rectifies some of the colonial injustices to forest dwellers by providing relief and rehabilitation in case of illegal eviction and forced displacement.

6.4 Pathways to Conflict

Despite such protections, indigenous communities were heavily affected by the recent rise in mining activity. Since, there is also a substantial overlap between the Naxalite insurgency, mining and tribal areas, there is a strong possibility that one reason for this violence can be found in resource-linked grievances (GoI 2019).

Discussing such violent responses of tribal populations, Gadgil and Guha (1992) maintain that the adaptations by different groups who come to occupy resource niches create competitive exclusion and conflicts. This could be seen in the conflicts linked to natural resource extraction, including Odisha, where the present case study was carried out, by highlighting the causal mechanism linking resource extraction, grievance articulation and conflict. Odisha had no Naxalite insurgency in the early decades following the country's independence from colonial rule. But as a consequence of mining-related displacements of local tribes in the state, the presence of Naxalite insurgents could increasingly be seen in large tracts of the state (Gadgil and Guha 1992).

Recent studies have established how Naxalite conflict in some parts of the country is linked to mining activities and their negative consequences for the local community (Hoelscher et al. 2012; Gadgil and Guha 1992; Ghatak and Oliver 2017). The scale of these conflicts is higher in places where mining activities coincide with higher levels of grievances, for instance, due to denial of habitat rights, increased livelihood insecurity, land scarcity, destruction of traditional agricultural system and spiritual connection to the ancestral land. Further, the likelihood of conflicts in the mining areas is higher where local communities have strong symbolic and material links with nature (Gadgil and Guha 1992).

These concerns point to the resource-conflict nexus, reminiscent of cultural ecology. Resource extraction by 'outsiders' affects local communities with historical ownership claims built from long-standing, century-old settlements, causing in them a sense of grievance and its consequent articulation, very often through violent mechanism.

6.5 Case Study: Bauxite Mines in Odisha

For the purpose of the present case study in Odisha, the mining-linked extraction of resources and the Naxalite insurgency seen in the district of Rayagada were analysed. The focus in this case study is the mining-induced land conflicts witnessed in the Niyamgiri[9] hill range of the district, which is home to two subgroups of the Kondh tribe, the *Dongria* and *Kutia Kondh*. Their livelihoods and spirituality are inextricably linked with the land in question: while the *Kutia Kondh* inhabit the foothills, the *Dongria Kondh* live in the upper reaches of the Niyamgiri hills which is their only habitat. The highest hill peak is considered to be the home of their revered god, *Niyam Raja* while other hilltops and their associated forests are regarded as supreme deities (Fig. 6.1).

This hill region in the Rayagada district of Odisha has rich deposit of bauxite, the primary raw material for aluminium. It was witness to one of the biggest land conflicts in the country that saw the landmark decision protecting the tribes' rights by the Supreme Court on 18 April 2013, which rejected the appeal of the mining ban and decreed that the *Dongria Kondh* would have a decisive say in the permission for undertaking the mining project. The court recognized that the *Dongria Kondh's* right to worship at their sacred mountain must be 'protected and preserved' and that the religious and cultural rights of the local communities must be heard in further mining-related decision-making processes. The Supreme Court, subsequently, in its judgement in May 2016, again reiterated its April 2013 decision while rejecting the plea of the state government for a reconsideration of its decision not to allow bauxite mining in the Niyamgiri hills.

In order to better capture the links between natural resource extraction and the Naxalite conflicts seen in India, we use this case of Odisha and the Niyamgiri hill conflict to trace the contestation between the local tribal communities and the mining company. Previously, a link from resource extraction to Naxalite conflict had been established: thereby, mining activities create a vicious circle amongst the various stake holders, resulting in the areas becoming an arena of contention leading to Naxalite-inspired conflicts (Ghatak and Eynde 2017). Using resource-related grievances as a cover, the rebels are able to get accepted by the displaced locals which strengthen their power position.

In this analysis, we follow the conceptualization outlined in Fig. 6.2, showing vertical and horizontal connections between context, stakeholders and power relations. In a first step entitled 'context and dimensions', we introduce to the analysis the social, legal, political and economic backstory which looks at the historical claims over the land as well as the traditional property rights of the community. Subsequently, we introduce

6 INDIA CASE STUDY   137

Fig. 6.1 Rayagada district in Odisha. Highlighted are the bauxite mines in the area. *Source* Open Government Data (OGD) platform

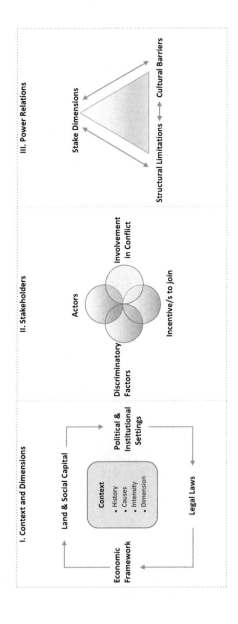

Fig. 6.2 Context, stakeholders and power relations in natural resource conflicts

the different stakeholders, their characteristics and interests, followed by an analysis of their different power relations which provides an insight into how the actors take part in the conflict. This conceptualization allows us to sketch the actors and their differing objectives which situates this resource conflict in the context of the Niyamgiri Hills in Odisha.

6.5.1 Context and Dimensions

As natural resource extraction and conflict are multi-layered, multidimensional and temporal in nature, it should be best understood in the light of their historical, social, economic and political context. This section presents a general overview by analysing these four key dimensions.

An important focus here lies on the Adivasi's lands, since they play such a significant role in their lives and culture as it is not just an economic asset but the basis of their livelihoods and subsistence. Access to Niyamgiri Hills was shaped by the culture and identity of the Dongaria Kondhs and in the end also secured through their strong social capital networks: the trust among Adivasis is a major element of social capital and is especially effective for the exchange of information and providing insights into sources of conflict-related matters. Their traditional structure is built on an informal system of norms and compliance with unwritten tribal community rules.

Whereas these social networks are an important factor in mobilizing the communities into action, there are other factors which fuel the emergence of such conflicts like competing claims to land ownership between Adivasis and mining companies. Since such tribal societies see the land as a common property, private rights given to companies by the state are not viewed as legitimate in their eyes. These competing claims to ownership have been heavily politicized by both sides which have produced a fertile ground for the Naxalites. They are able to exploit the discontent among the tribes to strengthen their presence and harm the interests of the state.

In the past, Naxalites have forayed into the region by taking advantage of the terrain to hide from the security forces and mobilize resistance of the tribes against mining in the hills. This has led to a fierce confrontation between the rebels and security forces in which many tribal communities have suffered. On the one hand, they have been killed by the Naxalites on the suspicion of being police informers. On the other, police have also harassed tribals on suspicions that they are providing shelter to the Naxals and by attributing to them the unlawful activities carried out by them (such as, burning down vehicles and stopping road construction and infrastructure works in the area). These examples highlight the crucial role played by the state. Whereas natural resources have the potential to cause conflicts, there is a strong argument in the literature which argues that states are an important mediation factor, determining whether certain resources lead to conflict or not. Thereby, potential problems of conflict and rent-seeking behaviour can be countered by well-functioning institutions (Venables 2016; Boschini et al. 2007). Given the right institutional framework, resource wealth can be translated into economic growth. At the same time, however, resource dependence also tends to influence governments themselves, by making them less able to resolve conflicts and more likely to exacerbate them. This can occur through three mechanisms: corruption, state (bureaucratic) weakness and reduced accountability (Ross 2003).

In this context, it is important to understand that political institutions are not just important mediating factors, but can also be potential sources of conflict themselves, especially when subject to substantial changes over time. In our case, extensive rights were given to the mining enterprise by the Odisha state government, in disregard of two statutory provisions provided under the Constitution of India protecting land rights of local communities—the Forest Rights Act, 2006, and Land Acquisition, Rehabilitation and Resettlement Act, 2013.

The Forest Rights Act, 2006, concerns the rights of forest dwelling communities to land and other resources and provides for relief and rehabilitation in cases of eviction and forced displacement. The Land Acquisition, Rehabilitation and Resettlement Act of 2013 provides for fair compensation and transparency when land is claimed for a public cause and mandates the need for the consent of land owners for both private (80%) and public–private-partnership (70%) projects.

Besides such protections, these two statutory provisions do not make a reference to the traditional collective property rights that tribal groups have over land and forests. If these rights were violated, then how can community ownership be compensated? The empirical application of these acts shows how governance changes may lead to the outright dispossession of tribals, and that the indirect benefits made available in the form of compensations to the displaced may or may not translate into guaranteed rights and policy-based entitlements.

In this regard, it was primarily the non-issuance of *pattas* (land titles) to the Adivasis that gave rise to the land conflicts in the region: the potential for land conflicts is greater when there are contradictions in the law, gaps in the land issues covered by the law and competition over the mandates of state institutions. These problems create confusion and uncertainty over land rights and increase tenure insecurity on the side of the Adivasis. The latter is not only based on the legality of the land rights, but also on the interests of the authority that is issuing and protecting the rights. In the Niyamgiri land conflict, the Dongaria Kondh tribes felt that they have been denied equity in their efforts at claiming their land rights, as opposed to the rights that were given to the mining enterprise to mine the hill and surrounding locality.

Stakeholder Analysis
Apart from their cultural significance, the land is also the only source of income for the Adivasis. Analysing the local economy provides useful information on livelihoods, commons and villages resources of the tribal communities. In addition, investigating the economic differences between the stakeholders reflects the power hierarchy and structure. Thereby, we will focus on two important sub-questions: first, how important is the economic factor in this conflict and second, how much does the conflict cost the individual stakeholders?

Through a stakeholder analysis, we identify the key actors and assess their respective interests in the context. The key stakeholders in the Niyamgiri mining conflict are the Adivasis, Naxalites, the mining enterprise and state institutions. These four stakeholders had direct interest in the lands around which the discussion is based: Adivasis are primarily threatened by the actions of mining enterprises. Their primary point of contention was their right to and historical ownership of the land. The Naxalites, on the other hand, saw a potential in using the mining-induced grievances as recruiting opportunities for their movement (Ghatak and Eynde 2017). Apart from private mining enterprises, motivated by profit, state institutions also (to a great extent) supported the mining activities because they are seeing them as an opportunity to bring economic growth to the state.

The stakeholder analysis is based on stakeholder's attributes, inter-relationships and interests in a conflict. All the four stakeholders are directly involved as their interests collide. Understanding why and to what degree they are involved in the resulting conflict is therefore an important element in determining its high intensity.

The Adivasis lose the most from the conflict. The stake 'land' includes elements of livelihood as well as traditional legacy. Adivasis are unheard, discriminated and prevented from participating freely in the mediating process. Their status, identity, ethnicity and limited access to information provides them with a weak negotiating position. This exclusiveness and unrepresentative position in the process have made their grievances systematic and structural, paving the way for them to be mobilized into protests, marches, sit-downs, public campaigns as well as network-based action through national and international organizations.

Power Relations

The conflict in the mining context in the Niyamgiri region was the result of the powerlessness of Adivasis in protecting their ownership rights. The mining enterprises were powerful in influencing the government to get permission to the forest clearances which they needed for their mining projects. Being powerless, Adivasis resorted to violence in order to oppose the mining activities fearing that there would not be a fair and just hearing of their case and that there was no other recourse.

At stake in this conflict was the land, associated lifestyle and livelihoods for Adivasis, while it was the economic gains for the mining enterprise from the bauxite extracted from Niyamgiri Hills. The fact that customary practices are not tangible and subjective too, the Adivasis saw their culture and identity as a part of the land and therefore considered it to be non-negotiable in its entirety. The relative importance attached to the Niyamgiri hills was, thus, based not only on the Adivasis' economic interests, but also on their feelings and perceptions.

The power relations between stakeholders involved are based on different sources of power: on the one hand is their power-position within the country through which mining companies have a big advantage as they possess a much closer and direct channel to the government. On the other hand, these companies also have much more resources at their disposal through which they can promote their interests. Such organizational and institutional settings that precluded the Adivasis from exercising their traditional rights, resulted in their systematic discrimination. Adivasis, Naxalites and mining enterprises have extremely unequal levels of power, political influence over state institutions and ability to negotiate agreements. Acknowledging the differences between all the stakeholders involved, their particular interests in the issue and their differentiated access to power, is hence essential to comprehend the relationships involved in the land conflict.

The Niyamgiri Mining Conflict
This case study throws light on the tribal groups who have been fighting for their land, which had been taken away for mining activities. The tribal communities have not only been protecting their land but also worshipping a part of it for generations. The cultural attachment, social life and economic well-being of two tribal groups—*Dongria* and *Kutia Kondh*— in the Niyamgiri hill region of the state of Odisha have come under direct threat due to the mining of bauxite from the area by a private multinational company. The tribal groups have been resisting this move of the Odisha state persistently.

Odisha state is a preferred investment destination for its abundant natural resources such as iron ore, bauxite, chromite and manganese. To obtain large revenues from its mineral resources, the Odisha government has invited many private multinational companies for mining and extraction of resources with promises of land, cheap electricity and speedy approvals.

The Niyamgiri hill region in the state of Odisha has received much attention because of the state government's decision to allow one of the largest aluminium companies in the world—Vedanta Aluminium Limited[10]—to mine bauxite from region. This move had a potential of displacing eight thousand local indigenous communities who have been living in the mountainous region for centuries. They also worship the *Niyamgiri* hill-top, which is seen as the seat of their God—the '*Niyam raja*', which is why they have been protesting the move of the government to give the hill region to the aluminium company for mining. Their opposition to mining in the Niyamgiri range for bauxite got momentum through their collective participation to celebrate their age-old traditional cultural festivals, which turned the festivities into a show of unity by the indigenous community. A Niyamgiri three-day annual festival has become an expression of self-assertion of the tribes that the hills are theirs and that they won't allow any kind of mining in the bauxite-rich hills. The festival has become a platform for the Kondhs (both Dongria and Kuttia Kondhs)—the dominant inhabitants of the hills—for renewing their pledge to fight the companies keeping an eye to mine the bauxite of the hills. The festival has grown in importance since anti-Vedanta agitation by the *Niyamagiri Suraksha Samiti* (NSS—the Niyamgiri Protection

Committee) gained momentum. However, despite multiple legal appeals to stop mining activities in the region, Vedanta Enterprise went ahead and constructed an aluminium refinery in in the region (the Langhigar Aluminium Refiniry) in 2006–2007.

With the enactment of the 2006 Forest Rights Act, an important shift regarding the rights of traditional forest inhabitants took place. While the law does not grant a formal legal title to forest dwellers, it guaranteed perpetual rights to those who show their own or forbearer's pre-existing occupancy or use of the land. Following this, in 2007, India's Supreme Court puts a hold on the Niyamgiri hills mining project based on evidences of severe environmental and labour issues at other Vedanta-owned facilities. Yet, Vedanta was granted permission to refine bauxite from already operating mining sites. In 2008, the Supreme Court approved the mining clearances for a joint operation by the state government Odisha Mining Corporation and Vedanta. However, this joint venture, too, was halted due to violations of environmental laws and of the Forest Rights Act, 2006. Soon, a four-member committee (the Saxena Committee) was convened to review the project. A thorough investigation was conducted by the central government under the eyes of its Minister of Environment and Forests (MoEF), which concluded that the mining should not be allowed in the Niyamgiri Hills and that the environmental clearances given to the Vedanta Enterprise were unlawful (Saxena et al. 2010). The Forest Rights Act, 2006, grants village councils (the Gram Sabhas) the right to take decisions on activities that could damage the environment, biodiversity and natural or cultural heritage. According to the report of this committee (Saxena et al. 2010), Vedanta and the state government had not received proper approval from the village councils of villages located in the affected region. The Supreme Court thus ordered voting in the village councils of all the twelve villages in the Niyamgiri hill region. In April 2013, all twelve village councils voted to deny mining rights to Vedanta thus winning the battle to protect their homes, culture and the '*Niyam Raja*'.

Implementation Concerns
Focusing on grievance articulation, there are multiple challenges that both the Indian State and the local communities face. One of these concerns the lacking documentation of grievances related to land rights issues. This becomes a major implementation challenge as encroachment of tribal lands have higher chances of being rejected. Not only are grievances

related to land not well-documented, there are also no documents stating their entitlement to the lands. Though it is the responsibility of the officials to provide required land records to individuals and the community, the majority of the locals do not have any authentic land records. There is also a lack of awareness about the different policy-based entitlement for the tribes among the frontline forest officials and also the forest dwellers, themselves.

In the Niyamgiri mining conflict case, despite having laws that protect the rights of local communities, the State Mining Corporation of Odisha (a state government subsidiary) along with the Vendanta mining enterprise started mining without due clearance from the village councils of the affected villages. At the same time, it is noticeable how different agencies of the state, functioning under the Indian Constitution, acted in a contradictory manner, as was seen with the Supreme Court ruling in favour of the voting rights of the village councils even though it previously allowed extraction to take place. What this showed is that a community-based focus can sometimes be more effective. When the official mechanism to address grievances fails to protect the rights of indigenous communities, their lands and livelihood, alternate mechanism emerges which can take the shape of protests, rebellion or even a Naxalite insurgency.

The Cost of Mining
The J B Shah Commission of Inquiry[11] observed that the mining operations of iron and manganese ores in the State of Odisha are carried out in the areas belonging to the local and indigenous people who are displaced from their homes and villages. In the State of Odisha, 130 mining projects were noted to be operating without approval of the authorities and some of them are in clear violation of Environmental Impact Assessment (EIA) Notifications, 1994 and 2006. It is estimated that 277.9 million MT iron ore for an approximate value of USD 6066.20 million and of 3.7 million MT of manganese ore for an approximate value of USD 412.35 million was extracted illegally. The number of lessees along with the quantity of illegal production in violation of environmental and forest clearances, and the operational mines with encroached area is listed in Annexure 1.

When looking at the development broad about by mining, tribal communities seldom feature at the center of the discussion. The local communities who are hurt, displaced and staying in bad conditions in the affected areas are not in a position to raise their voice. Even though the Constitution's provisions give guarantees to indigenous populations, many are observed to be in breach of the guaranteed provisions. For example, the Fifth Schedule of the Constitution of India says that no non-tribal can buy or lease land in a tribal area. But, through devious means, all kinds of activities go on despite these protections.

6.6 Concluding Remarks

This chapter has underlined the conflict risks in mining resource-rich areas in the state of Odisha which has triggered widespread *resentment* among the local indigenous communities. A major cause of conflict that arises due to extraction of resources is land alienation, unemployment, cultural or religious grievances, lack of proper implementation of government policies and programmes, manifested inequalities and lack of inclusive governance.

Formal and informal forms of institutions can play a strong role in avoiding conflicts in such regions, provided that the state machinery and grassroot level institutions function effectively. Institutions play a crucial role in mobilizing and keeping a check on the local population alongside providing a platform to make claims and negotiating with different civil society organizations, state and non-state agencies. Informal institutions contribute to common resources management through joint decision-making via socially shared rules and trust and remain ideally placed to help resolve local conflicts over land. The formal institutions, like the Forest Rights Act, 2006, or the Land Acquisition, Rehabilitation and Resettlement Act 2013, are paradigm shifts impacting the communities favourably by ensuring access to resources and thereby facilitating self-governance. However, despite the enactment of these acts, legislation has frequently failed to positively impact the livelihoods of tribals. The attempts to dilute the Forest Right Act have become more blatant in recent years with the settlement of rights conducted by Forest Settlement Officers instead of the village council (Gram Sabhas), the creation of land banks as well as the conversion of revenue forests. This shows that even with favourable institutional provisions, implementation challenges continue to pose a threat to the local communities.

Therefore, the forest rights question remains unresolved and caught somewhere in between the political recognition of land use, and the bureaucratic exercise of settling the claims. Ignoring these local rights has led to more discontent and exacerbates the internal security threat of Naxalite conflict. There is a need for dialogue to examine governance issues and the functioning of existing institutions, as well as looking at the current infrastructural and industrial development in tribals areas. Mining is a developmental requirement which sustains the need of the economy. But the repercussions of mining should not create negative externalities for the local communities residing in the region or the environment. Any kind of development project in the name of justifying national or state interests should therefore not make the local communities bear the brunt of the costs. This problem has drawn attention because of the rapid expansion of mining projects which the state promoted as a push for increasing growth and development in the rural areas of the state. The essential debate on forests and development calls for a recognition of diverging interests between the gains from mining and the needs of locals. Integrating the rights of local people and ensuring that they gain from local development opportunities therefore requires an integrated approach that involves all stakeholders.

Notes

1. Source: South Asian Terrorism Portal. https://www.satp.org/datasheet-terrorist-attack/fatalities/india-maoistinsurgency-odisha.
2. Socio-Economic and Caste Census of 2011. https://secc.gov.in/welcome.
3. State governments began to 'bank lands' allowing government to offer land to private investors right away, rather than having to wait for the lengthy process of land acquisition each time an investor wants land.
4. With the exception of coal, lignite and sand.
5. The Times of India, 24 June 2016, States Richest in Mineral Resources (https://timesofindia.indiatimes.com/india/States-richest-in-mineral-resources/articleshowprint/52896978.cms) Accessed on 25 May 2020.
6. The Government of India, under its 'Aspirational Districts' program, which is aimed to remove this high heterogeneity in living standards seen in the country, has identified backward districts taking 49 indicators from the 5 identified thematic areas—health and nutrition; education, agriculture, basic infrastructure and financial inclusion and skill development, and identified 115 districts as backward. For details, refer (GoI 2018).
7. The Simon Commission was a group of 7 MPs from Britain who were sent to India in 1928 to study constitutional reforms and make recommendations to the government.
8. Local government institutions.
9. For details, see Seetharam (2018) and Bera (2015).

10. London based multi-national mining company.
11. The Commission of Inquiry was appointed for the purpose of making inquiry of illegal mining of iron ore and manganese ore in contravention of applicable Central and State Acts and rules (Mines and Minerals (Development and Regulation) Act, 1957 (67 of 1957), the Forest (Conservation) Act, 1980 (69 of 1980), the Environment (Protection) Act, 1986 (29 of 1986) and notifications and guidelines issued under the aforesaid enactments) in the state of Odisha on 22nd November 2010.

References

Bera, S. 2015, June 11. *Niyamgiri Answers*. Retrieved from DownToEarth: https://www.downtoearth.org.in/coverage/niyamgiri-answers-41914.

Boschini, A. D., J. Pettersson, and J. Roine. 2007. "Resource Curse or Not: A Question of Appropriability." *The Scandinavian Journal of Economics*: 593–617.

Chandra, S. 2015, June. "The Vulnerable Mining Community." *International Journal of Environmental Planning and Management*: 41–47.

Gadgil, M., and R. Guha. 1992. *This Fissured Land*. New Delhi: Oxford University Press.

Ghatak, M., and O. V. Eynde. 2017. "Economic Determinants of the Maoist Conflict in India." *Economic and Political Weekly*: 69–76.

Ghatak, M., and V. E. Oliver. 2017. "Economic Determinants of the Maoist Conflict in India." *Economic and Political Weekly*.

GoI. 2018. "Transformation of Aspirational Districts:Baseline Ranking & Real-time Monitoring Dashboard." Retrieved from Niti Ayog, Government of India. https://niti.gov.in/sites/default/files/2018-12/AspirationalDistrictsBaselineRankingMarch2018.pdf.

GoI. 2019. "Districts Affected by Left Wing Extremism (LWE)." Retrieved from Press Information Bureau, Ministry of Home Affairs, Government of India. https://pib.gov.in/newsite/PrintRelease.aspx?relid=188075.

Gough, K. 1974. "Indian Peasant Uprisings." *Economic and Political Weekly*: 1391–1412.

Hoelscher, K., J. Miklian, and K. C. Vadlamannati. 2012. "Hearts and Mines: A District Level Analysis of the Maoist Conflict in India." *International Area Studies Review*: 141–160.

Mathur, L. 2004. *Tribal Revolts in India under British Raj*. New Delhi: Aavishkar Publishers.

Padel, F., and S. Das. 2010. *Out of This Earth: East India Adivasis and the Aluminium Cartel*. New Delhi: Orient Blackswan.

Ross, M. 2003. "The Natural Resource Curse: How Wealth Can Make You Poor." In *Natural Resources and Violent Conflicts*, edited by I. Bannon and P. Collier, 17–22. Washington: The World Bank.

Saxena, N. C., S. Parasuraman, P. Kant, and A. Baviskar. 2010. *Report on the Four Member Committee for Investigation into the Proposal Submitted by the Odisha Mining Company for Mining in Niyamgiri*. New Delhi: Ministry of Environment and Forests.

Seetharaman, G. 2018, April 18. "The Story of One of the Biggest Land Conflicts: No Mine Now, but Is it all Fine in Niyamgiri?" Retrieved from *The Economic Times*, https://economictimes.indiatimes.com/industry/indl-goods/svs/metals-mining/theres-no-mine-but-is-it-all-fine-on-niyam-hills/articleshow/63763978.cms?from=mdr.

Shiva, V. 1991. *Ecology and the Politics of Survival*. London: Sage.

Simhadra, V. C. 1979. *Ex-Criminal Tribes of India*. New Delhi: National Publishing House.

Stokes, E. 1978. *The Peasant and the Raj*. Cambridge: Cambridge University Press.

Suryanarayan, M. A. 2011. *Inequality-adjusted Human Development Index for India's States*. New Delhi: United Nations Development Programme (UNDP).

Venables, A. J. 2016. "Using Natural Resources for Development: Why Has It Proven So Difficult?" *Journal of Economic Perspectives*, 161–184.

Worsdell, Thomas, Kumar S. Shrivastava, Ankur Paliwal. 2020. "Mapping Land Conflicts and Their Impact on Human Rights and Investments in India" (Land Conflict Watch, India). Paper presented at Annual World Bank Conference on Land and Poverty, Washington DC, March 16–20, 2020 (URL: https://www.landconflictwatch.org/#home.

CHAPTER 7

Indigenous Mobilization and Resource Extraction in Guatemala

Alejandro Quiñonez and Ricardo Sáenz de Tejada

Guatemala is a small country located in northern Central America. According to data from the most recent population census, the number of inhabitants of Guatemala amounts to fifteen million people. Of these, just over 44% consider themselves indigenous and belong to different ethnic groups (INE 2018, 3–9).[1] Historically, indigenous peoples in Guatemala have been subjected to racial discrimination, exclusion, and exploitation. During the colonial period, oppression against indigenous peoples included slavery, various forms of forced labor, dispossession of their lands, and forced conversion to new religious and spiritual beliefs.

After independence from Spain in 1821, Central America experienced a prolonged period of civil wars, mainly among urban elites, which was followed by an era of relative calm among indigenous peoples and the development of strong local communities. This period of ethnogenesis contributed to the strengthening of local identities. In the second half of the nineteenth century, with the expansion of coffee cultivation, indigenous communities were subjected to new forms of dispossession.

A. Quiñonez · R. S. de Tejada (✉)
University of San Carlos of Guatemala, Guatemala City, Guatemala

© The Author(s), under exclusive license to Springer Nature Switzerland AG 2022
H. E. Ali and L.-E. Cederman (eds.), *Natural Resources, Inequality and Conflict*, https://doi.org/10.1007/978-3-030-73558-6_7

Through policies executed by the powerful white/mestizo elite, much of the land suitable for growing grain were taken from them through spurious legal mechanisms and forms of forced labor were re-established. Responding to these acts of dispossession, which included the best lands both in the flatlands as well as at the foot of the mountains, the indigenous communities moved to areas of refuge mainly in mountainous areas in the center and northwest of the country and in the northern jungle areas.

Since the end of the twentieth century, the indigenous communities had to confront a new type of threat, namely extractive projects, including metal mining, the construction of large hydroelectric plants, and the expansion of monocultures for export. These threats have put both the territories and the reproduction of life of these peoples at risk. Faced with these challenges, the communities have responded with a series of resistance strategies. This chapter analyzes these responses to extractive efforts and the way in which using both traditional and modern forms of organization has allowed these communities to contain these projects.

7.1 MILITARY GOVERNMENTS, THE PEACE PROCESS, AND THE MAYAN MOVEMENT

This section seeks to contextualize the development of indigenous communities during the second half of the twentieth century. The period from June to October 1944 saw the emergence of a movement that ended the liberal dictatorships of the nineteenth century. This movement, which was initially urban but subsequently spread to the rest of the country, forced the resignation of the dictator Jorge Ubico Castañeda, who was a coffee producer, as well as his successor, General Ponce Vaides (Sáenz 2015, 96–98).

Known as the October Revolution of 1944, this civic military movement initiated a set of reforms that transformed the state, society, and the indigenous communities. Among the reforms targeting indigenous peoples were the expansion of political citizenship, and the election of municipal mayors, who had formerly been appointed directly by the executive, as well as the promotion of education and training programs, cultural "missions," and economic measures intended to improve the living conditions of these communities.

During the government of President Jacobo Arbenz Guzmán (1951–1954), the Agrarian Reform Law (*Ley de Reforma Agraria*) was approved and implemented. This reform sought to end the power of oligarchy, distribute unused land to peasants, and lay the foundations for a capitalist model of production. However, the reform affected not only the interests of large national landowners, but also those of the United Fruit Company, an American company with strong influence in the US Department of State. A campaign of attacks was launched against the Arbenz government, which was depicted as communist, so that a political intervention that led to the fall of the government was justified (Sáenz 2015, 115–123).

President Arbenz Guzmán resigned from the presidency in June 1954. The new government banned all organizations that had supported the revolutionary policies. In rural areas, it persecuted the leaders of the agrarian movement, many of whom were of indigenous origin. The victims were either killed, imprisoned, or went into hiding.

After the fall of the revolutionary governments, a prolonged political crisis began that ended with a coup d'état in March 1963, which enabled the military high command of the Guatemalan army to seize power. From then on, a hybrid political regime was established, in which elections were held, some fraudulent and others not, and opposition parties and legislative blocks existed. Yet, the regime systematically violated human rights, banned and persecuted the left-wing opposition, and murdered political opponents.

The army's escalating repression targeting its opponents led to political radicalization and the emergence of armed guerrilla organizations, which sought to change the state of affairs via an armed struggle. Initially formed and led by the ladino/mestizo population, the insurgency spread to indigenous areas, where it drew on grievances held by indigenous peoples in response to long-standing racism, discrimination, and exclusion. Between 1979 and 1983, an indigenous uprising emerged that included the mobilization of entire communities. Supported by the oligarchic elites and the US government, the response of the army was brutal, and included mass execution of hundreds, the destruction of 440 villages, and acts of genocide against several indigenous communities (Sáenz 2015, 192–195).

Despite these events, a powerful Mayan movement emerged in 1984, which articulated both organizations defending indigenous language, traditions, and ancestral knowledge, and those advancing claims for political rights and land redistribution. Reaching its peak with the counter-celebration of the fifth centenary of Columbus' discovery of America, this movement had a decisive influence on peace negotiations between the government and insurgent groups. Signed in March 1995, the Agreement on Identity and Rights of Indigenous Peoples, among other things, recognized the existence of the Maya, Garifuna, and Xinca peoples, guaranteed their participation at all levels as well as the use of indigenous languages and practice of spirituality (Sáenz 2005, 56–66).

The legal recognition of indigenous peoples constituted important progress. Yet these advances were blocked by the implementation of neoliberal reforms, the further weakening of the state, and the holding of a popular consultation in which some of the strategic changes established in the Peace Accords were rejected. While the Maya movement as such was fading at the national level, a community movement emerged, which managed to revive municipal governments, the de facto recognition of customs and ancestral authorities, and the establishment of a dense organizational network.

The strengthening of indigenous communities and their ancestral authorities contributed to a set of institutional reforms that included legislation of decentralization the consolidation of municipal budgets, and the ratification of ILO Convention 169 (Sáenz 2005, 67–70). All the same, the conditions of poverty, marginalization, and political exclusion of indigenous peoples remain.

7.2 Indigenous Community Organization

The indigenous communities survived the plundering of their communal lands during the liberal reform of the nineteenth century, resisted the counterinsurgency policies after 1954, and recovered from acts of genocide in the 1980s. Fundamental in sustaining the local autonomy and the survival of community life in these most difficult conditions were the maintenance of communities and of the dynamics of political organization, which combine ancestral elements (e.g., traditional authorities, civic religious, and indigenous municipal institutions) with republican practices (e.g., town hall meetings, development councils, and "progress committees"), and making use of the state institutions in their favor (Tzul 2016).

Furthermore, inaccessible geography and domestic policy contributed to this development. Thanks to their remote and mountainous location, relatively far from agricultural production areas and with little road infrastructure, many areas inhabited by indigenous communities were unattractive for investment projects. In addition, these communities developed strategies to maintain control of municipal governments, regardless of the elected mayors' party affiliation. In the municipalities with an indigenous majority, most of the mayors are of Mayan origin (Sáenz 2005).

The relationship between the state and the communities exhibits major contradictions. On the one hand, the state is largely absent in areas relating to public goods provision, such as education, health, food, and security. On the other hand, the state presence tends to be disruptive and, in many cases coercive, as it is expressed through corruption, military interventions, and attempts to control strategic resources such as water, forests, and land.

Moreover, the state does not respond uniformly to the demands of indigenous peoples. As a result of the negotiations of the peace agreements and the signing of ILO Convention 169, a series of institutional entities and mechanisms have been established that offer the indigenous groups certain levels of influence over public decisions. The establishment of the Commission against Racism and Discrimination,[2] the Ombudsman for Indigenous Women,[3] and the Presidential Commission on Human Rights[4] are some of the public institutions serving to defend indigenous rights. Along these lines, the struggle to assert indigenous rights has been transferred to the courts, where activists and human rights law firms have won several cases. In response, the central government, however, relies on a repressive institutional framework that includes constitutional provisions that give the army responsibility for the country's internal security and the Public Order Law that enables the participation of the army and the suspension of rights in the name of restoring public order.

Extraction projects that operate in indigenous areas are diverse in nature and thus affect communities differently. These include metallic and non-metallic mining, large hydroelectric plants, agricultural monocultures for export, in particular palm oil and cane sugar, and infrastructure megaprojects, such as highways and electric transmission lines. Such projects have encountered rejection by the affected communities, by threatening the sustainability of community life, by limiting the access to water, and by damaging the environment, including community forests and agricultural land. The companies that promote these projects have different characteristics and their capitals have different origins, including the United States, Canada, Spain, Switzerland, Italy, and Russia.

In order to measure the depth of the social and political impact generated by resource extraction in Guatemala, we need to analyze its local repercussions. Thus, the following sections trace the community response to extractive projects, in particular the cases of hydroelectric companies in Huehuetenango and mining companies in other parts of the country.

7.3 Hydroelectric Extraction and the Ancestral Plurinational Government of Northern Huehuetenango[5]

Located in the northwest of the country, Huehuetenango is one of the departments with the greatest cultural diversity of Mayan communities in Guatemala. Since the colonial period these ethnic groups have successfully defended their territories from threats to their ancestral way of life and natural assets. During the most critical period of the civil war, from 1981 to 1984, the Guatemalan army resorted to persecutions, massacres, selective assassinations, and disappearances to undermine the will of the guerrilla organizations operating in these territories. Yet, the main victims in this conflict were the impoverished civilian population. According to the Guatemalan Truth Commission, the army bore the main responsibility for human rights violations (CEH 1999). To confront counterinsurgent violence, the indigenous communities drew on ancestral knowledge to preserve the sustainability of community life. From knowledge to manage food production to processes of election and appointment of political functionaries, ancestral knowledge has contributed to sustain the country's communities facing multiple threats of violence (Quiñonez Monzón 2018).

Represented and sheltered by elders and community leaders who are recognized as Ancestral Authorities (Tzul 2017), this ancestral knowledge gave rise to the Plurinational Ancestral Government, in the midst of the escalating resource conflict. For centuries, the territory of Northern Huehuetenango has been inhabited by the indigenous groups Chuj, Akateko, Q'anjob'al, and Poptí as well as by a significant number of Mestizos. The social and economic dynamics of this region depend critically on the daily interaction with related communities across the border in southern Mexico. Despite the limitations imposed by the interstate border, constant communication with the Tzotzil, Tzeltal, Tojolabal, and related groups has been maintained for generations. Nevertheless, the border has not been an impediment in the signing of agreements between peoples at both sides of the frontier.

Yet, massive migration of Central Americans seeking to reach the United States poses a serious problem to cross-border communications. There is also a rapid increase of criminality in the border area with Mexico because of trafficking of drugs, weapons, and humans. The state's inability to address these problems contrasts with its attentive collaboration with extractive companies in the same area. The presence of state institutions, such as the National Civil Police, Courts, the Public Ministry, or the army, generates tensions leading to a confrontational and violent attitude toward the organized civilian population, when the latter stages protest actions against extractive companies. In recent years, the violence targeting civilians has increased in this region of the country, causing some to question the participation of the state in a model of development that goes against the needs and practices of the communities.

Three municipalities in Northern Huehuetenango stand out in terms of conflict intensity. These projects are Hidroelectrica Cambalam I y II in Santa Cruz Barillas, Hidroeléctrica San Luis in Santa Eulalia and Hidroeléctrica, Pojom II and San Andrés, San Mateo Ixtatán (see Fig. 7.1). The involved companies enjoy the support by foreign capital and Guatemalan partners that handle the legal situation in the country. Despite some of them having been withdrawn, the projects located in these areas have triggered a socio-environmental conflict that has had major consequences for the affected communities.

In the case of Santa Cruz Barillas, the company responsible for the construction of the hydroelectric plant, Hidro Santa Cruz SA, is part of the Ecoener Hidralia consortium with operations in other Latin American countries and with headquarters in Spain[6] (Van Gelder y de Wilde 2015). This company arrived in Santa Cruz Barillas in November 2010. Although the population held a good-faith community consultation prior to the company's arrival, which rejected the extractive projects, the company continued with its extraction plan, thus generating friction with the population. In May 2012, amid a climate of protests and tensions in the region, an attack targeted local residents, which resulted in one fatality and two wounded. The local population blamed the hydroelectric company personnel for these events (Bastos et al. 2015), which triggered a series of violent events, including the attack on military installations. This prompted President Otto Pérez Molina, who is currently incarcerated for corruption, to declare martial law on the area, sending in

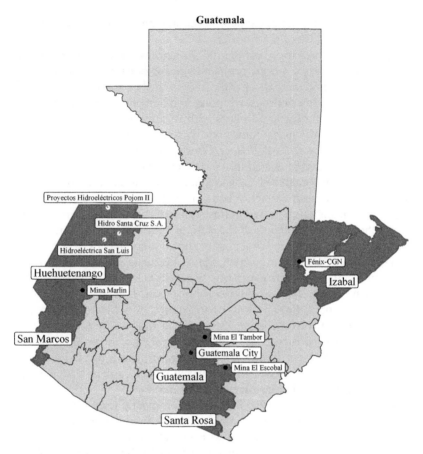

Fig. 7.1 Mining and hydroelectric projects analyzed in this chapter. *Source* Coordinadora Nacional Para La Reducción De Desastres

police and military units. These governmental actions were seen as highly controversial. Accusing the army of excessive use of force, the local residents reported these acts to human rights organizations (CDH 2012). Similar events recurred during the years that the company operated in Santa Cruz Barillas. For many community leaders, their opposition to the hydroelectric plant resulted in serious charges, leading to their imprisonment following lengthy legal proceedings. Finally, in 2016, the company

Hidro Santa Cruz SA abandoned its interest in building a hydroelectric plant in the area (Juárez, ElPeriódico December 22, 2016).

In 2004, the inhabitants of Santa Eulalia found out that the company Guatemala Cooper SA would try to initiate a mining project in their municipality. As the news spread throughout the area, community assemblies decided to conduct a good-faith community consultation. Inspired by the consultations conducted in previous years in the west of the country and other regions of Huehuetenango, the first consultation in Northern Huehuetenango was held in Santa Eulalia on August 29, 2006. This consultation marked a milestone in the struggle to protect the municipality and its natural assets. With this consultation, the communities made clear their rejection of any form of extractive activity in the municipality. In the consultation, 99% of the population voted against the planned mining activity (Antonio and Rivera, Prensa Comunitaria 30 Agosto 2016).

Ultimately, the mining project never materialized. In 2010, new conflicts erupted in the municipality following the activities of the Cinco M company, which sought to build a hydroelectric plant in the municipality of Santa Eulalia. Tensions began with the company's refusal to respect the popular decision. However, since the state authorities refuse to recognize the community consultations as binding and definitive, the company continued to advance its plans without giving any explanation to the community.[7] After several attempts to enter into dialogue, both the company and the government failed to respond to the demands of the population.

In a climate of uncertainty including indications of anomalies in the granting of construction licenses for the hydroelectric plant, the community leader and teacher Daniel Pedro Mateo was murdered on April 7, 2013. Recognized as a leading defender of the community's land and natural assets, he had played an important role in the 2006 community consultation. His murder raised many doubts after his body was found three days later with signs of torture in a place near the property of the hydroelectric plant. His death unsettled the local inhabitants, who accused the company's personnel of the murder. Yet, even several years following Mateo's death, those responsible for the murder have not been brought to trial.

Another critical moment in this conflict resulted from the closure of the Snuq Jolom Konob Community Radio. Since its foundation, it had become a resource for cultural expression and information for the population of Santa Eulalia, as a part of the nationwide network of community radio. Following the first news about new extractive projects in the region, the radio station began informing the population about the risks that this type of extractive activity would bring to their communities. This information crucially influenced the result of the community consultation of August 2006.

After the state authorities' capture of community leaders in the municipality of San Mateo Ixtatán, there was a series of violent attacks against inhabitants of Santa Eulalia in January 2015 (Prensa Comunitaria, February 4, 2015). These events involved Diego Marcos Pedro, the Municipal Mayor of Santa Eulalia at that time, who on October 20 ordered the closure of the Snuq Jolom Konob radio. A severe blow to the community organization, this action was seen as a retaliation against its information campaign. After an attempt to reopen the radio station on March 19, 2016, which provoked attacks on the population and journalists covering the event, the broadcaster remained closed until December 2016 (Quiñonez Monzón 2018).

The construction of the San Luis hydroelectric plant was interrupted in 2018 after

> the municipality of Santa Eulalia requested to the Judicial Body (OJ) that the hydroelectric license granted by the Ministry of Environment and Natural Resources (MARN) be suspended, because the Mayan people Q'anjob'al had not been consulted about the project. The municipal autonomy was also violated, because the MARN approved the Environmental Impact Study (EIA) without the participation of the municipality, and in addition there is not a single document confirming that the company Cinco M, Sociedad Anónima had carried out this management before this institution. (Rivera 2018)

The Municipality of Santa Eulalia's request was granted. However, in 2019, the company filed a legal action in the Constitutional Court to try to reverse this ruling and to allow it to continue with the construction of the dam. To date, there is no information on the final resolution of this legal body.

Another of the most conflictual cases in Northern Huehuetenango took place in the Ixquisis region in the municipality of San Mateo Ixtatán.

Here, as in previous conflicts, the extractive industry's attempts to manipulate the population, to superimpose its own interests over the welfare of the communities, are evident. Around 2009, representatives of the company Promoción de Desarrollo Hídrico SA (PDHSA) arrived in this municipality, located on the border with Mexico. Without identifying themselves as representatives of the extractive industry, they offered the not yet electrified community installation of electrical power. This situation caused uncertainty in the population, who had previously conducted a good-faith community consultation in which 99% of the population of the 59 villages in the municipality had rejected any type of extractive activity.

Evidently, the company knew that revealing its intentions relating to three hydroelectric projects, Pojom I, Pojom II, and San Andrés, would renew the population's opposition. It thus attempted to win over people who had served in the army during the civil war (Simón, Prensa Comunitaria, December 27, 2016). Taking advantage of this previous conflict, the company managed to gain the support of former military personnel, resuscitating the division and confrontation of those dark years. This strategy was accompanied by the offering of infrastructure projects that would benefit communities such as "projects providing potable water, and organization of sports and cultural activities in the villages. In addition, a booth with outlets and tables to connect telephones or computers was made available to the inhabitants of the area, and the company took on the task of paving the road that leads to San Francisco Nentón" (Pérez, Plaza Pública, June 23, 2014).

Without taking into account the results of the community consultation, the government authorized PDHSA in 2011 to begin the construction of the projects. Since then, the communities of San Mateo Ixtatán have experienced constant conflict. While the local population fears that project will cause environmental damage such as river diversion, forest depletion, and destruction of river biodiversity, the state has refused to take these fears seriously while maintaining a strong military presence in the area.[8]

The constant clashes between the population that opposes hydroelectric projects and those who support them reached a critical point, resulting in civilian victimization including homicide (Temper, del Bene y Martínez-Alier 2015; Business and Human Rights Resource Center 2019). The community members contend that the state and the company are mainly responsible for the escalating violence. According to several testimonies, the latter have won the support of municipal authorities through bribes and mobilized people who infiltrate peaceful protests to accuse community leaders of criminal acts. In the same way, the company and the state assert that community members, mobilized by ex-guerrilla fighters, have destroyed equipment and caused other disturbances in the vicinity of the company's property (Pérez, Plaza Pública 2014; Simón, Prensa Comunitaria 2016).

In 2018, the Agreement for Peace and Development of San Mateo Ixtatán was signed, which "is an instrument for overcoming social conflict through peaceful and legal means, using dialogue and negotiation to find points of understanding and agreement, from the perspective of a win-win for all parties" (Agreement for Peace and Development of San Mateo Ixtatán 2018). This agreement calls for participation of different groups and organizations representing the region, including the company that owns the hydroelectric projects, as its promoters through a "Peace, development and culture consortium" promoted by the companies Acdares y *Soluciones SA* (AYSSA) and *Fundación y Tecnológica para el Desarrollo de Guatemala* (Funtedegua).[9] Despite the fact that this agreement covers different points and areas regarding the development of the region, community leaders and Ancestral Authorities point out that "it does not have the support of the communities of the Maya Chuj people, who mostly inhabit the municipality, nor does it enjoy the support of the rest of the communities in the Yich Kisis microregion affected by the three hydroelectric projects, or the Q'anjob'al and mestizo communities on the border with Mexico" (Rivera, Prensa Comunitaria, January 25, 2020). Finally, as one of its first actions in January 2020, the government of President Alejandro Giammattei visited Northern Huehuetenango to present the "Verification and Follow-up Commission of the Peace Agreement and Development in San Mateo Ixtatán" through government agreement No. 30-2020.

Since the beginning of the resource conflict, the Plurinational Ancestral Government of Northern Huehuetenango has emerged as one of the most representative organizational efforts of the indigenous peoples in Guatemala. Thanks to its strong community base, it builds and maintains its legitimacy through extensive assembly processes and alliances at the regional level. It is important to understand how the network of social, political and cultural relationships that give rise to the Plurinational Ancestral Government works, to take distance from the classic concepts that Western politics has given to indigenous peoples, that is, "to think indigenous as political That produces strategy forces us to abandon an interpretation of indigenous politics surrounded by mythification, tradition, use and custom, and place it in the codes of a series of calculations to maintain, regulate and defend concrete wealth is what makes it possible for life to flow. We are facing another form of political rationality" (Tzul 2016, p. 50).

The ethnic groups of the region have been interacting closely for centuries. Following the first news of extractive activity, they started mobilizing to defend their land and communities. The analysis and discussions conducted by the ancestral authorities and other leaders of the region addressing the consequences of resource extraction in other countries and regions of Guatemala made apparent that these types of projects would not improve the living conditions of these communities and would, instead, bring conflict and environmental degradation.

In this context, the Ancestral Plurinational Government was created by local organizations in the municipalities that make up the northern region of Huehuetenango: Santa Cruz Barillas, San Pedro Soloma, San Mateo Ixtatán, Santa Eulalia, San Miguel Acatán, San Rafael la Independencia, San Sebastián Coatán, and San Juan Ixcoy, with the aim of resisting the state and extractive companies. In each of these municipalities there are different expressions of community representation, each with its own characteristics, such as peasant organizations, women's organizations, teachers, and established and new media outlets. These can be understood as Communal Government Systems, which are defined as "Plural plots of men and women that create historical-social relationships that have body, strength and content in a specific space: communal territories, and to govern it, the plots update government structures that they have inherited to conserve, share, defend and recover the material means for the reproduction of human life and of domestic and non-domestic animals, all this agglutinated in the territory" (Tzul 2016, p. 39). Especially important is the incorporation of local institutions recognized by the state of Guatemala. Recognized by the Law of the Councils for Urban and Rural Development (Decree 11-2002), the Community Development Councils (COCODES) play an important role in the management of community development projects. In this sense, COCODES have become an intermediary between the communities and the state. This shows that, rather than rejecting the state, the community organization and the Plurinational Ancestral Government are making active use of these state institutions in their struggle for influence.

Through its assembly, the communities of Northern Huehuetenango agreed to prioritize the defense of their land and natural assets, in light of the emergency situation produced by hydroelectric and mining firms having already received licenses for extraction. Despite tensions and permanent pressure from the companies and the government, the Plurinational Ancestral Government managed to create a broad community-based consensus to maintain a strong organizational base while relying on ancestral knowledge as an ethical and political basis for their actions. This political exercise has recognized the full ethnic diversity of the population and promoted its generational replacement, coordinated actions, and built legitimacy based on a strengthened Mayan identity.

Many of the extractive projects are currently on hold, while some companies, such as Hidro Santa Cruz, have withdrawn entirely from the region. This has been achieved by the political and legal pressure exerted by the communities. In their path, these companies have left a large list of aggressions against the communities and communal leaders, in addition to a latent conflict that is re-configured with each new government.

7.4 Mining Projects and the Response of Aggrieved Communities

The global demand for metallic minerals such as gold, nickel, and silver has encouraged transnational corporations to develop a special interest in those countries that, like Guatemala, possess these resources. State weakness and lax regulation, however, imply that resource extraction is likely to trigger socio-environmental conflicts (IRALEP 2010). The mining companies in Guatemala are typically transnational corporations with operations centers in industrialized countries and links to local interest groups and government officials willing to promote their operations.

According to recent information offered by the Ministry of Energy and Mines of Guatemala (2018), 305 mining licenses have been granted in the country, of which 117 correspond to construction materials, 152 to non-metallic minerals, and 36 to metallic minerals. In addition, 183 operating licenses and 236 exploration licenses are in process[10]. Exploration and exploitation licenses are distributed throughout the national territory. Most of them affect indigenous and ladino/mestizo communities. As we have seen in the case of hydroelectric projects, mining projects have been accompanied by repeated human rights violations, as well as the approval of states of emergency and the criminalization of community leaders opposed to extractive activities. Some opponents of the mining projects have been persecuted, intimidated, jailed on false charges, and even killed. In some communities, the extractive companies have actively supported the establishment of paramilitary groups that terrorize the population and put the preservation of community life at risk (Dary et al. 2018).

The mining projects also exert a negative impact on the environment. Among the effects of these activities are the contamination of water bodies, interference in the biological cycles of ecosystems, release of toxic gases and chemical waste, all in violation of industrial safety protocols. The lax and manipulable environmental legislation in Guatemala, and the low technical capacity of the authorities in charge of managing and protecting natural assets reveal persistent efforts to weaken institutional constraints in order to lower extraction costs and to inhibit interference by local communities and activist organizations (IRALEP 2010).

In many cases, mining projects violate the rights of indigenous peoples. From the perspective of the affected populations, mining activities pose a threat to the land and the living beings inhabiting it. The broad majority of the affected communities appreciate as a fundamental principle the balance between human beings and nature. On this view, extraction directly undermines the dignity and identity of the affected ethnic groups. Together with institutional withdrawal and local conflicts in rural regions that are particularly affected by mining, this situation has encouraged community-level mobilization. In order to articulate their grievances, the indigenous peoples have built extensive networks at the local and regional levels.

To illustrate these responses, we will analyze four cases of mining conflicts in Guatemala while focusing on racism and attacks against indigenous populations. In general, the introduction of mining projects in indigenous territories further exacerbates pre-existing conflict over land. Given this context, each one of the processes of territorial struggle of the indigenous communities involves, in itself, a struggle of the most marginalized populations in the country.

Illustrating how these projects operate in different regions of the country, these cases represent a sample of the way that large transnational corporations act locally. In particular, they show how the firms seek to manipulate and alter national and community-level politics. The alliance between the state and private interests reflects recurrent patterns, thus confirming that extractive processes in impoverished countries with weak institutions constitute a part of a global economic strategy which lets southern countries continue to supply raw materials at a low cost, regardless of the associated social, political, and humanitarian consequences.

In the following, we will illustrate these phenomena by exploring four prominent mining projects that have given rise to innovative resistance strategies (see Fig. 7.1).

7.4.1 The Marlin Mine, Sipacapa and San Miguel Ixtahuacán, San Marcos

The Marlin mine was one of the first extractive projects that showed the affected Mayan communities in Guatemala what it meant to face both a transnational corporation and the state. The Marlin mine, which is owned by Montana Exploradora SA, a subsidiary of the Canadian company Goldcorp Inc., operated in the municipalities of Sipacapa, San Marcos and San Miguel Ixtahuacán, Huehuetenango in western Guatemala for 12 years. In 2019, this company merged with the American Newmont Mining Corporation, thus forming what is currently one of the world's largest gold mining corporation.[11]

The scale of these extractive activities corresponds closely to the damage done to the local ecosystems and the social fabric of the affected communities. According to the Environmental Justice Atlas, "[b]etween 2005 and 2010, Montana Exploradora exported 1.2 million ounces gold and 18.2 million ounces silver," produced primarily by open pit mining with "water consumption in 2010 of 3.833 million cubic meters, of which 151,000 cubic meters correspond to water pumped from wells, the rest comes from recirculated water from the tailings tank" (Temper, del Bene y Martínez-Alier 2015).

In an evaluation of the human rights impacts of the mine operation, it was established that "Goldcorp considers the Marlin Mine to be one of its operations with the lowest operating costs: USD 192 per ounce of gold in 2009, compared to a cost average of USD 295 for the corporate" (On Common Ground Consultants Inc. 2010, 36). From before the start of its operations in 2005 to its closure in 2017, this mining project accumulated a series of lawsuits, which pitted the Mam and Sipakapense Mayan communities against the state and the company that owned the project.

The Marlin Mine was granted an operating license in 2003. The government took this step without respecting.

the provisions of the Political Constitution or ILO Convention 169 regarding the rights of indigenous peoples over their territories by not informing or consulting the Mam and Sipakapense people about the approval of projects that would undoubtedly affect their territories, natural resources and the rights of indigenous peoples. (Sánchez 2017, p. 21)

On June 18, 2005, the communities of Sipacapa conducted one of the first mining-related community consultations in Guatemala.[12] This process yielded a verdict according to which 98% of the population rejected any exploration and mining in its territory. This result was not respected by the central government. Yagenova (2012, 70) claims that "[t]he obligation of consultation regarding any legislative, administrative measure or in relation to an infrastructure project, exploration or exploitation of natural resources in indigenous territories, is based on international instruments ratified by the Guatemalan State." According to Special Rapporteur on Indigenous Peoples, "the consultation should not be interpreted as a one-off act, but as a process of permanent dialogue between the state and the indigenous peoples which must be on the basis of respect for the collective rights of peoples" (cit. in Yagenova 2012).

The Guatemalan Constitutional Court (CC) ruled that the consultation was legal, but not binding (Sánchez 2017, p. 21). In the case of the Marlin Mine, the consultation was carried out by the Montana Exploradora company itself, without the participation of the Guatemalan government, thus granting them the mining license. This triggered a vivid debate about the legitimacy of the consultation processes in cases such as San Marcos. The state's reaction to the consultation in Sipacapa revealed its reluctance to defend the interests of the indigenous population of the country, thus exposing its alliance with transnational corporations in an effort to evade compliance with international legal agreements.

The civil war that was fought in Guatemala 36 years ago has left a legacy of polarization, which has survived until today in many communities that were affected by the violence and repression, mainly in the west of the country. Exploiting this situation, the companies have tended to co-opt leaders who participated in the army or the police, as a way to spread disinformation, to discredit and intimidate the opposition, and even to perpetrate acts of physical violence against community leaders.

Thanks to the persistent national and international efforts of the affected communities to articulate their grievances, the debate about mining began to gain prominence in the national political debate. In

2010, this social pressure prompted the Ministry of Environment and Natural Resources to impose a fine on the company due to water pollution. This situation triggered an intervention of the Inter-American Court of Human Rights (IACHR), which mandated protection measures in favor of the affected communities, even ordering the state of Guatemala to temporarily close the mine (Véliz 2015; Yagenova 2012).

Despite the social conflicts and these legal sanctions, however, the Marlin Mine continued to operate profitably until its closure in 2017 (Bolaños, Prensa Libre, February 21, 2017). In 2012, the mining company entered an agreement with the government to readjust its royalties, which were to increase from the legal minimum of 1–5%. Despite this, it is calculated that before its closure in 2017, the Marlin Mine had extracted 62.3 tons of gold with an approximate profit of 4.4 billion US dollars (Escalón, Nómada, August 23, 2018).

Yet, after 12 years of operation, and a long struggle of the communities of San Miguel Ixtahuacán and Sipacapa, extraction has had profound social and environmental consequences, some of which remain until today. The two municipalities of the department of San Marcos are currently still debating how to repair its damaged social fabric. The economic crisis resulting from the socio-environmental conflict involving the Marlin Mine has already had serious repercussions for local development, not the least due to the loss of jobs and the financial weakening of the region.

7.4.2 The El Tambor Mine, Progress VII Derivative, San José Del Golfo, Guatemala

The municipalities of San José del Golfo and San Pedro Ayampuc are located 28 km from Guatemala City. These localities have experienced one of the conflicts that have generated the most media coverage and discussion at the national level around the issue of mining and the forms of political organization of the affected communities. In 2010, the local communities learned about the authorization of mining operations. Confusion followed since neither the extractor nor the state made any attempt to provide information or to organize community consultations. The affected population would never have imagined that they were living at the gates of one of the largest mining projects in the world, known as "El Tambor" and that Progreso VII Derivada was only one of the twelve licenses authorized by the Guatemalan government for this project.

Overnight life of these communities was turned upside down by the presence of a project that could cause serious social and environmental damage:

> At the beginning of the century, the Ministry of Energy and Mines gave permission to the Canadian company Radius Explorations Ltd. and the South African Gold Field Inc. to evaluate the subsoil of a geological area of 107,072 hectares. To get an idea, the Historical Center of Guatemala with its 300 blocks of extension, occupies 2010 hectares. In other words, the Historic Center would fit 510 times with ease on the surface designated for El Tambor. 107 thousand hectares equals more than 1000 square kilometers. Guatemala has 108 thousand square kilometers. (Hernández 2014, pp. 116-117)

In 2012, this project was sold to a US company called Kappes, Cassiday & Associates (KCA), which operated in Guatemala through its subsidiaries Exploraciones Mineras de Guatemala SA (EXMIGUA). With strong governmental support, the firm continued setting up the El Tambor and Progreso VII Derivada project. Since the exploration activities began, the company had been buying land dedicated to agriculture and livestock from the local inhabitants. The residents of these communities indicated that they were never informed about the buyer's intended use of the land. In order to acquire the land, in some cases they resorted to direct or indirect coercion. In other cases, community members were seduced by high purchase prices. Unidentified speculators approached the owners of the land to offer them double or triple the value established for the sale. This turned out to be a good business since it helped the company to take over the land necessary to realize an integrated project covering approximately 1% of the national territory (Hernández 2014, pp. 116-117).

After hearing the first news about the granting of exploration and exploitation licenses, the communities began a process of peaceful struggle that earned them national and international recognition. At the border between the aforementioned municipalities, in the middle of the road, they set up a protest camp in a location known as "La Puya." Located near the entrance to the Progreso VII Derivada mining project, this became an emblematic site of resistance to the mining project.

The main objective of the community camp was to prevent the entry of heavy machinery that was going to start mining in the area. Stopping the project would mean a multi-year struggle amid threats, repression, and fear of contamination of water sources. The resistance began after an event that was of great importance to the affected communities and that helped to mobilize resistance. On March 1, 2012, in the early hours of the morning, heavy machinery intended to enter the mining project to start the excavation work. At this moment, Ms. Estela Reyes of the El Carrizal community attempted to block the machinery from moving forward. The trucks and heavy vehicles had to stop, until other residents urged Ms. Reyes to withdraw to avoid further escalation. Yet, the example having been set, the inhabitants of the affected communities were now willing to do anything to prevent mining from taking place, including risking their own lives. This event would mark a before and after in this socio-environmental conflict, in addition to completely transforming the course of anti-mining struggle in Guatemala.

After this event, the residents took turns to monitor the entrance to the mining area 24 h a day and, if necessary, notify the communities to prevent any attempt to enter with machinery at the project site. The "La Puya" camp has been characterized by the use of peaceful means, the role of women and the use of religious symbols to oppose the extractive project. While traditionally the leadership of the protests had been male, the leadership assumed by the women of the communities of San José del Golfo and San Pedro Ayampuc constitutes a change in the social movements' action repertoires.

As a consequence, the security forces were unable to act violently in La Puya. Attempting to force the protesters to withdraw to make way for the heavy equipment, the police encountered women embracing religious images and clinging to their bibles while the men remained in the background rather than intervening in a confrontational manner. One of the leaders of the movement, Yolanda Oquelí pointed out the following:

> Here, the men wanted from the beginning to burn tires, dig deep ditches, confront the police. We told them that this was not going to happen, because if it happened they would be arrested and beaten. We were going to have to stand up and not let them take them away. If they take them, we falter. Instead it will be more difficult for us to be beaten. (Yolanda Oquelí, quoted in Véliz, Nómada August 18, 2014)

According to Valladares,

The Resistance is made up of people from various communities of San José del Golfo and San Pedro Ayampuc, organized in defense of the land, the territory and natural assets, including the Ladino population and, to a lesser extent, indigenous people from Nacahuil. With this sit-in, men and women of all ages have managed in an organized way to stop the claim of various Canadian companies. (Valladares and López 2015, 3)

In response to this peaceful resistance, an attack was perpetrated against Yolanda Oquelí, who was shot at a place near the La Puya camp, and she was seriously injured. "As a result of this event, the Inter-American Commission on Human Rights ordered the Guatemalan authorities to grant protection services to Ms. Oquelí. Since then, the activist lives with security guards. Still, she is exposed to persecution and the Guatemalan government has made several demands including a lawsuit accusing her of kidnapping" (Entrevista a Ana Sandoval (2016) citada en Temper, del Bene y Martínez-Alier 2015).

To authorize mining extraction, the authorities did not carry out the community consultations as legally stipulated. For this reason, the Environmental and Social Legal Action Center (CALAS) filed a legal action on August 29, 2014, requesting the suspension of any further mining activity. In response, the Supreme Court of Justice (CSJ) granted provisional protection in favor of CALAS, suspending the exploitation license of the mining project (Public Square, July 1, 2016). The company appealed this decision before the Constitutional Court (CC), which rejected the legal arguments presented by the company and ratified the CSJ decision. On June 29, 2016, the CSJ definitively confirmed its decision (Villatoro, Plaza Pública, July 1, 2016).

The company has defended itself by reinterpreting the country's laws, and by proposing that if the mining license were suspended, it would not view it as its own responsibility, but that of the state itself. Therefore, according to its legal representatives, the company should been seen as the aggrieved party and the country would thus be in breach of the Free Trade Agreement (FTA) between the United States, Central America, and the Dominican Republic. With this argument, the company filed a request for arbitration with the International Center for Settlement of Investment Disputes (ICSID), which was accepted. This could force the State of Guatemala to pay damages of up to approximate US $300 million as compensation for the suspension of activities at the El Tambor Mine (Bolaños, Prensa Libre, December 15, 2018).

Extractive companies have often resorted to legal means to pursue their operations despite the rejection of the affected communities. To this end, they have hired law firms both in Guatemala and in the United States. Despite community critique, chronic state weakness allows companies such as Kappes, Cassiday & Associates to exert pressure on judicial bodies. Accordingly, the legal intimidation campaign relies on often fabricated accusations framing local activists.

In sum, the experience of La Puya has set an example to follow for communities that are in a similar situation in other regions of the country. Making clear that despite various dispossession strategies, the community organization has emerged strengthened and has so far successfully adapted to the complex conditions posed by extractive activity in Guatemala.

7.4.3 *The El Escobal Mine, San Rafael Las Flores, Santa Rosa and Jutiapa*

Since the intensification of mining activities in Guatemala started in the early twenty-first century, the Mina el Escobal has belonged to the most controversial operations of its kind. This mining project has triggered numerous legal cases and brought forth a strong communication campaign in which the business chambers have tried to generate social and political pressure.

The El Escobal mine was acquired by Tahoe Resources Inc., a Canadian company based in Reno (Solano, Plaza Pública, April 07, 2015). The company received authorization to start its operations in 2013, despite the fact that no community consultation had been carried out in the area where it operated. Predictably, this situation unleashed conflict in the affected communities, who initiated actions to impede the operations of the mine. On April 27, 2013, during a demonstration, the mining company's security detail lashed out at people protesting outside the mine, which led to a complaint before a Canadian court years later.

Given persistent popular protests, the government decreed a state of siege in the communities near the mine on May 2, 2013. According to the viewpoint of the protest leaders, however, this measure merely served the purpose of stopping social protest and criminalizing the movement. Indeed, the decree "allowed, according to article 19 of the Public Order law, to intervene or dissolve, without the need for any prevention, any organization or association operating in the area; suppress any action, individual or collective, that would be contrary to the provisions taken to restore normality in the area; and the arrest without a warrant of any person suspected of conspiring against the government" (Baires, Plaza Pública, September 23, 2013).

Raising tensions in the area, the governmental response clearly favored the mining company, thus exposing its unwillingness to resolve socio-environmental conflict peacefully. As usual in these cases, knowing in exactly what happened at the site state is difficult, especially since the involved actors have their own particular version of what happened, and may hide or bias information to support their arguments.

Such was the case of the statements made by President Pérez Molina and his Minister of the Interior Mauricio López Bonilla, who repeatedly asserted that the state of siege had nothing to do with the interests of the mining company: "The issue of mining is not a major motivation for this operation and the state of emergency that we are implementing. Rather it is to restore order and care for the lives of Guatemalans who reside in these places" (Baires, Plaza Pública, September 23, 2013).

As we have seen from similar cases, the government's response has tended to be mostly repressive, by militarizing conflict zones rather than creating conflict-averting channels for dialogue. The systematic criminalization of community leaders serves several purposes. It damages those who organize peaceful protest in order to undermine their struggle. Moreover, it sends a message of intimidation thus intending to break the communities' will to continue demonstrating against the mining projects. By imprisoning community representatives, including those of the ancestral authorities and the organizations of the Mayan peoples, the measures have the potential of weakening the entire affected communities. Nevertheless, the communities have remained at the forefront of this anti-mining fight, facing companies and the state in court. The ensuing legal struggle has been one of the most complex of its kind. In 2017, the Environmental and Social Legal Action Center (CALAS) filed a legal appeal in order to immediately suspend the mine's activity referring to the absence of any prior community consultation as legally prescribed.

The legal process in which Xinca communities have faced the mining firm San Rafael is highly complex in the legal, the economic, and, especially, the political sense. One of the peculiarities in this case concerned the debate around the existence of members of the Xinca group in the area where the mining project is located. This controversy required anthropological expertise from the University of San Carlos de Guatemala and the Universidad del Valle, to scientifically verify the existence of this population (García, Nómada, July 26, 2018).

The repressive campaigns in response to mining protest constitute a clear violation of the affect communities' rights. Furthermore, they directly attack the social fabric of the communities by questioning their ethnic identity, which shows that the Guatemalan State continues to harbor deep-seated structural racism.

At the moment of writing, the San Rafael mining case is currently in process: "In 2018, the [Constitutional Court] of Guatemala issued a ruling stating that the mine can begin to operate as long as the community consultation with indigenous peoples is carried out, which was not carried out before the licenses were granted, but the process has not been achieved since it is stagnant due to discrepancies in the pre-consultation phase" (Bolaños, Prensa Libre July 30, 2019). This is the situation despite the multiple pressures received by business chambers in Guatemala. It has been reported that "Tahoe Resources paid different firms of lobbyists in Canada and the US $270 000. According to a report in the United States Senate's Public Records Office, the company hired the services of four lobbying firms that visited the United States Department of State, the House of Representatives and the Senate, the White House, the office of the vice president Mike Pence and of commercial representatives from that country" (García, Nómada, January 10, 2019a). In keeping with this account, several US politicians have imposed pressure to produce a ruling favorable to the mining project.

In 2019, the El Escobal project changed owners to Pan American Silver, a Canadian mining company that operates several mines in Mexico, Peru, Bolivia, and Argentina (García, Nómada, January 10, 2019a). The new owners have declared that they will adopt a different, less aggressive policy to manage this long and difficult conflict, promising that they will respect and comply with the orders of the Guatemalan justice agencies.

In addition, a Canadian court ruled in favor of the protestors who were attacked by the mining company (Bolaños, Prensa Libre, 30 July 2019). The ruling showed that the company was responsible for the attack on the neighboring protesters and that the security director at the Alberto Rotondo mine gave the order to shoot at the protesters. For this case, the new owners of the mine were forced to apologize publicly while adopting an attitude different from their predecessors. The President and CEO of Pan American Silver made the following statement:

As part of due diligence, we are evaluating how consistent our human rights and security practices are with the Voluntary Principles on Security and Human Rights, as well as the Rights of the Child and the Security checklist. In our Escobal operation in Guatemala, we have already reviewed our security practices as indicated by the Human Rights Officer, who reports to our Legal Counselor". (Bolaños, Prensa Libre, 30 July 2019)

With the case of the El Escobal mine, it remains to be seen how the relationship between community, state, and company will be transformed with this change of ownership. In any case, it will be difficult to repair the social damage that this process has left behind, and if its operation is completed, the environmental impact can be expected to do harm to the region's communities and ecosystems.

7.4.4 The Fénix-CGN Mine, El Estor, Izabal

Located in the municipality of El Estor in the northeastern department of Izabal, the mining project known as Compañía Guatemalteca de Níquel (CGN) is one of the most durable in Guatemala. Surrounded by controversy, this nickel mine continues to operate despite the environmental problems that it has caused for decades. Multiple court cases, many of which still in process, have included attempts to frame a community journalist and the murder of three students from a private university.

"This mine began its operation in 1970, when the Carlos Arana Osorio government granted a concession for the exploitation of nickel, cobalt, iron and chrome during 40 years to the company Explotaciones y Exploraciones Mineras de Izabal (EXMIBAL), a subsidiary of the Canadian company International Nickel Company (INCO)" (Escalón, Nómada, August 23, 2018). From the beginning, the affected communities have always resisted the extension or renewal of mining permits in the area. The grievances concern both the appropriation of community land and damage caused to the natural environment of the region. In response, the national government has consistently responded with repression and criminalization of the protest leaders.

In 2004, the Canadian company Sky Resources-Hudbay Minerals acquired shares in INCO and intended to acquire permission to continue operating the mine for another 40 years. At the same time, a violent attempt was made to evict the affected communities. Representatives of the local population denounced serious human rights abuses, including the rape of Q'eqchí women. In 2011, the mine was purchased by the multinational company Solway Investment group that is registered in Switzerland, with its parent company located in Malta (Escalón, Nómada, August 23, 2018).

With the arrival of this company in Estor Izabal, the conflict escalated. Shortly after this point, there was a murky case that remains unclear to this date and that belongs to the mining cases that have had the greatest media impact in Guatemala. During a field visit to an area near the Fénix mine, a group of biology students from the Universidad del Valle was found dead while conducting an exploration in search of crocodiles. The only survivor was the students' professor, who also worked for the mining company. His version of the events, however, did not align with the forensic evidence. This incident provoked a wave of public outrage, but the Guatemalan justice system never resolved the case (García, Nómada, June 25, 2019b).

The Solway mine extracts ferronickel, a high-quality material. Its extraction requires the use of strong chemical substances, which, according to the community, have contaminated Lake Izabal in the mine's vicinity. In 2017, fishermen noticed a change in color of the lake's water. This was of great concern since fishery constitutes the only source of their subsistence. After filing complaints that were ignored by the authorities, the fishermen held a demonstration on the road to the mine, to prevent the entry of machinery. During these protests there were clashes between residents and the national civilian police that caused the death of a fisherman called Carlos Maaz. No clarity was ever gained about those responsible, however, but the protests led to criminal prosecution of several protesters. Among those affected is Carlos Choc, a journalist who belongs to the Prensa Comunitaria network. While reporting on the event, Choc took a photograph in which Maaz can be seen lying on the ground. As a result of his reporting, Choc and another journalist were persecuted for imputed links to organized crime. These accusations forced Choc to live in hiding (Guégan y Schilis-Gallego 2019).

Criminal prosecution belongs to the mining companies' repertoire of action when responding to local opposition to their activities. The conflict in the area has been escalating, amid a significant increase of drug-trafficking. Moreover, palm oil monocultures in the area have equally led to the displacement and repression of the population. For its part, the government has been unable to control the situation, reacting to the conflict through the militarization of the entire area. This development became even more pronounced in September 2019, after the Jimmy Morales government decided to decree a state of siege in 22 municipalities in the northeast area of the country, ostensibly in order to persecute drug-trafficking. The local population, however, viewed these governmental measures as a sign of a tightening link between the state and companies, since constitutional guarantees were suspended during the siege.

The situation in this region being extremely complex, the crisis is likely to persist. The government persists in its militarization of the area, which human rights organizations view as an attack against the freedom of expression and movement of thousands of inhabitants. By contrast, organized crime does not appear to have been seriously affected. Therefore, there is a lingering suspicion among mining opponents that these actions are being taken to clear the ground for the mining companies, which have never had to interrupt their operations. Meanwhile, environmental and social deterioration continue to pose high costs for those affected by mining.

7.5 Conclusion

The objective of this chapter has been to analyze how extraction projects, specifically those involving hydroelectric and mining resources, affect indigenous groups in Guatemala and how these groups respond to these threats. Despite being a relatively small country, there are around twenty ethnic groups that reside within its borders, most of them being of Mayan origin, yet with several internal differences. This ethnic diversity, which is associated with geographic conditions and a historical legacy of colonial domination, produces two phenomena that interact in response to the threat of extractive projects. On the one hand, indigenous communities share a set of grievances derived from their long-standing historical situation that subjects them to political oppression as well as socio-economic exclusion. This is visible in chronically underdeveloped political representation in parliament, the executive and judicial bodies. Furthermore, there are also major differences in social indicators between indigenous and non-indigenous, including differences in access to public goods, such as education and health services. These inequalities result from an economic system that remains biased in favor the white elite to the detriment of the rest of the population.

As noted, there are differences between and within the ethnic groups in Guatemala. Internally, the differences are expressed along the political, religious, and social class dimensions. Indigenous communities tend to be divided within themselves. Nevertheless, they share a strong sense of local identity, which differentiates communities from each other and in some cases manifests itself in strong inbreeding. Furthermore, there are territorial disputes over strategic resources such as water between neighboring communities, which sometimes cause violent conflicts.

The intrusive challenge posed by extractive projects, however, has allowed the communities to overcome internal differences and divisions in defense of their territories. An example of this at the local level are the results of good-faith community consultations. Having been held in more than 80 municipalities, these consultations have shown that typically more than 90% of the affected populations oppose these projects. At the regional level, local differences have been set aside to establish a common front to confront extractive companies. The case of the plurinational government of Northern Huehuetenango illustrates how the affected communities managed to overcame their differences in their struggle against extractive projects.

It should also be highlighted that, in the defense of their territories, indigenous communities have tended to strengthen and renew their ancestral authorities. Since forms of self-government were established in the period of colonial domination in the so-called Indian villages, the affected communities have been forging structures of political authority—in some cases linked to religion—that have made it possible to maintain internal political and social order while negotiating with external authorities and actors.

As shown by the cases analyzed in this chapter, foreign international companies that operate were the main extractors, often in an alliance with local groups. This alliance is built through the establishment of supply chains that benefit local companies and the lobby of business chambers, which act as local agents for the foreign-based corporations. Another strategy of the corporations has been to take advantage of institutional weaknesses, such as the lack of regulation and the absence of a solid bureaucratic apparatus, to obtain licenses without fully complying with legal requirements.

In the areas of resource extraction, transnational companies employ various strategies that include bribery of municipal authorities, employment of security companies that carry out intelligence operations and other illegal activities, alliances with local businesses and different funding forms of local projects. For the affected population, however, the environmental costs of these projects are frequently much greater than their potential benefits.

Likewise, the cases presented in this chapter show how local communities have adjusted their repertoires of political action by adapting them to the twenty-first century. First, they increasingly rely on community consultations in good faith. Second, they use ethnic identity as a mobilizational and political resource. Finally, they systematically challenge the state and transnational corporations through legal means.

As regards the first set of strategies, community consultations are the result of the application of ILO Convention 169. Based on the recognition of the right of indigenous peoples to be consulted in those decisions that affect them, the communities independently managed and organized good-faith consultations. The governmental attitude to such consultations has evolved from a failure to recognize their existence, to the standpoint that they are legally valid but not binding, all the way to recognizing the need of improving their regulation. In these respects, the actions of indigenous communities have caused changes in the legal system that are favorable to their peoples.

The second change relates to the communities' political and strategic use of ethnic identity. In the areas affected by resource extraction, the inhabitants have used their ethnic identity to claim rights as indigenous peoples and to take advantage of the national and international framework protecting indigenous peoples. This dynamic has even produced re-ethnicization dynamics, as is the case in the southeastern region of Guatemala, where the Xinca identity (a non-Mayan ethnic group) has been revitalized, which has allowed the strengthening of community ties and the establishment of new authority structures, as Xinca parliament for example (Dary et al. 2018). These developments have even been visible in population censuses that report that the Xinca population went from less than 2000 people in 2002 to 200 000 people in 2018 (Vásquez 2019).

Finally, indigenous communities have successfully used the judicial system to block extractive projects. In the last five years, based on the legal action by the Mayan communities, with support from law firms and human rights defenders, most mining projects in Guatemala have been suspended in the absence of a valid and binding consultation. Through these means, the communities have managed, at least for the moment, to contain the threat of extractive projects and to preserve their land and their relative autonomy.

Notes

1. These numbers are disputed. According to some Maya leaders, the percentage is as high as 60%.
2. La Comisión contra el Racismo y la Discriminación (CODISRA).
3. La Defensoría de la Muyer Indígena (DEMI).
4. La Comisión Presidencial de Derechos Humanos (COPREDEH).
5. This section is based on the BA thesis in anthropology "Community Autonomy and political subject in the notion of Ancestral Plurinational Government in the North of Huehuetenango" by Alejandro Quiñonez Monzón 2018.
6. The company's capital also comes mainly from Spain.
7. It should be noted that "[t]he Cinco M Sociedad Anónima company has strong links with the Magdalena Group, one of the main economic groups in the commercial generation of energy in the country, production of sugar for export and biofuels in the Central American region, owned by the Leal family" (Rivera, Prensa Comunitaria, 28 de Noviembre 2013).
8. As indicated on its official Web site, PDHSA, which has subsequently been renamed Energía y Renovación SA, is a Guatemalan company dedicated to the development of hydroelectric projects with renewable energy sources, which currently operates the San Andrés (10.8 Mw) and Pojom II (20 Mw) projects through generator San Andrés SA and generator San Mateo SA, respectively, the latter benefiting from financing provided by the Inter-American Development Bank (IDB 2020). See https://energiayrenovacion.com/nosotros/#section-bfff7c45-8f70-10.
9. According to Janiot y Hernández (2018), "Both companies sell services to 'solve' social problems wherever they go. Since 2015, both try to become decision makers for the communities. AYSSA tried to install a team of promoters in an office, but its link with a businessman accused of corruption and his attempt to bring people closer to the hydroelectric plant forced his exit from the territory".
10. https://www.mem.gob.gt/mineria/estadisticas-mineras/licencias-vigentes-y-solicitudes-en-tramite/.
11. This merger was carried out for an approximate amount of US $10 billion. See https://www.mining.com/newmont-goldcorp-10b-merger-close-week/.
12. The legal basis was provided by rights granted in the United Nations Declaration on the Rights of Indigenous Peoples, the ILO Convention

169 on indigenous and tribal peoples in independent countries, the International Convention on the Elimination of All Forms of Racial Discrimination, and the International Covenant on ESCR and the American Convention on Human Rights (Yagenova 2012).

REFERENCES

Antonio, Simón y Rivera, Nelton. 2016. Santa Eulalia a diez años de la Consulta Comunitaria. *Prensa Comunitaria*. 30 de Agosto. Recuperado de: https://www.prensacomunitaria.org/santa-eulalia-a-diez-anos-de-la-consultacomunitaria/.
Baires Quezada, Rodrigo. 2013. Las mentiras del estado de sitio.*Plaza Pública*. 23 de Septiembre. Recuperado de: https://www.plazapublica.com.gt/content/las-mentiras-del-estado-de-sitio.
Bolaños, Rosa María. 2017. Mina Marlin cerrará producción en mayo, debe empezar fase de recuperación ambiental. *Prensa Libre*, 21 de Febrero. Recuperado de: https://www.prensalibre.com/economia/mina-marlincerrara-produccion-en-mayo/.
Bolaños, Rosa María. 2018. Abren arbitraje internacional por mina El Tambor contra Estado de Guatemala, demandarían Q2 mil millones. *Prensa Libre*. 15 de Diciembre. Recuperado de: https://www.prensalibre.com/economia/abren-arbitraje-contra-guatemala-por-la-puya/.
Bolaños, Rosa María. 2019. Propietaria de Minera San Rafael emite disculpa pública por incidente del 2013. *Prensa Libre*. 30 de Julio. https://www.prensalibre.com/guatemala/comunitario/propietaria-de-minera-san-rafaelemite-disculpa-publica-por-incidente-del-2013/.
Bastos, Santiago, de León Quimy, and Rodr.guez Dania Rivera Nelton y Lucas, Francisco. 2015. *Despojo, Movilización y represión en Santa Cruz Barillas. En: Dinosaurio Reloaded*. Coordinadores Manuela Camus, Santiago Bastos y Julián López García. Facultad Latinoamericana de Ciencias Sociales y Fundación Constelación. Guatemala.
Business & Human Rights Resource Center. 2019. *Guatemala: Asesinan a dos integrantes de la resistencia en contra de una hidroeléctrica de Energía y Renovación*. 02 de Enero de 2019. Recuperado de: https://www.business-humanrights.org/es/%C3%BAltimas-noticias/guatemala-asesinan-a-dos-integrantes-de-laresistencia-en-contra-de-una-hidroel%C3%A9ctrica-de-energ%C3%ADa-y-renovaci%C3%B3n/.
Comisión para el Esclarecimiento Históricao CEH. 1999. *Guatemala: Memoria del Silencio: Informe de la Comisión para el Esclarecimiento Histórico*. Guatemala: UNOPS.
Convergencia por los Derechos Humanos. (CDH). 2012. Comunicado ante el estado de sitio en Barillas, *Guatemala*. 16 de Mayo. Recuperado de:

https://movimientom4.org/2012/05/comunicado-ante-el-estado-de-sitioen-barillas-guatemala/.
Dary, Claudia et al. 2018. *Pensar Guatemala desde la resistencia. El neoliberalismo enfrentado*. Guatemala: Prensa comunitaria y FyG Editores.
Escalón, Sebastián. 2018. Viaje al pueblo tras la Mina Marlin: la debacle económica y moral (1/2). *Nómada*. 23 de Agosto. Recuperado de: https://nomada.gt/identidades/guatemala-rural/viaje-al-pueblo-tras-la-mina-marlin-ladebacle-economica-y-moral-1-2/.
García, Jody. 2018. La CC preguntó a la UVG si hay xinkas para decidir sobre la Mina; esta fue la respuesta. *Nómada*. July 26. https://nomada.gt/identidades/guatemala-rural/la-cc-pregunto-a-la-uvg-si-hay-xinkas-para-decidir-sobre-la-mina-esta-fue-la-respuesta/.
García, Jody. 2019a. La Minera San Rafael tiene nuevos dueños con otra actitud sobre la consulta. *Nómada*. 10 de Enero. Recuperado de: https://nomada.gt/identidades/guatemala-rural/la-minera-san-rafael-tiene-nuevos-duenos-con-otra-actitud-sobre-la-consulta/.
García, Jody. 2019b. Un sentenciado por imprudencia, una multa de Q51 millones, la UVG exonerada, pero el crimen de los estudiantes continúa sin resolverse. *Nómada*, 25 de Junio. Recuperado de: https://nomada.gt/pais/actualidad/un-sentenciadopor-imprudencia-una-multa-de-q51-millones-la-uvg-exonerada-pero-el-crimen-de-los-estudiantes-continua-sin-resolverse.
Guégan, Marion y Schilis-Gallego, Cécile. 2019. En Guatemala, una foto comprometedora para una mina ruso-suiza. *Forbidden Stories*. Recuperado de: https://forbiddenstories.org/es/en-guatemala-una-foto-compro metedora-para-una-mina-ruso-suiza/.
Hernández, Oswaldo J., and Ochoa José Andrés. 2014. El oro tan cerca de la capital. *En Compilación de investigaciones y análisis de coyuntura sobre la conflictividad socioambiental en Guatemala*. Instituto de Agricultura, Recursos Naturales y Ambiente (IARNA). Universidad Rafael Landívar.
Instituto Nacional de Estadística. (INE). 2018. *XII Censo Nacional de población y VII de vivienda*.
Instituto Regional de Altos Estudios Políticos. (IRALEP). 2010. *Comprendiendo la conflictividad por minería en Guatemala para tender puentes de gobernabilidad*. Guatemala: IRALEP.
Juárez, Tulio. 2016. Hidro Santa Cruz desiste de su proyecto Cambalam a raíz del rechazo significativo en Santa Cruz Barillas.*ElPeriódico*. 22 de Diciembre. Recuperado de: https://elperiodico.com.gt/nacion/2016/12/22/hidros anta-cruz-desiste-de-su-proyecto-canbalam-a-raiz-del-rechazo-significativo-en-santa-cruz-barillas/.
On Common Ground Consultants Inc. 2010. "Evaluación de Derechos Humanos en la mina Marlin de Goldcorp. Informe comisionado por el

Comité de Gestión para la Evaluación de Impactos en los Derechos Humanos en la Mina Marlin." Report.
Pérez, Alejandro. 2014. La chispa que encendió la conflictividad en San Mateo Ixtatán. *Plaza Pública*, 23 de Junio. https://www.plazapublica.com.gt/content/la-chispa-que-encendio-la-conflictividad-en-san-mateo-ixtatan.
Prensa Comunitaria. 2015. "Informe de los sucesos acaecidos los días 18, 19 y 20 de Enero del año 2015en los municipios de San Mateo Ixtatán y Santa Eulalia, departamento de Huehuetenango." *Prensa Comunitaria*, February 4. https://comunitariapress.wordpress.com/2015/02/04/informe-de-los-sucesos-acaecidos-los-dias-18-19-y-20-de-enero-del-ano-2015-en-los-municipios-de-san-mateo-ixtatan-y-santa-eulalia-departamento-de-huehuetenango/.
Quiñonez Monzón, Alejandro. 2018. *#Autonomía Comunitaria y Sujeto Político en torno a la noción de Gobierno Ancestral Plurinacional en el Norte de Huehuetenango*. BA Thesisi in Anthropology. Escuela de Historia. Universidad de San Carlos de Guatemala.
Rivera, Nelton. 2016. Pojom, la historia de una agresión: la llegada de la empresa, engañando y falseando. *Prensa Comunitaria*. http://www.prensacomunitaria.org/pojom-la-historia-de-una-agresion-la-llegada-de-la-empresa-enganando-y-falseando/.
Rivera, Nelton. 2018. Una hidroeléctrica irrespeta el derecho de consulta del pueblo Q'anjob'al. *Prensa Comunitaria*. https://www.prensacomunitaria.org/una-hidroelectrica-irrespeta-el-derecho-de-consulta-del-pueblo-qanjobal/.
Rivera, Nelton. 2020. En San Mateo Ixtatán hablan de un acuerdo entre el Estado y una empresa, y se olvidan de la población. *Prensa Comunitaria*, 25 de Enero. Recuperado de: https://www.prensacomunitaria.org/en-san-mateoixtatan-hablan-de-un-acuerdo-entre-el-estado-y-una-empresa-y-se-olvidan-de-la-poblacion/.
Sánchez Monge, Geiselle Vanessa. 2017. *Las dimensiones económicas de la actividad minera (El Caso de Mina Marlin)*. Instituto de Análisis e Investigación de los Problemas Nacionales (IPNUSAC). Universidad de San Carlos de Guatemala y Diakonia.
Sáenz, Ricardo. 2005. *Elecciones, participación política y pueblo maya en Guatemala*. Guatemala: INGEP, Universidad Rafael Landívar.
Sáenz, Ricardo. 2015. "Modernización y conflictos (1944–2000)." In *Los caminos de nuestra historia: estructuras, procesos y actors*, Vol. II, edited by B. Arroyo. Guatemala: Editorial Cara Parens, Universidad Rafael Landívar.
Simón, Francisco. 2016. Pojom, la historia de una agresión: la llegada de la empresa, engañando y falseando. *Prensa Comunitaria*. 27 de Diciembre. Recuperado de: https://www.prensacomunitaria.org/pojom-la-historia-de-una-agresion-la-llegada-de-la-empresa-enganando-yfalseando/.

Solano, Julio. 2015. Una red cuasi militar para proteger la mina Escobal. *Plaza Pública*. 07 de Abril. Recuperado de: https://www.plazapublica.com.gt/content/una-red-cuasi-militar-para-proteger-la-mina-escobal.
Temper, Leah, Daniela Del Bene, and Joan Martinez-Alier. 2015. "Mapping the frontiers and front lines of global environmental justice: The EJAtlas." *Journal of Political Ecology* 22: 255–278. https://jpe.library.arizona.edu/volume_22/Temper.pdf.
Tzul, Gladys. 2016. *Sistemas de Gobierno Comunal Indígena*. Mujeres y tramas de parentesco en Chuimeq'ena'. Sociedad Comunitaria de Estudios Estrat.gicos y Centro de Investigaciones y Pluralismo Jurídico Tz'ikin. Editorial Maya Wuj. Guatemala.
Valladares, Rafael, and Carmen López. 2015. *Inorme final Mujeres, minería y migrantes de San José del Golfo, Guatemala. 2012–2014*. Guatemala: Dirección General de Investigación, USAC.
Vásquez, Diego. 2019. "Los cinca: ciclos históricos e invisibilización censal." *Plaza Pública*, September 26. https://www.plazapublica.com.gt/content/los-xinka-ciclos-historicos-e-invisibilizacion-censal.
Van Gelder, Jan Willem y de Wilde. (2015). Joeri Company profile of Ecoener and Hidralia Energía. *Amigos de la Tierra*. Profundo Research and Advice. Amsterdam, Países Bajos.
Véliz, Rodrigo. 2014. Mujeres a la delantera (por fe y estrategia). *Nómada*. 18 de Agosto. Recuperado de: https://nomada.gt/pais/mujeres-a-la-delantera-por-fe-y-estrategia/.
Véliz, Rodrigo. 2015. *El Extractivismo en Guatemala. En El Extractivismo en América Central*. Un balance del desarrollo de las industrias extractivas y sus principales impactos en los pa.ses centroamericanos. Fundación Friederich Ebert, Centroamérica.
Villatoro García, Daniel. 2016. La Puya: una comunidad en resistencia, una empresa insistente. *Plaza Pública*, 01 de Julio. Recuperado de: https://www.plazapublica.com.gt/content/la-puya-una-comunidad-en-resistencia-una-empresa-insistente.
Yagenova, Simona. 2012. *La industria extractiva en Guatemala: Políticas públicas, derechos humanos y procesos de resistencia popular en el período 2003–2011*. Facultad Latinoamericana de Ciencias Sociales. FLACSO. Guatemala.

CHAPTER 8

Fueling Conflicts by Sharing Benefits? Qualitative Evidence from a Mining Conflict in Burkina Faso

Selina Bezzola

8.1 INTRODUCTION

Over the last two decades, a large number of mining companies operating in developing countries have started to engage in "Corporate Social Responsibility" (CSR) activities (Dashwood 2012). CSR refers to a set of voluntary actions taken by mining companies to mitigate negative externalities of their operations and improve the social, economic and environmental impact on the areas in which they operate (Campbell 2012; Frederiksen 2018). This can involve investments in public services and infrastructure in extraction areas, contributions to local agricultural and other economic activities, as well as payments to support social, cultural or political activities of communities in mining areas (Bauer et al. 2016; Steinberg 2019). Funds that companies allocate to such CSR or "benefit-sharing" activities can be substantial. For example, in Peru, the amount of money mining companies invested in CSR activities between 2008

S. Bezzola (✉)
Center for Development and Cooperation, ETH Zürich, Zürich, Switzerland

© The Author(s), under exclusive license to Springer Nature Switzerland AG 2022
H. E. Ali and L.-E. Cederman (eds.), *Natural Resources, Inequality and Conflict*, https://doi.org/10.1007/978-3-030-73558-6_8

and 2011 corresponded to one-third of the international development aid flowing into the country during the same period (Amengual 2018). In Africa, quantitative data on CSR in the mining industry are scarce. A recent study finds that mines across 17 African countries spend on average approximately half a million US$ on CSR activities per mine and year, which corresponds to about 1% of the export value of these mines (Bezzola et al. 2020).

Arguably, by improving the social and economic well-being of mining-affected communities, CSR measures can compensate for negative externalities, redress grievances related to an unequal distribution of costs and benefits of resource extraction and thereby reduce the risk of local conflict (Bauer et al. 2016; Davis and Franks 2014). Yet, the increasing number of reported company-community conflicts over the past two decades raises doubts about whether those increased efforts to improve the performance of mining operations are able to curb tensions. Some observers have pointed to the existence of a "paradox," according to which the proliferation of these new policies was ineffective, and potentially even contributed to the emergence of more tensions in some cases (Brereton 2014; Hodge 2014).

This chapter aims to shed light on this apparent paradox by discussing whether and how CSR measures can produce additional conflict-inducing "externalities," such as elite capture of CSR rents and community-based grievances over deprived benefits. The focus of this chapter lies on step four of the theoretical framework introduced in Chapter 2 in this volume and analyzes a particular case of how "the extractors reaction" can fail to appease the situation.

Empirically, this study builds on a qualitative case study analysis of a mining conflict in Perkoa village located in center-western Burkina Faso. While the CSR program of the multinational mining company was initially well perceived, it eventually turned into a focus of tensions between the mining company and the local population. Methodologically, I apply a process-tracing method to inductively assess the sequence of events leading from CSR to conflict (George and Bennett 2004). I analyze primary and secondary data collected during repeated field visits between 2017 and 2019.

The resulting causal mechanism links to existing theoretical work and combines insights from the "private politics" literature with grievance-based accounts of social mobilization and conflict. The private politics literature emphasizes the role of multinational companies in engaging in direct contestation and negotiations with affected populations, especially when state authorities are weak or absent (Amengual 2018; Bebbington et al. 2008). A key argument is that mining companies have an interest in directing CSR funds mainly to those members of the local community that are either able to threaten their operations or to silence opposition (Amengual 2018; Frederiksen 2019). Yet, these studies tend to overlook the potential of such targeted approaches of benefit-sharing to produce grievances. By drawing on grievance-based accounts of social conflict (Cederman et al. 2013; Stewart 2008; Tilly 1978), I extend this argument by emphasizing how group-level grievances and deprivation can lead to mobilization and conflict.

The results of the case study analysis suggest that the CSR funds were directed to and then captured by the corrupt local elite, thereby excluding large parts of the local population from benefiting from the mine's benefit-sharing system. Awareness about deprivation of benefits contributed to the emergence of grievances among the excluded groups. I identify the recent political transition in Burkina Faso as an important enabling factor for those grievances to manifest themselves as open confrontations between the excluded community and the mining company. Analyzing the course of action of the mining company, the case study moreover identifies factors explaining why the mining company failed to accommodate grievances among the excluded group, including financial and knowledge constraints. After the occurrence of costly protests and the temporary halt of mining operations, the mining company adopted a new benefit-sharing system. The new system builds on more democratic and participatory processes, arguably contributing to more peaceful company-community relations.

Although based on evidence from one conflict only, the argument presented here can produce practical learning beyond this particular case. This chapter concludes with a discussion of the viability of different strategies to share benefits with local communities.

8.2 Theory: Benefit-Sharing in Mining Areas

8.2.1 *The Motivation to Share Benefits with Local Communities*

Compared to other industrial sectors, the extractive sector causes the most significant and often irreversible damage to the natural environment (Jenkins and Yakovleva 2006; Kapelus 2002). While the benefits of resource extraction mainly accrue to the extractive companies and the state, the population living in the areas where extraction takes place is confronted with a set of negative effects such as health and safety issues, expropriation of land assets and violations of human rights (Manzano and Gutiérrez 2019). In the extremes, such local environmental and social effects of mining manifest themselves in conflicts involving local communities, mining companies and government authorities (Andrews et al. 2017; Bebbington et al. 2008).

States and mining companies have a strong interest to prevent conflict around mining sites to occur. Conflicts can lead to interruptions or even closures of mining sites with costly consequences for governments in terms of loss of taxes and royalties, and for mining companies to loss of profits and threats to their large capital investments and their need to access resources (Steinberg 2019). The cost of a conflict with the local community is estimated to be at roughly US$ 20 million per week of delayed production for a large-scale mining operation (Davis and Franks 2014). Furthermore, news about conflicts and mine closures can deter future potential investors (Haslam 2018), or spur conflicts elsewhere in the country (Berman et al. 2017). In general, the two stylized options governments and companies have to respond to such threats of mobilization are to either use violence and repression to quiet opposition (Steinberg 2018), or win the consent of those affected by mining operations by proactively addressing their grievances and generating more positive outcomes in resource extraction areas (O'Faircheallaigh 2015). This chapter focuses on this second option.

In political science literature, the dominant approach is to focus on the role of the state in converting rents from resource extraction into benefits for local communities (Arellano-Yanguas 2011; Ross 2007). Yet, in many resource-rich countries, efforts to attract foreign investments have led to the adoption of liberal mining laws in the 1980s and 1990s that have, as a consequence, reduced government regulation, taxation of private profits and the capacity of states to redistribute rents and prevent conflict in mining areas (Campbell 2012; Dashwood 2012). In contexts of weak state institutions in remote mining localities, state authorities have thereby little capacities to implement collectively binding rules and to provide certain common goods (Hönke 2010). If companies depend on the provision of certain collective goods to be able to operate, they have major incentives to step in and fill the governance gap by providing these goods and services themselves (Börzel, Hönke, and Thauer 2012). In this context, direct contestation and negotiations, so-called private politics, between mining companies and communities have come to play an essential role in explaining local outcomes (Bebbington et al. 2008; Amengual 2018).

The increasing importance of mining companies' behavior in research on mining-related conflicts is also mirrored in the CSR literature. While largely absent until the late 1990s, the terms "responsibility" and "sustainability" have increasingly come to the agenda in the extractive sector (Frederiksen 2019; Jenkins and Yakovleva 2006). Preventing and managing tensions with surrounding communities is thereby an important, yet not the only factor explaining why mining companies increasingly engage in benefit-sharing activities. Dashwood (2012) identifies the emergence of a global normative consensus around sustainable development in general, together with the spread of transnational and home country regulation as an important driver of CSR adoption (see also Campbell 2012). Moreover, international financial institutions increasingly require companies to adhere to standards of social conduct, involving community consultation, compensation and sustainability reporting (GRI 2013; IFC 2012). Others suggest that companies voluntarily comply with social business practices as they are increasingly concerned with potential reputational damages resulting from public exposure of misconduct and shaming campaigns by transnational nongovernmental organizations (Börzel et al. 2012). Finally, CSR can be driven by a legislative threat by host states to enact more stringent legislation for company behavior. Such a "shadow of hierarchy" can act as an incentive for companies to voluntarily commit to reaching better outcomes in order to avoid state regulation (Börzel et al. 2012).

8.2.2 *The Consequences of Local Benefit Sharing Activities*

While a number of studies have focused on the drivers of CSR adoption, less scholarly attention has been devoted to studying the consequences of CSR on local communities and local conflict in particular. Proponents of CSR argue that such benefit-sharing activities can play an important role in preventing or mitigating conflict. They can compensate communities for negative externalities associated with resource extraction that are not, or badly, addressed by mandatory compensation schemes. In addition, they can promote economic development and reduce tensions related to the distributional effect of resource extraction by sharing benefits from resource extraction more evenly among communities and regions (Bauer et al. 2016; O'Faircheallaigh 2015). In contrast, scholars in business ethics and critical social sciences typically criticize benefit-sharing for being insufficient, a mere PR stunt, empty of content and used as a form of "green-washing" to divert attention from or cover up misdeeds (Calvano 2008; Gardner 2015; Slack 2012). Lower-impact benefit-sharing activities of mining companies can thereby be misused to divert attention from more significant needs and undercut the ability of communities to make additional demands (Genasci and Pray 2008).

A somewhat different take on the consequences of CSR is discussed in the private politics literature. These studies suggest that in order to mitigate operational risks and prevent local conflict, mining companies tend to deliberately use their benefit-sharing activities in a targeted way to "socially engineer" the political terrain in their favor (Brock and Dunlap 2018; Frederiksen 2019). Profit-seeking private companies attempt to adopt these strategies at minimal cost. They therefore bargain with communities to determine which types of concessions are most likely and at minimal costs to "buy-off" or "silence" potential opponents of the company's operation, therefore contributing little to overall development. In doing so, benefit-sharing activities are likely to end up privileging those actors with significant holding power, mostly elites, or actors, which are most likely to inflict costs and harm to their operations (Amengual 2018; Calvano 2008). Literature has thereby documented how mining companies have used CSR to generate support from local elites, by, for instance, supporting local traditional leaders' ceremonies, using local leaders to recruit labor and using companies owned by local political leaders as contractors (Frederiksen 2019). Similarly, in a similar case study on a mining community in Guatemala, Costanza (2016) argues that the mining company provided luxurious private gifts to opponents to the mining project to render them powerless and prevent conflict. Amengual (2018) further explains that the use of such targeted benefit-sharing strategies depends on the local context. In a comparative case study on four mining communities in Bolivia, he finds that when local communities are fragmented in terms of economic interests and social identities, companies are more likely to be confronted with requests for targeted and private spending. In cohesive societies, companies are in turn more likely to provide public goods for all.

These studies have in common that they understand targeted benefit-sharing activities as a cost-effective and viable strategy to silence tensions and prevent conflict, especially in fragmented local communities. Yet, these studies largely ignore the limitations of these strategies and their potential to trigger, rather than reducing, local grievances and conflict. In this study, I build on literature on grievances and conflict (Cederman et al. 2013; Gurr 1993; Stewart 2008) and argue that such targeted approaches to sharing benefits with local communities can lead to grievances and feelings of deprivation among those members of the local population that do not benefit from CSR. Arguably, even small shifts in local power structures could empower formerly excluded and discriminated groups and transform the previously established targeted benefit-sharing system into major cause for community mobilization and conflict.

8.3 Context: Mining and Political Transition in Burkina Faso

Burkina Faso is one of the poorest countries in the world. According to the Human Development Index, Burkina Faso ranks 183rd out of 189 countries. 71% of the population live in rural areas and 44% of the population are considered to live in extreme poverty (HDI 2018). The country's mining sector was long dominated by artisanal and small-scale gold mining, but the contribution of the sector to the national revenue was not substantial.

Starting with the first large-scale industrial mine in 2007, Burkina Faso has undergone a significant change toward an export-led economy (Zabsonré et al. 2018). The country is one of the fastest growing industrial mining sectors in sub-Saharan Africa and currently ranks as the fifth largest gold exporter on the continent (after South Africa, Ghana, Tanzania and Mali) (U.S. Geological Survey 2017). By the end of 2017, eleven industrial mines were active and nine under construction. In 2017, 71% of the total export earnings and 16% of the government's state budget came from natural resource extraction, which contributed to 8.5% of Burkina Faso's gross domestic product (GDP) (EITI Burkina Faso 2019).

The Burkinabé mining sector was considered attractive for multinational corporations because of a comparably low taxation by international standards: in the 2003 mining law, corporate tax for the mining industry was set at 20% (Engels 2018; KPMG 2017; Laporte and Quatrebarbes 2015). The central government is the main beneficiary of taxes and royalties from mining as all revenues are entirely collected by the central administration. Since 2010, the government transfers 20% of the mining land taxes levied on mining companies to municipalities and regions that host a mining activity (Zabsonré et al. 2018). In relation to total government income from mining, the sum transferred to municipalities and regions corresponds to less than one percent (EITI Burkina Faso 2019). The 2003 mining law set little binding obligations in terms of company-community engagement, consultation, local employment and procurement and contributions to local development (Torche 2014). Several observers of the mining sector in Burkina Faso note that the state has been largely absent in local mining communities (Newspaper: Kabore 2016). It has therefore been at mining companies' own discretion to decide whether and how to engage with local actors to secure their social license to operate (Report: ORCADE 2016, 72).

In 2017, all eleven mining companies reported having conducted CSR activities, as reported by the Extractive Industries Transparency Initiative (EITI Burkina Faso 2019). The total value of these CSR activities conducted by the eleven mining companies in Burkina Faso amounted to 17 million US dollars per year, which is equivalent to 5.3% of the total government income from mining. This is a substantially higher amount of money than the one percent of the government income from mining that was redistributed back to the mining municipalities in the same year, as required by the national mining law (2.71 million USD) (EITI Burkina Faso 2019). Typical benefit-sharing activities conducted by mines in Burkina Faso involve investments in health, water and education infrastructures; direct contributions to local communities to support agricultural or other income-generating activities; donations to sport activities and cultural festivities; and contributions to the administrative functioning of municipalities (EITI Burkina Faso 2019). Some mining companies have set up own foundations through which they channel their benefit-sharing activities, such as the Nantou Foundation of the Perkoa mine that is introduced in the next section and discussed in the case study. Other mines, such as Essakane, directly contribute financially to the official local development plans of the neighboring municipalities. Financed activities include the provision of clean water, electricity, support to agriculture and construction of schools (Newspaper: Da Hien 2015; Kabore 2016).

The concept of benefit-sharing or CSR features quite prominently in the national debate on natural resource governance in Burkina Faso (Interviews 27, 29). Since 2014, a coalition of civil society organizations awards a prize every year to the best performing mining company. On the other side, civil society organizations criticize companies' social activities and argue that they are scarcely more than PR campaigns or at best attempts to pacify the local population (Engels 2018). Mining companies also seek to use their CSR activities to push against what they see as expanded government regulation. A recent revision of the mining law that aims at increasing the role of the state in creating benefits for local mining communities received strong opposition from mining companies operating in Burkina Faso. Concretely, a new directive signed in 2017 stipulates the establishment of a new fund for local development, to which in addition to 20% of mining land taxes, mining companies are obliged to contribute one percent of their monthly turnover. This fund is seen as an institutionalization of benefit-sharing efforts by mining companies. Many companies have argued that they would be forced to reduce their own social activities if this law came into force. In addition, mining companies voiced concerns over the capacity of the municipal governments to effectively manage the money. They preferred to engage directly with local communities and manage the money from the fund themselves (Newspaper: Kabore 2016; Werthmann and Ayeh 2017 own interviews).

Mining areas in Burkina Faso have repeatedly experienced tensions and conflicts in the past, involving mining companies, local communities and state authorities. Some disputes are related to the fact that many mining companies operate in areas where artisanal and small-scale mining have been present for many years, therefore causing displacement and loss of income-generating opportunities for small-scale minors (Côte and Korf 2018). Other disputes are related to the broader environmental and social impacts of the installment of industrial mines and the lack of benefits accruing to the local communities (Report: Engels 2018; ORCADE 2016). A well-documented conflict is the one around Canadian-owned Karma gold mine in the north of Burkina Faso that experienced violent demonstrations by the population due to the mine's potential infrastructure damage to an important mosque nearby (Engels 2018; Werthmann and Ayeh 2017). The conflict around the Perkoa mine, as presented in this chapter, has not been documented so far in academic literature but in news outlets (e.g., Africa Mining Intelligence 2015; Burkina24 2015).

In October 2014, Burkina Faso's long-term president Blaise Compaoré was forced to resign his presidency following mass demonstrations in the capital Ouagadougou against his attempt to change the constitution to suspend term limits (Freedom House 2018). A transitional government of representatives from opposition parties, the military and civil society was established in late 2014 and administered multiparty presidential and parliamentary elections in 2015. In September 2015, the presidential guard, loyal to Compaoré, attempted to stage a military coup, which failed due to massive popular protests and the fact that segments of the military backed the transitional government. The failed coup delayed the elections for several weeks but they were eventually held in late November 2015 and ushered in a new civilian government presided by Roch Marc Christian Kaboré that laid a foundation for the development of more democratic institutions. The government of Burkina Faso has been pursuing the decentralization of public administration since the 1990s. Following the popular uprising in 2014, all elected municipal governments were dismissed and temporarily replaced by centrally appointed special delegations until local elections were held again in May 2016 (Lierl and Holmlund 2017). In spite of improvements in terms of development of democratic institutions, Burkina Faso's security situation has worsened since the political transition. In the last three years, Islamic militants carried out regular attacks especially in the north and east of the country, but also in the capital Ouagadougou. Despite extreme poverty, terrorism, and corruption, civil society and the media remain strong forces for democracy and for the respect of civil liberties (Freedom House 2018).

8.4 Methodology

To better understand how and under what circumstances targeted CSR activities can become a driver of company-community conflicts, I conduct a heuristic case study. Compared to other types of case studies, the heuristic case study is useful to refine or adjust theoretical propositions and generate new hypotheses inductively (George and Bennett 2004). The case selected for the analysis should provide a sort of "crucial experiment" in which certain variables of interest happen to be present in a special way (Lijphart 1971). The Perkoa crisis constitutes an interesting case for generating a new theory on how CSR can lead to conflict. The company engaged in extensive CSR activities but faced community conflicts related to CSR. We hence know that a correlation exists between CSR and conflict, but are in the dark regarding how the two are linked to each other.

Process-tracing is a well-suited method to perform such a heuristic function in a single-case research design (George and Bennett 2004).

Theory-generating process-tracing starts with empirical material and uses a structured analysis of this material to detect a plausible hypothetical causal mechanism. It often also involves a deductive element, in which inspiration from existing theoretical work is sought and integrated in the causal mechanism (George and Bennett 2004).

In this chapter, I use primary data collected during three different field visits between 2017 and 2019 and secondary data collected from newspapers, administrative and company data. During field visits, I conducted 37 semi-structured interviews with mining representatives, village leaders, traditional chiefs, public authorities, key informants and experts. The unstructured interviews included questions regarding the respondents' perception of the positive and negative effects of the mining operation on the local communities, the relationship between the mine, the government and the population over the years, and the factors leading to the conflict in 2015. In addition, I analyze official company and government reports such as the mine's environmental impact assessment (EIA). Other secondary sources include press reports, documents from international organizations such as UNICEF and The World Bank, documents from national administration such as from the national Ministry of Mines and Energy, mining companies, trade unions and NGOs.

As the topic around benefit-sharing in Perkoa is still politicized, a conflict-sensitive approach was necessary to study the topic. Trust between the researcher and the interviewees was particularly important and an informal approach to conversations with key informants and local stakeholders was required. Also, as the conflict occurred several years prior to this study, interview questions had to be asked bearing in mind the risk of recall biases in respondents' answers. A major advantage was that the author was able to visit the area three consecutive times. This helped establishing trust and ask key questions several times to compare reliability and properly understanding the events that led to the conflict.

8.5 CASE STUDY: BENEFIT-SHARING AND CONFLICT IN PERKOA

8.5.1 Background

The Perkoa zinc mine is located in the department of Réo in the center-western region of Burkina Faso, 135 km from the capital Ouagadougou. The existence of the zinc deposit was already documented back in 1982 but became economically attractive only following the zinc price boom in the early 2000s (Newspaper: Aimé 2016). In 2006, the Australian-based company Blackthorn Resources carried out a feasibility study to exploit the deposit and requested an exploitation license granted by the government in early 2007 to their locally registered subsidiary "Nantou Mining SA." Construction works on the mine started soon after but were interrupted in 2008 until early 2011 due to the international financial crisis and the decline in global zinc prices. With investments and new leadership by the Swiss group Glencore International, in a joint venture with Blackthorn Resources and Burkina Faso's government, the "Perkoa mine"—named colloquially after the village nearby—was finally constructed in 2012 and exported its first batches of concentrates in early 2013 (S&P market intelligence data). In April 2014, Glencore bought Blackthorn Resources' remaining interest but sold all its share two years later, in 2016, to the Canadian company Trevali Mining Corporation, of which it owns a 25% direct interest and two seats on the company's board of directors (Drechsel et al. 2018). Trevali is a zinc-focused, base metals company that owns three other mines in Namibia, Peru and Canada. It owns 90% of the shares of Perkoa mine, while the government of Burkina Faso owns the remaining 10% (Fig. 8.1).

The environmental impact assessment—a document commissioned by the company as an obligation to obtain the exploitation license from the government in 2006—identifies Perkoa as the village most affected by the mining operation due to its geographical vicinity. The report presents the expected risks of the mining project for the socio-economic environment of the approximately 5000 inhabitants of Perkoa as follows. It identifies adverse effects on the environment, the local economy and the employment structure as well as an increased stress on the administration and public service provision, notably health services, due to the influx of job-seeking migrants. The document explicitly mentions that these effects could lead to conflict between social groups as well as between local groups and the mine. With regard to displacements, the report notes that 396 people will lose access to land and housing due to the mining project. The mine elaborated a resettlement and compensation plan for these physically impacted households and stated that it would implement these mandatory compensation activities in the Perkoa village directly through its own technical staff.

In addition, the mine communicated early on that it would promote and contribute to local development in Perkoa village and beyond,

8 BURKINA FASO CASE STUDY   197

Center-Western Region of Burkina Faso

Sanguié-Province in the Center-Western Region

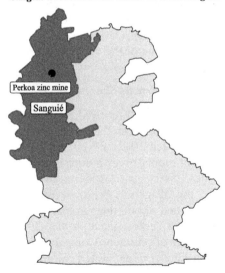

Fig. 8.1 Map of Sanguié-Province in the Center-Western Region of Burkina Faso in which the department of Réo and the Perkoa mine is located. *Source* Institut Géographique du Burkina

including in Réo town and other villages in the area. For these social benefit-sharing activities, the management of the mine established a separate body, the "Nantou Foundation" (Interviews 8, 9, 10). The official purpose of the foundation was to contribute to local welfare in the mine's local impact area (Newspaper: Le Quotidien 2015). During initial meetings between managers of the mine and the village chiefs, numerous promises were made such as the construction of a health center or the renovation of the school (Interview 14, 34). Villagers of Perkoa therefore expected to be showered with large handouts from the foundation (Newspaper: Africa Mining Intelligence 2015 Interviews, 14, 34).

Since its creation in 2006, the Nantou foundation was headed by Rosalie Bassolé, serving for many years as a provincial deputy in the national parliament. Conversations with mine representatives suggest that the mine chose to align with Bassolé at the time as she represented the province in the national parliament and signaled the capacity and willingness to translate mining benefits into local development (Interviews 8, 30). In addition, Rosalie Bassolé's husband, Djibril Bassolé, a citizen from Perkoa village, served at that time as minister of foreign affairs in the Compaoré government. Hence, channeling benefit-sharing funds through a foundation managed by the Bassolé family seemed a promising strategy in the eyes of the mine to establish a favorable local business environment. Figure 8.2 sketches the timeline of the conflict in Perkoa.

8.5.2 *From Benefit-Sharing to Grievances*

While its creation was initially well received, the foundation soon turned into a major point of friction between the population in Perkoa village and the mining company. Between 2012 and 2014, the company transferred a considerable amount of money every month to the Nantou Foundation for its various activities (Newspaper: Modeste 2015a; Batao 2016). Yet, throughout this time, the villagers in Perkoa were not aware about those transfers. They only learned about their existence during the visit of a parliamentary delegation in Perkoa village in May 2015.

Months after the ouster of president Compaoré, a parliamentary delegation of the transitional government visited Nantou mining and different actors of the municipality and the villages to inform them about the planned revision of the mining code (Newspaper: Modeste 2015a). After meeting with the managers of the mine, the delegation also met with the village chiefs of Perkoa to discuss their relations with the mine. During

8 BURKINA FASO CASE STUDY 199

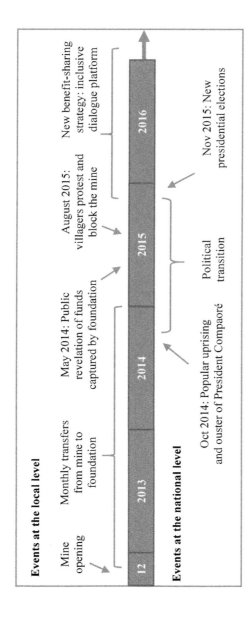

Fig. 8.2 Timeline of conflict in Perkoa. *Source* Own visualization, based on primary and secondary data analysis

this meeting, the population voiced complaints about the failure of the mine to contribute to local development in spite of the many promises made. The parliamentarians then told the population about the monthly transfers from the mine to the Nantou Foundation and that these were intended to finance development activities in their locality. This revelation took the villagers by surprise. They claimed to not have benefited from any investments from the foundation in their village. The chiefs started to suspect that the directors of the foundation must have misused and misappropriated the funds received from the benefit-sharing arrangement with the mine (Interviews 14, 15, 28, 32, 34). It was only over a year later that a report commissioned by the national parliament to investigate mismanagement in the mining sector confirmed that the foundation had indeed embezzled funds received from the mine (Report: Commission 2016). Rosalie Bassolé and her husband were convicted for receiving money from the mine "under cover of the foundation" for the realization of social projects for the benefit of the inhabitants without the knowledge of the latter (Newspaper: Batao 2016; Fitzgibbon 2017).

Back in 2015, subsequent to this revelation by the parliamentary delegation, the village chiefs of Perkoa asked for several meetings with the mine and the foundation to ask about the whereabouts of the funds dedicated to local development. While both, the mine and the directors of the foundation, confirmed the regular payments, they refused to present detailed accounts or records of funds transferred. They later explained that no official charter, mandate or written contract between the mine and the foundation existed and that the foundation did not have a registered, physical office, to which community members could go and submit requests or proposals for funding (Interviews 8, 30, 33). Hence, the villagers had no way to participate in decision-making and allocation of resources of the mine or the foundation. Instead, serving as its president, Mrs. Bassolé appointed members of her family and close friends to form a loose board of directors of the foundation (Newspaper: Bama 2015). This blurry legal status of the foundation, its corrupt and clientelist management and complete lack of community participation and consultation facilitated the emergence of serious discontent and grievances among the Perkoa villagers over unmet expectations and deprivation of benefits. They were convinced that the mine and the foundation were operating in a co-opted manner, thereby causing unequal outcomes between the direct beneficiaries—the people around the Bassolé-family—and the villagers in Perkoa excluded from this inner circle of beneficiaries.

8.5.3 Form Grievances to Conflict

Following the awareness of the corrupt management of the foundation and the deprived benefits, the village chiefs started to voice new demands for direct investments in development activities in their village. For example, they pointed to the long overdue construction of the access road to the village, the extension of the electrification of the village and the renovation of the primary school buildings and its roofs (Newspaper: Modeste 2015b Interviews 32, 34). On the other hand, they demanded the immediate suspension of payments from the mine to the foundation (Newspaper: Le Quotidien 2015). Yet, the company refused to enter into negotiation and to meet these demands. By pointing to the low zinc prices at the time, the management of the Perkoa mine publicly explained that its profits were close to zero and that given these financial constraints, it was not possible to expand its benefit-sharing activities (Interviews 8, 30; Fitzgibbon 2017). The villagers then demanded the immediate halt of payments from the mine to the foundation. The representatives of the mine communicated, however, that the mine's benefit-sharing policy stipulates that all its local development projects ought to be channeled through and managed by the foundation, and that this cannot be easily changed (Interviews 8, 30). This gave the ultimate impetus for the disruption of relations between the mine and the Perkoa village chiefs and the mobilization of hundreds of inhabitant from Perkoa village against the mine (Interviews 32, 34).

In late August 2015, a large number of villagers from Perkoa joined the village chiefs to protest against the mine. Several hundred people held a sit-in in front of the gates and blocked the road access to the entrance to the mine for several days (Newspaper: Burkina24 2015). Workers of the mine were kept inside the mine and started running out of food. The company was forced to suspend production for several days (Newspaper: Africa Mining Intelligence 2015). Following the announcement of the mine that it would have to close for good if the protests went on, government authorities ordered special security forces to disperse the roadblock (Engels 2018). The interference of the security forces incited additional fury among the protesters and many of them were arrested. In addition, about 40 people from Perkoa village, who by the time were employed by the mine, were arrested while on their way to work the day the mine opened again, causing additional protests (Interviews 16, 34).

Following these incidences, the mine communicated that it would stop supporting the foundation financially. Instead, it decided to establish a new platform for dialogue and community consultation (the CCMP: "cadre de concertation minier de la province de Sanguié") at the provincial level. The meetings of this new platform take place four times a year at the High-Commissary offices in Réo since early 2016 and are seen as the primary exchange forum through which all information and exchanges run between the mine, the local authorities and the population. The main purpose of this new platform is that representatives of the mining-affected villages, civil society leaders, representatives of the municipal governments, of the central government and of the mining company meet and discuss priorities, needs and concerns of the local communities. Also, it serves to identify possible areas where the mining company could financially contribute to the local development plans or where the communities demand direct investments from the company (Interview 36). In terms of tensions, some grievances related to lack of employment opportunities in the mine still persist but no overt threats have been voiced against the mine since then (Interviews 30, 35). The village chief and members of the community agree that the mine has since created a better and more peaceful environment and that it contributes to better development outcomes, such as through providing training, building health centers, water wells and schools (Interviews 28, 34).

8.6 Analysis: From Benefit-Sharing to Grievances and Conflict

This section links the events leading to the conflict in Perkoa to the theoretical arguments stemming from grievance-based accounts of social mobilization, as well as from the private politics literature. The discussion is structured along the four steps introduced in Chapter 2 of this volume. First, I identify the main groups involved in the bargaining over the benefits from resource extraction. Second, I show how group-based grievances emerged and how they were articulated by community leaders. Third, I discuss the factors that facilitated community mobilization, and finally, I examine explanations for why the company failed to react to grievances and prevent conflict.

First, an important hypothesis regarding the causes of violent conflict is the presence of horizontal inequalities between groups (Stewart 2008).

These inequalities can thereby run along ethnic, religious, regional, class-based lines or other group boundaries that might be socially constructed and separate groups into camps with different salient identities and common interests (Ostby et al. 2009). In the case of the Perkoa crisis, the population was divided into two major identity-based groups. One group consisted of the people involved in the management of the foundation, i.e., the Bassolé family living in Réo together with other members of the local elite. They interpreted the arrival of the mine back in 2006 as a personal achievement as it was thanks to them that the foreign investors of the mining project became interested in the subsoil resources in Perkoa (Interviews 32, 33). The second group consisted of the people around the village chiefs and the wider population of Perkoa. As Perkoa was the village most affected by the mining operation, they perceived to be the rightful beneficiaries of the contributions from the mine. In this socially fragmented context, the mining company decided to entrust the members of the local elite with the management of their benefit-sharing system. By doing so, they enabled and favored the generation of private benefits over the provision of public goods for the wider population.

Second, social mobilization theory suggests that when identity-based differences coincide with economic and political differences, they can become salient and translate into politically consequential grievances (Cederman et al. 2013). A related argument suggests that grievances can emerge from disparities between aspirations to benefit from economic progress and the perceived realities, as suggested by Ted Gurr's (1993) "relative deprivation" concept. The Perkoa case illustrates how the villagers expected to be showered with handouts after the mine opening and the establishment of the foundation. Yet, as benefits were captured by the directors of the foundation, inequalities between beneficiaries of the system and the excluded parts of the population increased. The disparity between aspirations to benefit from benefit-sharing activities and the observation that no investments were done in their village generated feelings of deprivation and shared frustrations among villagers of Perkoa and, as a consequence, politically consequential grievances.

Third, identity-based grievances are particularly likely to lead to mass mobilization when state authorities are weak, as this limits the capacity of the state to accommodate grievances either economically or politically (Basedau et al. 2014). In the case of Perkoa, the presence of the state during the second half of 2015 was very limited. Following the ouster of President Compaoré in late 2014, all elected municipal governments were dismissed and temporarily replaced by special delegates until early 2016. This has caused a governance void at the local level (Lierl and Holmlund 2017). Moreover, during the political transition, Rosalie Bassolé lost her deputy mandate and her husband his ministerial post. This tilted the power balance in favor of the village chiefs and created a window of opportunity for them to capitalize on government weakness (Interviews 28, 34; Engels 2018). These factors paved the way to openly denounce and accuse elites of wrongdoings and to mobilize a large number of villagers to march against the mine.

Finally, the private politics literature suggests that mining companies have an interest to continuously adjusting their benefit-sharing activities to new groups threatening their operation (Costanza 2016; Amengual 2018). The Perkoa case shows, however, that company-led targeted benefit-sharing systems bear serious limitations when it comes to their capacity to react to empowered groups. The first limitation is the financial capacity to expand CSR budgets. CSR activities are likely to be among the first of being downsized when mineral prices go down (Andrews et al. 2017). The mine claimed that due to the low zinc prices at that time, it was financially constrained to meet the additional demands of the villagers. Instead, it emphasized its continuous support to the foundation as this was its official benefit-sharing system (Interview 32). This strategy failed since the power balance was changing and formerly discriminated groups became empowered and able to mobilize against the mine.

The second limitation refers to the fact that the Perkoa mine, as many other industrial mines operating in developing countries, is a foreign-owned and foreign-managed mine. This can limit their capacity to acquire a thorough understanding of who the local power holders are and which actors the mine should target, especially when power structures are changing. The Perkoa case illustrates that the management of the Perkoa mine largely ignored the political dynamics that arose after the ouster of President Compaoré. It appears that the mine management was overwhelmed by the events and underestimated the importance of engaging with empowered groups. Directing the benefit-sharing activities to members of the local elite, who lost power due to their association with the former regime, turned into a non-viable option any more to ensure local peaceful relations.

In the aftermath of the Perkoa crisis, the mining company adopted a new benefit-sharing system that involves more democratic and participatory processes. This is arguably a more viable strategy to react to political dynamics. In the next section, we discuss implications of the mechanism identified here for other forms of sharing benefits from mining with local communities.

8.7 Discussion: Generalizability and Implications Beyond Perkoa

This section discusses the generalizability of the argument presented above and the implications for other benefit-sharing strategies. In a first step, I discuss whether the identified mechanism is unique to the case of Perkoa or whether I can be extended to other settings too. While the mechanism is in line with existing literature on grievance-based accounts of conflict and private politics and hence theoretically plausible, there exists little documentation of other cases where benefit-sharing activities have contributed to conflict in general, and particularly through the mechanism identified in the analysis. The question of whether the mechanism holds for other cases can therefore only be answered vaguely. Based on the case study, I can, however, identify contextual factors that make the mechanism particularly likely to hold elsewhere.

The first factor concerns the structure of the local population. While in cohesive local communities, mining companies have to bargain with groups that request public goods and shared benefits for all, companies are inclined to adopt targeted and exclusionary benefit-sharing systems, the more fragmented local societies are, as this reduces their costs (based on Amengual 2018). The existence of fragmented local populations, for instance also ethnically distinct groups, makes it therefore particularly likely that benefit-sharing is conducted in a targeted way, thereby favoring the emergence of group-based inequalities and grievances. Second, an important enabling factor for mobilization in the case study was the political transition. Political events that change the power balance and empower formerly excluded and voiceless groups to speak up therefore seem to be particularly likely for targeted benefit-sharing activities contribute to conflict. Support for this argument is provided by Thomas (2013), who documents that the political transition in Guinea in 2010 and 2011 enabled and empowered local communities to overtly voice their grievances and protest against the exclusionary and clientelist ways of company engagement with local mining communities. Yet, given the lack of appropriate counterfactual, I cannot determine the deterministic character of these two factors. In other words, I cannot claim that the Perkoa crisis would not have happened without the fragmentation in the local population and without the political transition. Given the limited number of documentations of similar cases, I conclude that more comparative and quantitative research is needed to identify the validity of these arguments for cases beyond the Perkoa case.

In a second step, I discuss the implications of this argument for other forms of benefit-sharing. Concretely, are other approaches more promising in terms of accommodating grievances and preventing conflict? In the Perkoa case, benefit-sharing activities were channeled through a local foundation. Compared to more "ad hoc" ways of sharing benefits with local communities, establishing local foundations can arguably shift responsibility for community development away from the company to the managers of the foundation, which are typically members of the local community (The World Bank 2010). By placing decision-making power in the hands of the local community, the activities of a foundation are expected to be implemented in a more democratic, participatory and community-needs focused way than ad hoc spending. This was, however, not the case in Perkoa. The blurry legal status of the Nantou foundation, its opaque management and lack of community participation and consultation produced discontent and grievances among the local population. Moreover, the establishment of private-funded governance entities can alter the role and importance of more politically embedded and legitimate governance entities provided by local authorities and public institutions (Frederiksen 2019). Private entities might become the target of different interests and provoke different expectations among the local population. Moreover, as private expenditures are typically outside the normal budget process, traditional local oversight bodies cannot properly monitor how they are spent or whether the community is benefiting as a whole. Hence, even when designed in a more participatory way, foundations are at risk of being used as a system through which rents can be distributed to local elites with significant holding power or control over access to important resources.

An alternative way to share benefits is by collaborating and aligning with existing local institutions and local authorities. Such an approach was pursued by another mine in Burkina Faso, the Canadian-owned Essakane gold mine in the north of Burkina Faso, the biggest mine in the country.

Similar to the Perkoa mine, it has established a benefit-sharing scheme early on to improve living conditions of the local population. Contrary to the Perkoa case, however, the Essakane mine has decided to financially contribute to the formal multi-year municipal development plans ("Plans communaux de développement," PCD) of the three municipalities directly affected by the mining operation. Specific investments conducted by the mining company through the municipal government were the construction of school infrastructure, market stalls and water infrastructure (Newspaper: Kabore 2016). To promote regular exchanges and information flows between local communities, the local administration and the managers of the mine, a dialogue platform (the "Comité de communication de la mine d'Essakane," CCME) was established already back in 2010 (Newspaper: Nombre 2015). This strategy to collaborate with existing local institutions, instead of setting up an own foundation, has proven successful during the political transition. The CCME meetings were canceled for some time during the height of the political crisis in late 2014, but they resumed again in March 2015 and continue since to function as a platform to negotiate over the contributions of the mine to the local development plans (Report: ORCADE 2016). Similarly, after the open confrontation in Perkoa, the mining company has also adopted a more institutionally embedded benefit-sharing system. No overt conflict has since then taken place. This can be seen as support for the claim that aligning benefit-sharing approaches with local institutions seems to be more promising approach to adjust to local power dynamics.

Finally, a major criticism of company-led benefit-sharing is that mining companies are not the actual legitimate actor to invest in local development (Hönke and Thauer 2014). The argument goes that state-led forms of benefit-sharing are more legitimate and development-oriented. Yet, research on state-led forms of redistribution of the mining rent concludes with a sobering note. Such decentralization policies imply a significant inflow of money to municipalities in mining regions, often characterized by low capacities to efficiently absorb the money and to prevent it from being misused for clientelistic politics (Arellano-Yanguas 2011; Caselli and Michaels 2013; Ross et al. 2012). With regard to Burkina Faso, the government has recently adopted a new mining law that stipulates a formalization and institutionalization of benefit-sharing efforts by mining companies. The law requires companies and the state to contribute to a state-managed fund for local development, which should finance activities elaborated in mining municipalities' local development plans. While this new law creates hopes for a more democratic and inclusive distribution of rents from resource extraction, it has also raised concerns about the capacity of municipal governments to manage these funds in a development-oriented way (Interviews 25, 27, 37). Moreover, political systems can be corrupt and political dynamics can influence who holds power and who is excluded. For instance, analyzing mining revenue distribution policies in Sierra Leone and Ghana, Dupuy (2017) finds that the redistribution of the mining rent to mining municipalities did not translate into development, as funds were diverted to the private pockets of local authorities and invested in projects that primarily benefited the elites.

In sum, institutionally more embedded benefit-sharing strategies are likely to create more peaceful outcomes than private transfer systems. However, there is no guarantee for this to hold. More evidence is needed to better understand different approaches to share benefits with mining communities, how they interact with local contexts and which policy options work best in a given context. Possibly, benefit-sharing strategies that are managed in a transparent way and that allow communities to participate in an inclusive way are promising approaches.

8.8 Conclusion

This study presents a novel causal mechanism linking benefit-sharing activities to social conflict via grievances. Empirically, the study builds on a case study of a benefit-sharing strategy adopted by a foreign-owned industrial mine in Burkina Faso. The analysis uses process-tracing methods and a mix of qualitative data collected during several rounds of fieldwork. The mechanism extends and refines existing arguments from the private politics literature and literature on grievance-based explanations of social mobilization and conflict. The results of the case study suggest that company-led benefit-sharing strategies can contribute to grievances and conflict when benefit-sharing activities are directed to and captured by corrupt local elites and not distributed to the wider population. This can then create grievances among populations deprived of these benefits and provide fertile grounds for group-mobilization. Moreover, the analysis shows that the political dynamics in Burkina Faso, as well as the financial and knowledge constraints of the mining company, enabled grievances to transform into open confrontation between the mining company and the local population.

The Perkoa case is not a unique case and the mechanism identified is likely to hold in other contexts too. In many mining communities, companies adopt targeted and exclusionary benefit-sharing systems to limit costs and manage risks. Remote mining regions in developing countries are often marked by the existence of different class- or identity-based groups, including ethnic minorities, with unequal access to power and politics. This makes it likely that benefit-sharing activities are captured by certain groups, hence depriving other groups and facilitating the emergence or accentuation of group-based inequalities and grievances. Moreover, political events can change local opportunity structures and empower formerly excluded and voiceless groups to speak up (Engels 2018). This is not unique to Burkina Faso and literature has documented how political transitions in other countries encouraged local communities to overtly voice their grievances and protest against the exclusionary outcomes of resource extraction (see Thomas 2013, on Guinea).

This study also presents arguments suggesting that more institutionalized forms of benefit-sharing strategies can produce more broader public benefits for all members of the local population, while more private CSR systems are conducive to being captured and generating private rents. However, literature also suggests that neither public, private, nor combined approaches to share benefits from mining with local communities are completely exempt from corruption and mismanagement. This is mainly due to the presence of weak state institutions and the existence of particular interests in mining regions. From a policy perspective, this exploratory analysis calls for more transparent and participatory benefit-sharing systems, and for measures to improve government capacity in the management and oversight of resource revenues.

REFERENCES

NEWSPAPER ARTICLES AND PUBLIC REPORTS

Africa Mining Intelligence. 2015. "Nantou Sinks Deeper Into Turmoil at Perkoa." https://www.africaintelligence.com/Ama/Exploration-Production/ 2015/10/06/Nantou-Sinks-Deeper-into-Turmoil-at-Perkoa,108104842-Art. Accessed October 17, 2019.

Aimé, Florentin. 2016. "Perkoa: Première mine de Zinc d'Afrique de l'Ouest avec 6,3 millions de tonnes." *Ecodufaso*. March 15, 2016. http://ecodufaso. com/Perkoa-Premiere-Mine-de-Zinc-Dafrique-de-Louest-Avec-63-Millions-de-Tonnes/. Accessed October 17, 2019.

Bama, Ladji Y. 2015. "Mine de zinc de Perkoa - Une si longue arnaque !" *Le Reporter.* https://www.reporterbf.net. Accessed February 5, 2018.

Batao, Joachim. 2016. "Enquête sur les titres miniers: François Compaoré et Rosalie Bassolé auteurs de malversations financières." *Burkina Demain.* 26 Octobre 2016. https://www.burkinademain.com/2016/10/26/Enquete-Sur-Les-Titres-Miniers-Francois-Compaore-et-Rosalie-Bassole-Auteurs-de-Malversations-Financieres/. Accessed October 17, 2019.

Burkina24. 2015. "Cri de coeur : Il faut sauver la mine de Perkoa." 3. September 2015. https://www.burkina24.com/2015/09/03/Cri-de-Coeur-Il-Faut-Sauver-La-Mine-de-Perkoa/. Accessed October 17, 2019.

Commission. 2016. *Rapport General de la Commission d'enquete parlementaire sur la gestion des titres miniers et la responsabilite sociale des entreprises minieres.* Assemblé Nationale Burkina Faso.

Da Hien, Donald. 2015. "PRIX de récompense des meilleures pratiques RSE/Entreprises minières." *Réseau Afrique Jeunesse.* http://www.afriquejeunesse.com/Spip.php?Article134. Accessed October 5, 2019.

Fitzgibbon, Will. 2017. "Development Dreams Stand Still While Mining Money Moves Offshore." *ICIJ.* November 8, 2017. https://www.icij.org/Investigations/Paradise-Papers/Development-Dreams-Stand-Still-Mining-Money-Moves-Offshore/. Accessed October 17, 2019.

Kabore, Elie. 2016. "Nouveau Code minier: Le fonds de développement local divise." *L'Economiste Du Faso.* April 11, 2016. https://www.leconomistedufaso.bf/2016/04/11/Nouveau-Code-Minier-Le-Fonds-de-Developpement-Local-Divise/. Accessed October 17, 2019.

KPMG. 2017. "Corporate Tax Rates Tables." https://Home.Kpmg.com/Xx/En/Home/Services/Tax/Tax-Tools-and-Resources/Tax-Rates-Online/Corporate-Tax-Rates-Table.html. Accessed January 9, 2018.

Le Quotidien. 2015. "Bras de fer entre les populations de Perkoa et la fondation Nantou: Les habitants de PERKOA ne veulent plus de la Fondation." September 2, 2015. http://News.aouaga.com/H/74222.html. Accessed October 17, 2019.

Modeste, Bationo. 2015a. "Explication du nouveau code minier a Perkoan: La population remontée contre le CNT." *Le Pays.* July 28, 2015. http://Lepays.bf/Explication-Du-Nouveau-Code-Minier-a-Perkoan-La-Population-Remontee-Contre-Le-Cnt/. Accessed October 17, 2019.

Modeste, Bationo. 2015b. "Tension entre populations de perkoan et nantou mining: Des manifestants arrêtés." *Le Pays.* September 7, 2015. http://Lepays.bf/Tension-Entre-Populations-de-Perkoan-et-Nantou-Mining-Des-Manifestants-Arretes/. Accessed October 17, 2019.

Nombre, Souaibou. 2015. "Burkina Faso: Comité de communication de la mine d'Essakane." *AllAfrica.* April 8, 2015. https://Fr.allafrica.com/Stories/201504091032.html. Accessed October 5, 2019, No. 4: 2015.

ORCADE. 2016. "Rapport d'enquete: Sondage sur la cohabitation entre les communautes des sites miniers et les entreprises minieres au Burkina Faso." *Organisation Pour Le Renforcement Des Capacités de Développement.*

Academic Articles and Technical Reports

Amengual, Matthew. 2018. "Buying Stability: The Distributive Outcomes of Private Politics in the Bolivian Mining Industry." *World Development* 104: 31–45.

Andrews, Tony, Bernarda Elizalde, Philippe Le Billon, Chang Hoon Oh, David Reyes, and Ian Thomson. 2017. "The Rise in Conflict Associated with Mining Operations: What Lies Beneath?" *Technical Report. Canadian International Resources and Development Institute (CIRDI).*

Arellano-Yanguas, Javier. 2011. "Aggravating the Resource Curse: Decentralisation, Mining and Conflict in Peru." *Journal of Development Studies* 47 (4): 617–638.

Basedau, Matthias, Annegret Mähler, and Miriam Shabafrouz. 2014. "Drilling Deeper: A Systematic, Context-Sensitive Investigation of Causal Mechanisms in the Oil-Conflict Link." *Journal of Development Studies* 50 (1): 51–63.

Bauer, Andrew, Uyanga Gankhuyag, Sofi Halling, David Manley, and Varsha Venugopal. 2016. "Natural Resource Revenue Sharing." *Natural Resource Governance Institute—Report.*

Bebbington, Anthony, Denise Humphreys Bebbington, Jeffrey Bury, Jeannet Lingan, Juan Pablo Munoz, and Martin Scurrah. 2008. "Mining and Social Movements: Struggles Over Livelihood and Rural Territorial Development in the Andes." *World Development* 36 (12): 2888–2905.

Berman, Nicolas, Mathieu Couttenier, Dominic Rohner, and Mathias Thoenig. 2017. "This Mine is Mine! How Minerals Fuel Conflicts in Africa." *American Economic Review* 107 (6): 1564–1610.

Bezzola, Selina, Isabel Günther, Fritz Brugger and Erwin Lefoll. 2020. "CSR and Local Conflicts in African Mining Communities" In *The consequences of Corporate Social Responsibility in African mining communities*, PhD Dissertation. Zurich: ETH Zurich.

Börzel, Tanja A., Jana Hönke, and Christian R. Thauer. 2012. "Does it Really Take the State?" *Business and Politics* 14 (3): 1–34.

Brereton, David. 2014. "Is the Seeming Paradox Resolvable? Some Reactions to Professor Hodge's Paper." *Journal of Cleaner Production* 84 (1): 37–38.

Brock, Andrea, and Alexander Dunlap. 2018. "Normalising Corporate Counterinsurgency: Engineering Consent, Managing Resistance and Greening Destruction Around the Hambach Coal Mine and Beyond." *Political Geography* 62: 33–47.

Calvano, Lisa. 2008. "Multinational Corporations and Local Communities: A Critical Analysis of Conflict." *Journal of Business Ethics* 82 (4): 793–805.

Campbell, Bonnie. 2012. "Corporate Social Responsibility and Development in Africa: Redefining the Roles and Responsibilities of Public and Private Actors in the Mining Sector." *Resources Policy* 37 (2): 138–143.

Caselli, Francesco, and Guy Michaels. 2013. "Do Oil Windfalls Improve Living Standards? Evidence from Brazil." *American Economic Journal: Applied Economics* 5 (1): 208–238.

Cederman, Lars-Erik, Kristian Skrede Gleditsch, and Halvard Buhaug. 2013. *Inequality, Grievances, and Civil War*. Cambridge: Cambridge University Press.

Costanza, Jennifer Noel. 2016. "Mining Conflict and the Politics of Obtaining a Social License: Insight from Guatemala." *World Development* 79: 97–113.

Côte, Muriel, and Benedikt Korf. 2018. "Making Concessions: Extractive Enclaves, Entangled Capitalism and Regulative Pluralism at the Gold Mining Frontier in Burkina Faso." *World Development* 101: 466–476.

Dashwood, Hevina S. 2012. *The Rise of Global Corporate Social Responsibility*. Cambridge: Cambridge University Press.

Davis, Rachel, and Daniel Franks. 2014. *Costs of Company-Community Conflict in the Extractive Sector*. Cambridge, MA: Harvard Kennedy School.

Drechsel, Franza, Bettina Engels, and Mirka Schäfer. 2018. "Les mines nous rendent pauvres: L'exploitation minière industrielle au Burkina Faso." *GLOCON Country Report*.

Dupuy, Kendra. 2017. "Corruption and Elite Capture of Mining Community Development Funds in Ghana and Sierra Leone." In *Corruption, Natural Resources and Development*, edited by Aled Williams and Philippe Le Billon. Cheltenham: Edward Elgar Publishing.

EITI Burkina Faso. 2019. "Country Report 2017." *The Extractive Industries Transparency Initiative*.

Engels, Bettina. 2018. "Nothing will be as before: Shifting political opportunity structures in protests against gold mining in Burkina Faso." *Extractive Industries and Society* 5 (2): 354–362.

Frederiksen, Tomas. 2018. "Corporate Social Responsibility, Risk and Development in the Mining Industry." *Resources Policy* 59: 495–505.

Frederiksen, Tomas. 2019. "Political Settlements, the Mining Industry and Corporate Social Responsibility in Developing Countries." *Extractive Industries and Society* 6 (1): 162–170.

Freedom House. 2018. "Freedom in the World 2018." *Burkina Faso Profile*. https://Freedomhouse.org/Report/Freedom-World/2018/Burkina-Faso. Accessed October 20, 2019.

Gardner, Katy. 2015. "Chevron's Gift of CSR: Moral Economies of Connection and Disconnection in a Transnational Bangladeshi Village." *Economy and Society* 44 (4): 495–518.

Genasci, Matthew, and Sarah Pray. 2008. "Extracting Accountability: The Implications of the Resource Curse for CSR Theory and Practice." *Yale Human Rights and Development Journal* 11 (1).

George, Alexander L., and Andrew Bennett. 2004. *Case Studies and Theory Development in the Social Sciences*. Cambridge, MA: MIT Press.

GRI, Global Reporting Initiative. 2013. *G4 Sector Disclosures: Mining and Metals*.

Gurr, Ted Robert. 1993. "Why Minorities Rebel: A Global Analysis of Communal Mobilization and Conflict Since 1945." *International Political Science Review* 14 (2): 161–201.

Haslam, Paul Alexander. 2018. "Beyond Voluntary: State-Firm Bargaining Over Corporate Social Responsibilities in Mining." *Review of International Political Economy* 25 (3): 418–440.

HDI. 2018. *Human Development Indicators Burkina Faso*.

Hodge, R. Anthony. 2014. "Mining Company Performance and Community Conflict: Moving Beyond a Seeming Paradox." *Journal of Cleaner Production* 84 (1): 27–33.

Hönke, Jana, and Christian R. Thauer. 2014. "Multinational Corporations and Service Provision in Sub-Saharan Africa: Legitimacy and Institutionalization Matter." *Governance: An International Journal of Policy, Administration, and Institutions* 27 (4): 697–716.

Hönke, Jana. 2010. "New Political Topographies. Mining Companies and Indirect Discharge in Southern Katanga (DRC)." *Politique Africaine* 120 (4): 105–127.

IFC. 2012. "Performance Standards on Environmental and Social Sustainability." *IFC's Sustainability Framework*, 72.

Jenkins, Heledd, and Natalia Yakovleva. 2006. "Corporate Social Responsibility in the Mining Industry: Exploring Trends in Social and Environmental Disclosure." *Journal of Cleaner Production* 14 (3–4): 271–284.

Kapelus, Paul. 2002. "Mining, Corporate Social Responsibility and the Community: The Case of Rio Tinto, Richards Bay Minerals and the Mbonambi." *Journal of Business Ethics* 39 (3): 275–296.

Laporte, Bertrand, and Céline de Quatrebarbes. 2015. "What Do We Know About the Sharing of Mineral Resource Rent in Africa?" *Resources Policy* 46: 239–249.

Lierl, Malte M., and Marcus Holmlund. 2017. "Performance Information and Voting Behavior in Burkina Faso's Municipal Elections: Separating the Effects of Information Content and Information Delivery." *Innovations for Poverty Action Working Paper* 35.

Lijphart, Arend. 1971. "Comparative Politics and the Comparative Method." *The American Political Science Review* 65 (3):682–693.
Manzano, Osmel, and Juan David Gutiérrez. 2019. "The Subnational Resource Curse: Theory and Evidence." *The Extractive Industries and Society* 6 (2).
O'Faircheallaigh, Ciaran. 2015. "Social Equity and Large Mining Projects: Voluntary Industry Initiatives, Public Regulation and Community Development Agreements." *Journal of Business Ethics* 132 (1): 91–103.
Ostby, Gudrun, Ragnhild Nordas, and Jan Ketil Rod. 2009. "Regional Inequalities and Civil Conflict in Sub-Saharan Africa." *International Studies Quarterly* 53 (2): 301–24.
Ross, Michael L. 2007. "How Mineral-Rich States Can Reduce Inequality." In *Escaping the Resource Curse*, edited by Macartan Humphreys, Jeffrey D. Sachs and Joseph E. Stiglitz, 237–255. New York City: Columbia University Press.
Ross, Michael L., Päivi Lujala, and Siri Aas Rustad. 2012. "Horizontal Inequality, Decentralizing the Distribution of Natural Resource Revenues, and Peace." In *High-Value Natural Resources and Post-Conflict Peacebuilding*, edited by P. Lujala Rustad and S. A., 1: 251–259.
Slack, Keith. 2012. "Mission Impossible?: Adopting a CSR-Based Business Model for Extractive Industries in Developing Countries." *Resources Policy* 37 (2): 179–184.
Steinberg, Jessica. 2018. "Protecting the Capital? On African Geographies of Protest Escalation and Repression." *Political Geography* 62: 12–22.
Steinberg, Jessica. 2019. "Mines, Communities, and States: The Local Politics of Natural Resource Extraction in Africa." *Cambridge University Press* 5 (28 [3]): 13–15.
Stewart, Frances. 2008. *Horizontal Inequalities and Conflict: Understanding Group Violence in Multiethnic Societies*. Basingstoke: Palgrave Macmillan.
The World Bank. 2010. *Mining Foundations, Trusts and Funds: A Sourcebook*. Washington, DC: The World Bank.
Thomas, Esther. 2013. "When Multinational Gold Mining Companies and Neighboring Communities Meet: Why (Not) Engage?" *SFB-Governance Working Paper Series*, No. 59.
Tilly, Charles. 1978. *From Mobilization to Revolution*. New York: McGraw-Hill.
Torche, Laurent. 2014. "Le Burkina Faso face à la «malédiction des ressources naturelles»: Perceptions et analyse sous l'angle de la transparence et de la législation du secteur minier jusqu'au 25 octobre 2014." *Mémoire Professionnel. IHEID Geneve*.
U.S. Geological Survey. 2017. "2014 Minerals Yearbook." *Africa*.

Werthmann, Katja, and Diana Ayeh. 2017. "Processes of Enclaving Under the Global Condition: The Case of Burkina Faso." *Working Paper Series Des SFB 1199 an Der Universität Leipzig* 14.

Zabsonré, Agnès, Maxime Agbo, and Juste Somé. 2018. "Gold Exploitation and Socioeconomic Outcomes: The Case of Burkina Faso." *World Development* 109: 206–221.

PART IV

Conclusions

CHAPTER 9

Conclusions for Theory and Policy

Hamid E. Ali, Lars-Erik Cederman, and Yaron A. Weissberg

The overall goal of the book has been to analyze the link between resources and conflict, focusing in particular on how non-fuel resources may trigger both violent and peaceful protest. Inspired by a study of oil and conflict presented in Chapter 3, we have applied both quantitative and qualitative methods to analyze the resource-conflict nexus specifically for non-fuel minerals. While most of the existing quantitative literature has failed to find any conflict-inducing effect exerted by inequality and grievances, qualitative studies have documented such influences. By combining both quantitative and qualitative approaches, this book offers a more comprehensive perspective on this issue.

We started this volume with distinguishing between fuel and non-fuel resources. Motivated by the mining boom at the beginning of this

---

H. E. Ali
School of Public Administration and Development Economics, Doha Institute for Graduates Studies, Doha, Qatar
e-mail: hamid.ali@dohainstitute.edu.qa

L.-E. Cederman (✉) · Y. A. Weissberg
International Conflict Research, ETH Zürich, Zürich, Switzerland
e-mail: lcederman@ethz.ch

© The Author(s), under exclusive license to Springer Nature Switzerland AG 2022
H. E. Ali and L.-E. Cederman (eds.), *Natural Resources, Inequality and Conflict*, https://doi.org/10.1007/978-3-030-73558-6_9

century, the so-called commodity super-cycle (Berman et al. 2017), new publications have increasingly focused on non-fuel resources in order to understand their impact on conflict risk. Together with the strategies to decarbonize the world economy, this trend is expected to continue. We began our discussion with some expectations related to non-fuel mining and the political fallout it can create. Looking at grievances, we expected them to be less pronounced compared to oil and gas primarily because they generate lower revenues and do not involve the state to a similar degree. This was expected to lead to lower distributional and political grievances but as much, if not more, dangers arising through migration-based and environmental grievances.

Overall, we expected resource conflicts to be less intense for non-fuel minerals—as shown in previous analyses (Christensen 2019)—and with different grievances at play. This final chapter summarizes the main findings produced by this book and examines to what extent our expectations have been found to be correct. Furthermore, we discuss avenues of future research and end by reflecting on the general policy implications that can be drawn from the results.

9.1 Summary of the Main Results

What have we learned? Overall, we have found ample evidence that inequality can be linked to conflict and protest, whether violent or not. Specifically, our results show that extraction of non-fuel minerals contributes to conflict and protest through this link by reinforcing preexisting inequalities and causing new grievances. This represents a corrective to general claims that only "greed" or "opportunities" drive conflict rather than grievances associated with resource extraction.

Focusing on sub-Saharan Africa, Chapter 4 confirms that mining in Africa has triggered violent conflict between affected groups and the state in question. While the large-N analysis of that chapter cannot enter into details as regards the underlying causal mechanisms, it shows that political exclusion of ethnic groups makes mining conflict much more likely than for groups that are represented in the central government.

The qualitative chapters complement this initial analysis by offering a more detailed picture of the role played by grievances in conflict processes involving resource extraction. Our four-step framework that we introduced in Chapter 2 has helped us to manage the complexity of the individual cases.

9 CONCLUSION 221

Under the first step, concerning the identification of extracting actors and affected communities, the case study chapters suggest that the state is less involved in non-fuel extractive projects than in the case of oil extraction (cf. Chapter 3). Indeed, since the 1990s, there has been a major trend toward privatization and deregulation of the extractive industry more generally. Chapter 5 shows that Zambia is no exception from this trend. The shift of ownership from the state to private hands may in fact have increased tensions, especially since the chiefs have stood to gain more from privatized, large-scale copper mining than the workforce as a whole. Likewise, Chapter 8 shows that conflict reduction in the hands of private mining firms may do more harm than good. This finding challenges the claim that private schemes in the name of "Corporate Social Responsibility" can effectively substitute for state-led efforts to reduce inequality and protect the rights of the affected communities.

The second analytical step disentangles the grievances held by affected communities. Based on interview-based research, Chapter 5 offers a detailed picture of specific types of grievances held by members of ethnic groups in the copper mining areas of Zambia. In fact, this analysis finds clear evidence that extraction of non-fuel minerals can trigger distributional, migration-related, political, and environmental grievances, as anticipated by Chapter 2. Although the value involved in the case of copper mining is inferior to that of oil extraction, the former has generated distributional tensions in the Zambian case. Furthermore, Chapter 5 finds that locals repeatedly expressed migration-related grievances that follow ethnic lines. Local chiefs have even tended to reinforce these resentments in order to defect the attention from their own efforts to enrich themselves from the extractive projects. There is also a general perception of political inequality in favor of outsiders, with allegedly better support and representation in the country as a whole. Finally, as would be expected in the case of large-scale, open-pit mining operations, the environmental damage has been substantial, which has further fueled frustrations.

In many respects, the overall pattern of grievances does not differ dramatically from the grievances that were expressed in some of the cases driving the results of Chapter 3. In Aceh, for example, gas extraction triggered all four types of grievances, primarily because exploitation of Aceh's gas riches required a massive intervention by the state. It is plausible, however, that extraction of non-fuel minerals requires the state to play less of a prominent role, which means that distributional grievances may be more local than in the case of petroleum.

As opposed to copper mining in Zambia, the indigenous communities in India and Guatemala have exhibited an even more narrow set of grievances, focusing mostly on environmental ones (see Chapters 6 and 7). In these cases, the main source of resentment has been the disruption of the traditional lifestyle of peripheral populations rather than a feeling of being shortchanged in purely distributional terms. Thus, the main source of frustration concerns environmental damages and the threat to livelihoods that depend directly on free access to remote lands. As shown by Chapter 6, such grievances may also derive from perceived threats to symbolic values associated with natural landmarks, such as sacred mountains and other landscape features.

Turning to the third analytical step, it generally seems to be the case that grievance-driven mobilization processes are indeed more local rather than regional, although Chapter 7 suggests that there is a degree of national coordination and support among protest movements in Guatemala. The overall picture is one of grievances fueling outrage with aggressive exploitative tactics, both on the part of governments and extractive firms. In the Guatemalan case, the overwhelmingly peaceful resistance has drawn extensively on traditional community resources and informal institutions and practices. In India, the response has been less peaceful, mostly because the ideologically motivated Naxalites have been successful in mobilizing resistance based on widely held grievances in the local population. It should be noted that, in contrast to most of the oil-related conflicts discussed in Chapter 3, the case studies, as well as the cases underpinning the quantitative analysis in Chapter 4, hardly feature outright secessionist claims.

With governments less directly threatened, this may also explain why the governmental reaction has generally been less dramatic and violent than in case of oil extraction. In terms of the fourth step of our theoretical framework, however, we have found that the lower value generated by extraction of non-fuel minerals compared to hydrocarbons has not, as a rule, led to a more accommodating attitude on the part of the extractive parties. Confronted with resistance from indigenous communities, the Indian and Guatemalan states have often relied on coercive methods rather than compromise and dialogue. As illustrated by Chapter 7 on

Guatemala, it is overly optimistic to expect foreign firms to come under pressure from Western governments to adopt more cooperative stances, even when they are based in countries with a liberal tradition and arguably more respect for human rights than in the country of extraction.[1] Indeed, the case studies provide plenty of evidence of coercive and even violent suppression of local protest, including the assassination of the leaders of the resistance movement and even the deployment of troops. It is remarkable that such violent tactics have not triggered widespread armed resistance in the case of Guatemala.

Obviously, governmental reaction to protest is not always violent and oppressive. The Indian case illustrates that the state has attempted to reduce grievances through reforms granting local communities new rights, but more recently, the implementation of these rights has been increasingly diluted, as documented by Chapter 6. This case highlights the crucial role played by the state and its institutional strength in mediating the conflict-inducing effects of extraction: On the one hand, provisions to reduce grievances among the affected communities can help to mitigate violence. On the other, however, this only works if the institutions are strong enough to uphold these provisions against corporate interests. Without the guarantee of having one's rights protected, strong community organization has become an important substitute in order to redress grievances and upholding codified legal provisions. Even though the Indian case demonstrates how these rights can be upheld in the end, these mechanisms harbor dangers on their own since other less benign groups can build on similar grievances for more violent ends. For the Guatemala case (Chapter 7) we see a similar story.

Given these problems, it is fortunate that the mining companies themselves have been increasingly willing to engage in grievance-reducing activities. Whether for strict cost reasons or a genuine desire to improve the living conditions of the affected communities, these efforts have the potential of easing tensions and reducing the risk of violent conflict. Unfortunately, however, there is no guarantee that such favorable outcomes will follow. Looking at an example of benefit sharing in Burkina Faso, Chapter 8 shows that such efforts may even perversely fuel grievances and conflict if such schemes benefit particular elite groups, creating new inequalities and grievances. Thus, the distributional implications of benefit sharing need to be considered very carefully.

9.2 Future Research

What lessons for future research can be drawn from this book? While the findings should encourage students of resource conflicts to take inequalities and grievances seriously, they by no means imply that factors related to "greed" and "opportunities" are unimportant. In fact, self-interest happily coexists and interacts with grievance-based motivations. Likewise, there is no reason to separate grievances from mobilization, since the former clearly support the latter. Instead of pitting these ideal–typical explanatory logics of conflict against each other, future research needs to chart out how they interact, and in many cases even reinforce each other (Cederman and Vogt 2017). Resource conflict has for a long time belonged to the domain of materialist and grievance-skeptical scholarship, but it is becoming increasingly clear that such a crude division of labor makes little sense. Hopefully this volume contributes to making this point more obvious.

Methodologically, our main aim has been to take endogeneity seriously. Chapters 3 and 4 apply various techniques that address this challenge. Focusing on petroleum extraction, the former chapter relies on a geological instrument for oil extraction that indicates such activities are indeed negatively affected by conflict. Unfortunately, there is no easy way of generalizing this method to minerals, which is why our analysis of mining conflict in Chapter 4 uses a temporal strategy based on shocks.

In addition, this volume illustrates that a mixed-method approach combining quantitative analysis and qualitative case studies could yield insights that would help improve internal validity. Certainly, the latter type of studies is able to shed light on the overall plausibility of the postulated causal mechanisms of statistical studies, such as those presented in Chapters 3 and 4. Yet, a more extensive selection of case studies would be needed to fully close the gap between these two modes of analysis.

One of the most exciting areas of research pertains to the influence of the green-energy revolution. While fracking has helped boost the supply of oil, concerns with climate change combined with technological progress rendering alternative energy sources cheaper has led to a general shift of resource extraction away from petroleum toward minerals that underpin the green-energy revolution, see for instance Hund et al. (2020) and Bazilian (2018).

In the case of oil and gas, the discussion has shifted away from the debate around "peak oil"—i.e., the time when oil supply can no longer keep up with demand—to one surrounding "peak demand" (Scholten 2018). Future research therefore will have to focus more on declining oil and gas production and what it means for conflict in and around petroleum-exporting nations.

In order to understand the conflict risk of non-fuel extraction, future research can build on some of the findings of this volume. Just as previous publications, we too find that non-fuel resources lead to conflict at a lower level. Whereas oil and gas extraction motivated secessionist conflicts, non-fuel minerals are more likely to increase the threat of local riots and protests. Future research might tell us why we see these differences. Is it simply driven by the fact that non-fuel minerals are less strategically important because they produce fewer rents, or could the difference be explained by their local effects on development? Whereas oil and gas extraction benefit the local population almost exclusively through the allocation of rents, non-fuel resources have increasingly been shown to create local economic benefits (Benshaul-Tolonen, 2018).

9.3 Policy Implications

A scholarly consensus tells us that oil extraction can be linked to violent conflict (Ross 2015; Koubi et al. 2014). Confirming this general insight, Chapter 3 tells us, more specifically, that the risk pertains primarily to aggrieved secessionist groups. The case of Aceh also reminds us that such conflicts can be solved through grievance-reducing inclusive arrangements, such as governmental and/or territorial power sharing.

Since we have found that ethno-political equality increases the risk of mining conflict as well, there are good reasons to recommend similar conflict-reduction strategies in the case of non-fuel mineral extraction. While mining conflict tends to express itself in more local and less intense ways, implying that distributional grievances may be less salient than in petroleum-related conflicts, inclusive policies and practices could still be useful since they help empower affected communities in ways that channel conflict in peaceful ways.

Indeed, long-term reduction of both political and economic inequality afflicting peripheral communities is the safest way to prevent and resolve conflict. This main lesson is driven home by the general results of Chapter 4 which indicate that exclusion makes mining conflict in Africa more likely. The case studies offer further evidence that compromise and dialogue can reduce tensions, thus reducing the threat of violence.

Rather than merely strengthening state capacity, then, the policy implication is that issues of fairness and distribution need to be taken seriously as well. Yet, the implementation of such measures is critical. The analysis of benefit sharing presented in Chapter 8 reminds us that even well-intentioned, but poorly implemented, efforts aiming to reduce the risk of conflict through inclusion of local communities may backfire if local elites profit from these measures rather than affected populations. Clearly, inequality reduction and legal protection cannot be outsourced to private companies without running the risk that spotty and biased implementation may worsen the situation. While benefit sharing could in principle contribute to addressing distributional grievances, it is unlikely that private ad-hoc measures will be enough to prevent conflict. Ultimately, there is no substitute for governmental regulation with the full support of international organizations and the governments representing the mining companies' home countries.

NOTE

1. Looking at Chinese owned mines, Christensen (2019, 96) finds no evidence for a higher probability of protests.

REFERENCES

Bazilian, Morgan D. 2018. "The Mineral Foundation of the Energy Transition." *The Extractive Industries and Society* 5 (1): 93–97.
Benshaul-Tolonen, Anja. 2018. "Local Industrial Shocks and Infant Mortality." *The Economic Journal* 129(620): 1561–1592.
Berman, Nicolas, Mathieu Couttenier, Dominic Rohner, and Mathias Thoenig. 2017. "This Mine Is Mine! How Minerals Fuel Conflicts in Africa." *American Economic Review* 107 (6): 1564–1610.
Cederman, Lars-Erik, and Manuel Vogt. 2017. "Dynamics and Logics of Civil War." *Journal of Conflict Resolution* 61: 1992–2016.
Christensen, Darin. 2019. "Concession Stands: How Mining Investments Incite Protest in Africa." *International Organization* 73: 65–101.
Hund, K., D. L. Porta, T. P. Fabregas, T. Laing, and J. Drexhage. 2020. "Minerals for Climate Action: The Mineral Intensity of the Clean Energy Transition." *Climate Smart Mining*. Washington D.C.: World Bank Group.
Hunziker, Philipp, Lars-Erik Cederman and Yannick Pengl. 2018. *Digging Deeper: The Long-Term Effects of Mineral Resource Extraction in Africa.*

Paper presented at the Annual Meeting of the American Political Science Association, Boston.

Koubi, Vally, Gabriele Spilker, Tobias Böhmelt and Thomas Bernauer. 2014. "Do Natural Resources Matter for Interstate and Intrastate Armed Conflict?" *Journal of Peace Research* 51 (2): 227–243.

Ross, Michael L. 2015. "What Have We Learned About the Resource Curse?" *Annual Review of Political Science* 18: 239–259.

Scholten, Daniel, ed. 2018. *The Geopolitics of Renewables*. New York, NY: Springer.

Index

A
accommodation, 90
ACD2EPR dataset, 59, 73, 87
Aceh, 5, 7, 17–19, 25, 26, 44, 221, 225
Adivasis, 130, 132, 133, 139–142
Automatically Coded Oil Reserves (ACOR) dataset, 37, 49–53, 65

B
Bemba-speakers, 98, 100, 112–114, 117–119, 122, 123
benefit sharing, 8, 185, 187, 189–193, 195, 198, 200, 201, 203–209, 223, 226
Blaise, President Compaoré, 193
Burkina Faso, 8, 20, 186, 187, 191–197, 206–209, 223

C
case studies, 5, 7, 19, 20, 24, 43, 99, 102, 114, 121, 136, 143, 186, 187, 190, 192, 194, 205, 208, 221–225
chiefs, 98, 100, 102, 103, 108, 110, 112–114, 118, 120, 122, 123, 195, 198, 200–204, 221
Christensen, Darin, 11, 24, 26, 27, 73, 75–77, 82
civil war, 6, 7, 12–14, 21, 25–27, 39, 45, 46, 52, 64, 65, 75, 77, 151, 156, 161, 167
Guatemalan, 156
clean energy. *See* green technology/green-energy revolution
Collier, Paul, 12–14, 18, 25, 28, 41–43, 66, 74, 75, 120
conflict, separatist, 13, 121
contents analysis
qualitative, 104
Copperbelt, 97, 98, 100, 106, 107, 112–115, 118
corporate social responsibility (CSR), 22, 107, 108, 111, 112, 122,

185–187, 189–192, 194, 204, 209, 221
corruption, 24, 78, 140, 155, 157, 180, 194, 209
CRUST dataset, 48, 53, 59

D
deprivation, feelings of, 191, 203
difference-in-difference (estimation), 24
disaggregated data (disaggregation), 74, 81

E
endogeneity, 5, 7, 8, 24, 25, 38–40, 45, 48, 54, 59, 64, 74, 76, 224
environmental degradation, 4, 83, 85, 90, 163
ethnic diversity, 164, 177
ethnic group, 15, 19, 38, 39, 44–47, 50, 58, 59, 62, 64, 75, 77, 87, 100, 102, 118, 120, 121, 151, 156, 163, 165, 177–179, 220, 221
  excluded, 64, 79, 88, 89, 91
ethnic identity, 19, 44, 102, 174, 179
Ethnic Power Relations (EPR) dataset, 58, 87, 100
ethnic settlement areas, 73, 80, 83, 85, 88
Extractive Industries Transparency Initiative (EITI), 192
extractors, 14, 15, 17, 18, 21, 22, 26–28, 42, 78, 79, 168, 178, 186

F
Fearon, James, 12, 13, 18, 21, 42, 48, 74

focus group discussions, 103–105, 112
foreign direct investment (FDI), 3, 8, 11, 72

G
gas (extraction), 20, 39, 43, 74, 221, 225
genocide, 153, 154
geospatial data, 38
greed, 4, 13, 18, 20, 28, 73, 120, 121, 220, 224
green technology/green-energy revolution, 224
grievances, 4, 6–8, 12–21, 23, 25–27, 44, 58, 64, 65, 71, 73, 75, 77–79, 81, 85, 90, 91, 97–99, 102, 103, 105, 109, 114, 116, 117, 119–122, 130, 131, 133, 135, 136, 141, 142, 144–146, 153, 165, 167, 175, 177, 186–188, 191, 200, 202, 203, 205, 206, 208, 209, 219–226
  distributive, 7, 15, 99, 109, 119
  environmental, 7, 17, 25, 27, 77–79, 99, 109, 114, 119, 221
  migration-induced, 99, 109, 112, 119
  political, 6, 7, 17, 27, 64, 78, 79, 99, 109, 114, 119, 121, 221
Guatemala, 8, 27, 151, 156, 162–172, 174–179, 190, 222, 223
Guatemalan Truth Commission, 156
Guzmán, President Arbenz, 152, 153

H
historical claims, 15, 133, 136
Hoeffler, Anke, 12–14, 25, 41–43, 66, 74, 75, 120
hydroelectric plants/extraction, 152, 155–157, 159, 160, 180

I

ILO Convention 169, 154, 155, 167, 179, 181
inclusive growth paradox, 132
India, 8, 78, 129–134, 136, 140, 146, 222
indigenous communities, 131, 134, 135, 143, 145, 146, 151–154, 156, 165, 177–179, 222
inequality, 4, 7, 8, 12–16, 23, 26, 65, 71, 73, 75, 77, 79, 83, 91, 105, 110, 114, 121, 122, 133, 146, 177, 203, 205, 209, 219–221, 223–226
  horizontal, 13–15, 75, 77, 99, 202
  vertical, 13, 75
instrumental variables (IV), 40, 48, 52–54, 57–59, 64
internal colonialism, 28, 44
interviews, 103–105, 112, 118, 123–125, 192, 193, 195, 198, 200–204, 208
  in-depth, 103

K

Katanga, 6, 7, 26
Koubi, Vally, 4, 13, 38, 39, 72, 74, 121, 225

L

Laitin, David, 12, 13, 18, 21, 28, 42, 48, 74
local community, 8, 14, 17, 18, 27, 103, 105, 107, 108, 110, 111, 116, 118, 119, 129–133, 135, 136, 140, 144–147, 151, 165, 168, 179, 187–193, 195, 202, 205–207, 209, 223, 226
Lujala, Päivo, 13, 22, 46, 50, 74, 75

M

Mayan movement, 152, 153
minerals, 3, 12, 42, 72, 74, 91, 98, 121, 164, 224
  non-fuel, 4–6, 12, 25–27, 65, 71, 75–77, 129, 219–222, 225
mining, 3, 5, 6, 8, 11, 12, 20–27, 65, 72, 73, 75–80, 82, 83, 85–88, 90, 91, 97–99, 103–106, 108, 109, 111, 112, 115–119, 121, 122, 129–133, 135, 136, 139–147, 152, 156, 159, 164–177, 179, 185–193, 195, 196, 198, 200, 202–209, 220, 221, 223–226
  bauxite, 130, 131, 136, 142–144
  copper, 6, 7, 97–99, 102, 103, 105, 106, 109, 111, 115, 118–122, 221, 222
  gold, 98, 164, 166, 168, 191, 193, 206
  nickel, 164, 175
  revenues, 6, 22, 106–111, 114, 119, 191, 208
  silver, 164, 166
mining boom, 3, 8, 72, 99, 106, 112, 115, 118, 130, 219
mobilization, 4, 7, 8, 14, 18–20, 27, 44, 47, 73, 78, 80, 83, 85, 90, 98, 99, 103–105, 109, 117, 119, 120, 122, 131, 133, 153, 165, 186–188, 191, 201–203, 205, 208, 222, 224
  indigenous, 8, 20, 153, 165
Molina, President Pérez, 157, 173
multinational mining companies, 98, 102, 186

N

Naxalite insurgency, 135, 145
Niger Delta, 20, 44

Northern Huehuetenango, region of, 156, 157, 159, 160, 162, 164, 178

O
Odisha, 26, 130, 131, 135, 136, 139, 140, 143, 145
Odisha, state of, 8, 143, 145, 146
oil curse, 38–40, 45, 54, 58
 ethno-regional, 38, 44–47, 58, 64
 governmental, 39, 41–43, 45, 58
 individualist, 41–43
 resource curse, 4, 12, 18, 21, 23, 24, 66, 73–76
oil (extraction). *See* petroleum (extraction)
opportunity, 4, 16, 18, 23, 28, 43, 47, 73, 74, 79, 85, 97, 98, 104, 106, 117, 119, 120, 122, 132, 141, 147, 193, 202, 204, 209, 220, 224
opportunity-based explanations. *See* opportunity
opportunity costs, 12

P
peak oil, 224
PETRODATA dataset, 50, 52, 58, 63, 66
petroleum (extraction), 5, 7, 13, 23, 27, 38, 39, 46, 48, 64, 71, 78, 224
Plurinational Ancestral Government, 156, 162–164
private politics, 8, 186, 189, 190, 202, 204, 205, 208
protest, 4, 5, 8, 11, 17, 18, 20–22, 24, 27, 75, 76, 78, 80–83, 117, 130, 142, 145, 157, 162, 169, 170, 172–176, 187, 194, 201, 205, 209, 219, 220, 222, 223, 225, 226

R
repression, 21, 22, 27, 58, 153, 167, 169, 175, 176, 188
resource abundance, 4, 12, 18, 21, 65
resource curse. *See under* oil curse
reverse causality, 24, 38, 40, 41, 45, 76
Ross, Michael, 4, 13, 14, 22, 23, 38–40, 42, 43, 65, 66, 74–76, 121, 140, 188, 207, 225

S
secession, 6, 19, 39, 44, 46, 47
secessionist civil wars, 25, 45
sediment basins, 48
Social Conflict Analysis Database (SCAD) dataset, 73, 80
sons-of-the-soil, 16, 78
state weakness, 13, 164, 172
Stewart, Frances, 13, 23, 75, 187, 191, 202

T
traditional legacy, 142

U
Uppsala Conflict Data Program (UCDP), 52, 59, 80, 87

X
Xinca ethnic group, 154, 173, 179

Z
Zambia, 7, 97–100, 102, 103, 105, 106, 109, 115, 116, 119, 122, 124, 221, 222

Printed by Printforce, the Netherlands